Soviet and Post-Soviet Politics and Society (SPPS)
ISSN 1614-3515

Soviet and Post-Soviet Politics and Society (SPPS)
ISSN 1614-3515

Founded in 2004 and refereed since 2007, SPPS makes available affordable English-, German-, and Russian-language studies on the history of the countries of the former Soviet bloc from the late Tsarist period to today. It publishes between 5 and 20 volumes per year and focuses on issues in transitions to and from democracy such as economic crisis, identity formation, civil society development, and constitutional reform in CEE and the NIS. SPPS also aims to highlight so far understudied themes in East European studies such as right-wing radicalism, religious life, higher education, or human rights protection. The authors and titles of all previously published volumes are listed at the end of this book. For a full description of the series and reviews of its books, see www.ibidem-verlag.de/red/spps.

Editorial correspondence & manuscripts should be sent to: Dr. Andreas Umland, c/o DAAD, German Embassy, vul. Bohdana Khmelnitskoho 25, UA-01901 Kyiv, Ukraine. e-mail: umland@stanfordalumni.org

Business correspondence & review copy requests should be sent to: *ibidem* Press, Leuschnerstr. 40, 30457 Hannover, Germany; tel.: +49 511 2622200; fax: +49 511 2622201; spps@ibidem.eu.

Authors, reviewers, referees, and editors for (as well as all other persons sympathetic to) SPPS are invited to join its networks at www.facebook.com/group.php?gid=52638198614 www.linkedin.com/groups?about=&gid=103012 www.xing.com/net/spps-ibidem-verlag/

Recent Volumes

A. Salem, G. Hazeldine, D. Morgan (eds.)

HIGHER EDUCATION IN POST-COMMUNIST STATES

Comparative and Sociological Perspectives

ibidem-Verlag
Stuttgart

Bibliographic information published by the Deutsche Nationalbibliothek
Die Deutsche Nationalbibliothek lists this publication in the Deutsche Nationalbibliografie;
detailed bibliographic data are available in the Internet at http://dnb.d-nb.de.

Bibliografische Information der Deutschen Nationalbibliothek
Die Deutsche Nationalbibliothek verzeichnet diese Publikation in der Deutschen
Nationalbibliografie; detaillierte bibliografische Daten sind im Internet über http://dnb.d-nb.de
abrufbar.

Cover picture: UCL Institute of Education, taken in Bloomsbury,
London in March 2017 by A. Salem

ISSN: 1614-3515
ISBN-13: 978-3-8382-1183-1
© *ibidem*-Verlag / *ibidem* Press
Stuttgart, Germany 2018

Printed in the United States of America

For Danny Harvey

Contents

Contents

The Ends of Higher Education

A. Salem, Gary Hazeldine and David Morgan

1. University Education in a Neoliberal Climate

If we look at the English university system today, what we may see are the results of an all too familiar process: fees for students have greatly increased, with many facing a depressing mix of high debts and low-paid work; more and more academics, employed on casualised or short-term contracts, face economic insecurity;[1] the proportion of lecturers to students has almost halved,[2] with serious consequences for the quality, type and quantity of academic work; government auditing and managerial surveillance have become entirely standard, producing deep distrust, and fundamentally weakening academic freedom; above all, and this underlies all of the other developments, public subsidy for the universities is in continual decline—most clearly seen in the complete withdrawal of state funds for courses in all but the most business-friendly subjects.[3]

What has conditioned these developments? Part of an answer lies in the GBP 1000 fees for international students introduced in 1980 under the Thatcher administration. This was an early development of neoliberalising policy towards university education, partly because it suggested that academic study—which as a long history of student protests shows has always allowed some room for self-critique, and thus social critique—can be bought and sold like any other consumer product, and partly because it broke the social-democratic consensus that had held in the UK at large since

---

1   Noted in Anna Fazackerley, "Why are Many Academics on Short-Term Contracts for Years?", *The Guardian*, 4 February 2013, https://www.theguardian.com/education/2013/feb/04/academic-casual-contracts-higher-education (as of 1 September 2017).

2   As pointed out by Sarah Amsler and Joyce Canaan, "Whither Critical Pedagogy in the Neo-Liberal University Today? Two UK Practitioners' Reflections on Constraints and Possibilities", *Enhancing Learning in the Social Sciences* 1:2 (November 2008): 3.

3   The allusion is to science, technology, engineering and mathematics (STEM).

1945.[4] From being committed to funding universal access to higher education as part of a wider set of social benefits, and by extension to the idea that academic study is worthwhile in itself and necessary for self-development and self-expression, the main parties began to develop ways of making the universities more directly useful to state and economic interests.[5] There followed a marked shift of responsibility for funding university education away from the state to students. Over several decades, successive UK governments formed and maintained a policy of cutting back and finally withdrawing grants, while at the same time introducing and then gradually increasing loans and fees; in 2012, of course, the Cameron government greatly increased fees, opening the way for almost all universities to charge well over GBP 9,000 annually for access.[6]

---

4   The term 'neoliberalising' is used here to suggest that the neoliberal model, while it has certainly globalised itself and strengthened its hold, is not a once-and-for-all development but, as Joyce Canaan and others have argued, a varied and uneven process which brings about resistance to it, and which also opens the door to alternatives. For more on this use of the term see for instance Canaan, "Resisting the English Neoliberalising University: What Critical Pedagogy Can Offer", *Journal of Critical Education Policy Studies* 11:2 (March 2013): 19–23, http://www.jceps.com/wp-content/uploads/PDFs/11-2-02.pdf (as of 1 September 2017).

5   Northern Ireland, Wales and especially Scotland do not readily fit into this account, since from the late 1990s onwards these countries gained greater autonomy from the Union, and were able to make undergraduate study either free or much cheaper than it is in England, doubtless due in part to their commitment, within certain limits, to social-democratic governance. This illustrates Canaan's point that neoliberalism, or 'neoliberalisation' as she prefers to call it, is neither irreversible nor inevitable. See Canaan, "Resisting the English Neoliberalising University": 19–23.

6   There is a great deal of critical writing on this subject. See for example Roger Brown with Helen Carasso, *Everything for Sale? The Marketisation of UK Higher Education* (London: Routledge, 2013); Stefan Collini, *What are Universities For?* (London: Penguin, 2012); Stefan Collini, *Sold Out, London Review of Books* 35:20 (October 2013): 3–12; John Holmwood, *A Manifesto for the Public University* (London: Bloomsbury Academic, 2011); Fred Inglis, "Economical with the Actualité", *Times Higher Education*, 6 October 2011, https://www.timeshighereducation.com/features/economical-with-the-actualit/417654.article (as of 1 September 2017); and Andrew McGettigan, *The Great University Gamble: Money, Markets and the Future of Higher Education* (London: Pluto, 2013).

Unsurprisingly, once university education is rated at a specific monetary value, once it is sold and consumed like any other consumer object, it becomes harder to see it as a learning process (by definition more or less chaotic, unpredictable and uncontainable). Instead students may view their education as speculators looking for investment gains, and/or as consumers with regular expectations of their purchase. Such attitudes are generally encouraged by the universities: what course does not now mention its bearing on career plans, or sport a list of 'learning outcomes', as if it were a definitively finished mechanical product capable of delivering predictable and repeatable effects? The attempt to remake students as investors and consumers is also sharply enforced by state bodies like the funding councils and their successors. These require that universities publish 'key information sets' about courses to meet the 'needs' of prospective students and interested parents, information made up of little more than prices, and performance, and employment and salaries.[7] Of course, what is included in and excluded from these data sets makes them as much a matter of prescription as objective statement. They encourage a particular mentality among students and, in an exemplary piece of interpellation in Althusser's sense, play a role in creating the very student self-image that they claim to describe—one founded on consuming reliable, well-made goods, on speculative buying and, ultimately, on pursuing private wealth and comfort.[8]

Such tactics are bound up with vested interests, in that through them the neoliberal state may present what it has forced on students—costs, debts,

---

7   See for instance https://www.hefcw.ac.uk/policy_areas/learning_and_teaching/ information_for_students.aspx (as of 1 September 2017).

8   This is a very particular sort of freedom. In class-divided society, as Adorno notes, "the freedom of individuals is essentially private in nature": "this freedom consists essentially of acquisitions at the expense of others, in a specific kind of sovereignty in which the freedom of others is always offended against a priori, and which therefore contradicts the meaning of freedom from the outset". Theodor Adorno, *History and Freedom: Lectures 1964–1965*, ed. Rolf Tiedemann (Cambridge: Polity, 2006), 179.

risks, in short economic insecurity[9] – as a desirable consumer choice and a good investment opportunity. Whether students will buy into this attempt to refashion enforced poverty and insecurity as a choice and an opportunity is an open question, especially when set against what is happening now to so many who, in line with the state's commitment to neoliberal policies, have been condemned to unemployment, under-employment and workfare.[10] What can be said is that the neoliberal project elicits thoughts and actions appropriate to its development, in part by appealing to our sense of being free individuals with our own purposes and agency – in a process that Foucault, with what he calls "technologies of the self", would have found instantly familiar.[11]

---

9   See for instance Keith Burnett, "We Need to Talk About Free Education", *Times Higher Education*, 20 June 2017, https://www.timeshighereducation.com/blog/we-need-talk-about-free-education; Sean Coughlan, "Could Tuition Fees Really Cost £54,000?", *BBC Online*, 21 January 2017, http://www.bbc.co.uk/news/education-38651059; Angela Monaghan and Sally Weale, "UK Student Loan Debt Soars to More Than £100bn", *The Guardian*, 15 June 2017, https://www.theguardian.com/money/2017/jun/15/uk-student-loan-debt-soars-to-more-than-100bn (all as of 1 September 2017).

10   Bourdieu is clear that such "generalised precariousness", far from being a by-product of economic crisis, is the result of acts of political will, not least because it can serve as an effective tool of social control: "Generalised precariousness [...] is the basis of a new form of social discipline generated by job insecurity and the fear of unemployment". Its victims "are found almost as often among occupations requiring a high level of cultural capital", one example being "precariously employed teachers, overburdened with marginalised high school or university students who are themselves destined for casual work". Pierre Bourdieu, *Firing Back Against the Tyranny of the Market*, Vol. 2, trans. Loïc Wacquant (London: Verso, 2003), 61, 62. For an elaboration of this point see the chapter, "Job Insecurity is Everywhere Now", in Bourdieu, *Acts of Resistance: Against the New Myths of Our Time*, trans. Richard Nice (Cambridge: Polity, 2004), especially 85–86.

11   See for instance Michel Foucault, *Power: Essential Works of Foucault 1954–1984*, Vol. 3, trans. Robert Hurley et al. (London: Penguin, 2002), especially 201–222, 326–348, 403–417. See also Steph Lawler's insightful analysis in *Identity: Sociological Perspectives* (Cambridge: Polity, 2008), especially 61–63.

Such efforts to change *attitudes* towards being made to pay for undergraduate study are, we should not forget, very much linked with lessening government spending on higher education as a whole, spanning the GBP 100 million cut that occurred under Thatcher just after the 1979 election, all the way to Cameron's GBP 3 billion cut from 2010 onwards. The long decline of state funds has deeply affected students, as we have seen, but beyond this it has also had clear implications for universities. Above all, starving the universities of state funding has forced them to adopt corporate values, leading to micro-scrutiny and control by executives, market-managers, planners and administrators, and amounting to a Taylorisation of academic work. Now, as Louise Morley notes, "every academic activity is broken down into simpler and more manageable parts", resulting in "a fragmenting or fracturing" in which complex processes are translated into "empirically identifiable indicators, measures, competencies and outputs".[12] This reduction of complex processes to measurable quantities is of course entirely misleading. Think of the obsessive counting and recounting of 'contact hours', which tells you nothing about time spent with students outside the classroom, or the quality of conversation and thinking within it.[13] It does, however, say a great deal about the instrumental and classifying impulse that the Marxist philosopher Georg Lukács warned against a long time ago.[14]

---

12 Louise Morley, *Quality and Power in Higher Education* (Maidenhead: SHRE and Open University Press, 2003), 48.

13 As Paul Ashwin notes, "years of research have shown that the hours that students are taught does not directly relate to the quality of what they learn". Paul Ashwin, "'Bizarre' TEF metrics Overlook So Much about Teaching Excellence", *Times Higher Education*, 7 June 2016, https://www.timeshighereducation.com/blog/bizarre-tef-metrics-overlook-so-much-about-teaching-excellence (as of 1 September 2017). See also Camille Kandiko Howsen, "TEF: Don't Equate Contact Hours with Teaching Quality", *The Guardian*, 23 November 2016, https://www.theguardian.com/higher-education-network/2016/nov/23/tef-dont-equate-contact-hours-with-teaching-qua lity (as of 1 September 2017).

14 György Lukács put the same point in a more Marxist fashion, when he wrote that "capitalism promotes quantitative and calculative modes of thought governed by

Of course much more could be said, given more space. There is the apparent paradox that while less and less of its expenditure is devoted to funding academia, the state is more and more demanding of academics and universities. This is why Michael Burawoy, in analysing neoliberal policy towards universities, talks about "commodification plus regulation", and not simply one or the other.[15] Or there is the problem that higher education, as it becomes an offshoot of the economy, is not really there for students, but is rather a servant of business, fostering in its charges those qualities most appropriate to the ideal, productive and exploitable worker.

2. Neoliberalising University Education in Post-Communist States

Why begin a book on higher education in post-Communist states with a brief overview of the current state of higher education in England and to a lesser extent the UK?[16] Part of the answer involves the fact that we as editors are writing from the context of our own current experiences of UK higher-educational institutions, while also writing with a keen interest in

---

interests in profit, control, measurability and predictability, and thus constitutes science as a tool of its interests". György Lukács, *History and Class Consciousness: Studies in Marxist Dialectics*, trans. Rodney Livingstone (London: Merlin, 1990), 10. Similarly, as Douglas Kellner notes, Adorno and Horkheimer argued that "quantitative, abstract modes of thought are ruled by principles of equivalence and substitution whereby dissimilar things become comparable by reduction to abstract quantities which exclude individual quality on principle". Kellner, *Critical Theory, Marxism and Modernity* (Cambridge: Polity, 1989), 96.

15   Burawoy is surely right that if "The university as simultaneously participant in and observer of society is dissolving", and if "the university is losing its capacity to fend off pressures of instrumentalisation", it is because "These pressures come in two forms—commodification and regulation". Michael Burawoy, "Deliberative Democracy in a Global Context: A South African Model of Higher Education?", http://www.isacna.wordpress.com/2010/05/03/deliberative-democracy-in-a-glob al-context-a-south-african-model-of-higher-education/#more-437 (as of 1 September 2017).

16   This is a particularly pressing question in the context of Brexit and the increasing distancing of the UK from Europe.

developments in higher education globally and also specifically in the post-Communist context. But we also write with an enthusiasm for comparative sociology, and for what it can teach us about the key similarities and differences between educational institutions and systems in different countries and regions.[17] On the one hand, we want to avoid the assumption that higher education in post-Communist countries is, in any simplistic way, on an inevitable one-way journey towards greater Western-style neoliberalisation, regardless of national political interventions, specific histories and cultural differences. However, on the other hand, and supported by many of the chapters in this book, we also want to draw attention to the apparent shifts in this direction, along with the dangers of this process, and also its particular manifestations in the context of countries whose 'official' economic and political ideologies defined themselves against a marketised system until the late 1980s and early 1990s.

As has been outlined so far, what has appeared to be an unstoppable shift in higher education policy in the UK—despite strong and sustained protests and occupations by students,[18] often supported by staff, unions and the wider public—has led to a number of deeply worrying developments for universities and their staff and students, and there are many signs that these developments are increasingly impacting on, or already fully developed within, the educational policies and experiences of post-Communist universities. Although these significant changes have had a relatively long history in the UK, the impact of a number of recent changes have been

---

17 See for example Patrick Blessinger and John P. Anchan, eds., *Democratizing Higher Education: International Comparative Perspectives* (New York: Routledge, 2015); and Eleoussa Polyzoi, Michael Fullan and John P. Anchan, *Change Forces in Post-Communist Eastern Europe: Education in Transition* (New York: Routledge, 2003).

18 For more on the student protests see for example Sean Coughlan, "Students Protest Against Tuition Fees", *BBC Online*, 4 November 2015, http://www.bbc.co.uk/news/education-34721681 (as of 1 September 2017); and Paul Lewis et al., "Student Protest over Fees Turns Violent", *The Guardian*, 10 November 2010, https://www.theguardian.com/education/2010/nov/10/student-protest-fees-violent (as of 1 September 2017).

acutely felt in a very short space of time. Rising bureaucracy, managerialism, commodification and instrumentalism have had far-reaching consequences within all spheres of UK academic life, and a number of recent and important scholarly works have explored their impact on teaching, research and administrative duties.[19] These works also ask what the role of higher education and universities *ought* to be, who they belong to, whose interests they should serve, and the best ways to achieve this. They provide convincing, and damning, critiques of the ways in which marketisation and privatisation destroy the important *public* role of HE institutions by valuing them only in terms of economic growth and human capital, and of the ways in which new assessments of 'quality' and the broader audit culture fail to capture—or rather end up distorting—what it is they set out to measure. Importantly, these works not only outline what is at stake here, but also set out viable alternatives, and consider the ways in which the wider public, and those of us directly involved in higher education, can contribute to change; they make strong cases for how things might be different, given the political will.[20] Many of the chapters in this edited collection have been written by authors who also concern themselves with these issues, both at a national and institutional level, as well as at the wider theoretical level, and they explore the ways in which we can see similar, though often country-specific, manifestations of these economic and political processes in post-Communist states.

---

19 In particular see Andrew McGettigan, *The Great University Gamble: Money, Markets and the Future of Higher Education* (London: Pluto, 2013); Stefan Collini, *What are Universities For?* (London: Penguin, 2012); Stefan Collini, *Speaking of Universities* (London: Verso, 2017); John Holmwood, *A Manifesto for the Public University* (London: Bloomsbury, 2011); Michael Bailey and Des Freedman, eds., *The Assault on Universities: A Manifesto for Resistance* (London: Pluto, 2011); and Derek Sayer, *Rank Hypocrisies: The Insult of the REF* (London: Sage, 2015).

20 Germany's U-turn on tuition fees is a case in point. See e.g. Howard Hotson, "Germany's Great Tuition Fees U-Turn", *Times Higher Education*, 13 February 2014, https://www.timeshighereducation.com/features/germanys-great-tuition-fees-u-turn/2011168.article.

3. The Ends of Higher Education

In different ways, all the contributors deal with an unfolding process of transition in formerly Communist nations from one higher education system to another. Since the fall of Communism, higher education has found itself obliged to adapt to a radically different institutional and ideological environment. Previous political and ideological certainties have had to be abandoned, while entirely new sets of institutional values and practices have been adopted in their stead. Previously, universities in the region were pressed into the service of the state, part of a command-and-control apparatus defined by and devoted exclusively to the maintenance and furtherance of its Marxist-Leninist ideological underpinnings. Now, however, almost all of these universities find themselves obliged to incorporate and implement the structures and forms of Western free-market neoliberalism, with all the new ideologies accompanying them.

In practice, higher education has been swiftly commodified, to be regarded and marketed as a more or less luxurious consumer good. In this process any notion of studying for personal enrichment, or of education as a matter of personal and cultural self-fulfilment, has generally been sidelined. Instead the education system has been obliged to present its products in strictly functional, mercantile terms: as a means to the end of realising the career ambitions and professional aspirations of individual students. Of course the same process has been very much in evidence in Western culture, especially though not of course solely in the US and the UK, though in an arguably less traumatic fashion, since in those cases university education has long been treated as any other consumer product.

In former Communist countries, of course, education at all levels was centrally funded and administered by the state, usually resulting in direct subsidies for research and teaching in the case of universities and similar bodies. A dual institutional ethos developed whereby higher education came to be seen as both a universal service, to which all have access, and as a servant of the state—one that helped to maintain and ensure the state's continued existence through the constant supply of appropriately skilled graduates. Against this background, it is easy to appreciate the dramatic nature of the change which has now taken place. From being cost-free, universal in terms of access, and linked into the certainty and prescriptiveness of graduates' eventual employment in the public sector, higher education in post-Communist states now increasingly exists and operates within organisations dedicated to the competitive marketing of a readily saleable product. As a result, universities in these countries, alongside the staff who inhabit them, have had to comprehensively reinvent themselves.

These changes raise many questions with regard to the workings of the institutions involved, and to the wider political and historical context in which they operate. How have these institutions adapted to their new market conditions? What have been the tactics and techniques used to manage the transition from being publicly funded cultural establishments, open to all, to commercial organisations offering quasi-professional services only to those willing and able to pay for access, in the hope that their educational attainments may go some way to ensuring their future careers? What tensions and conflicts have risen as a result, and how effectively have these been negotiated? Who or what may be said to be the beneficiaries of this process of transformation — and who or what could be counted among its casualties? What lessons could be drawn from the experience, particularly but not only in countries like Britain, where the overt commercialisation of the universities is proceeding apace?

Such questions are directly addressed by the contributors, who bring the full apparatus of the sociology of education, discourse and empirical analysis, social theory, postcolonial studies and globalisation theory to the examination of diverse local situations. Olga Suprun argues that Lithuania's 2009 Law on Higher Education and Research has been complicit in the widespread and systematic implementation of a neoliberal model for Lithuanian universities. She considers the broader context which gave rise to this process of change, along with the current, and potential, impacts of the law, particularly in relation to issues of fair access and social equality. A range of alternative models for funding higher education – partially private, mass public and elite – are then explored alongside their main beneficiaries, while the role of different political ideologies in the funding model chosen and in the method of its implementation is spelt out. Notably, Suprun also makes the case for drawing finer distinctions within what she calls the "Anglo-American model"; that is, between a largely under-regulated system in the US and an arguably more egalitarian one in the UK as a whole. Finally, she considers the Constitutional Court's role in influencing legal reforms in this area, along with politically inflected definitions of what constitutes a 'good student' when laying down criteria for grants and fees, concluding with proposals that Lithuanian higher education is faced with a choice: either to fall more in line with the British model or, instead, to apply fair, uniform, reasonable and partial tuition fees.

In their statistical and empirical analysis of courses in social science at four Hungarian universities, Zoltán Ginelli, Attila Melegh, Sabina Csánova, Emese Baranyi and Rudolf Piroch seek to make visible the assumptions contained in specific curricula. Drawing, among others, on Foucault and his ideas about systems of discourse, the authors argue that while these curricula continually give the impression of a global culture and a globalised consciousness in their content and style, what lies unstated behind them is an ideal hierarchy of national economies and cultures, though one that navigates between Eurocentrism and conservative nationalism. There is no block, the authors go on to argue, between such egocentric cultural and political discourses and globalised, neoliberal economics, given how far universities in the country have become instruments of state policy – part of a national and nationalistic effort, that is, to situate Hungary at the top of a mythifying hierarchy of global competitiveness, development and progress.

Drawing on his own experience of teaching at universities in Azerbaijan, Piers von Berg explores the importance of, and potential for, civic education in the academy generally. Von Berg's case study work on a project for civic education, along with a youth forum that he was prominent in organising, demonstrate the importance, alongside the more traditional professional and academic skills, of personal and social awareness, agency and skills, and of how these might be further developed in British higher education. Using evidence from the case study, von Berg goes on to argue that civic education has a significant and lasting impact on the students involved in such alternative forms of teaching and learning, as illustrated in their future personal development, skills, social awareness and active citizenship.

Andreas Umland outlines what academics from Western Europe and the US may expect when working for the first time at educational establishments in countries like Russia and Ukraine, drawing on and appealing to his own experiences of teaching in the social sciences in those countries over many years. For Umland, much academic work in the region, not least in the social sciences, is marked by its exposure to a lengthy, drawn-out period of transition from one system to another, bearing the traces and after-effects of an education system operating for so long in isolation from global transformations — political, economic, social and cultural — while also being confined to and limited by a widespread intellectual and political culture of authoritarianism. This situation translates itself into a very particular set of circumstances where, for instance, teaching is quite didactic, the students being mute and passive objects of lecturers, institutionalised corruption is a regular feature to the extent that bribery is routinely used to influence grading, and where working conditions for academics are grossly oppressive. At the same time, Umland argues, such circumstances have been accompanied by some signs of change, particularly as academics from different countries help to globalise awareness of a quite different set of technical standards.

Marine Vekua traces changes in journalism studies in Georgia since the collapse of Communism, showing how the discipline has responded to extrinsic factors such as changes in state policy towards higher education as a whole, and the increasing influence of media companies on its structure and forms. In the process, she takes up issues of accreditation and institutional approval, the use of feedback systems for quality control purposes, methodological and technological distinctions in teaching, and working conditions for students and staff, arguing that Georgian universities offering courses in the discipline can be classified into three different types, depending on whether they take their inspiration from curriculum models coming out of Europe, the US or Georgia itself. For Vekua, the Georgian state's political efforts towards greater integration with Europe, not least its total commitment to the Bologna Process, has generally brought about a considerable improvement in academic training in journalistic practice. The results remain incomplete, however, such that Vekua's analysis creates a snapshot of a post-Soviet nation very much in the process of transforming its identity, in part by bringing its university system into line with more universal standards.

Joseph Backhouse-Barber attempts to do justice to the complexities of higher education in Russia, by rejecting any simplistic or reductive division between Russian and Western university systems, or between a politically muted Soviet model and a free-thinking post-Soviet one. Informed by Niklas Luhmann and systems theory, and in particular by the notion of dedifferentiation where the autonomy of a system with relation to its environment comes under threat,[21] Backhouse-Barber argues that business and state demands threaten the autonomy of the education system in different geographical areas at different times. Drawing also on Jürgen Habermas and aspects of Frankfurt School critical theory, a further argument is that rigid instrumentality and strategic considerations have penetrated to the base of the commonsense habits and predilections of students and staff, that is, their lifeworlds in Habermas's sense. These views are applied to the analysis not only of the distinctions but also of the continuities between Russia's higher education system in the Soviet period and in its current state. In the same way, the author establishes correspondences between university

---

21   For an account of this notion as it relates to the analysis of higher education in systems theory more generally, see Frans van Vucht, "Diversity and Differentiation in Higher Education Systems", paper given at the Centre for Higher Education Trust (CHET) Anniversary Conference, Cape Town, 16 November 2007: 1–22, http://www.universityworldnews.com/filemgmt_data/files/Frans-van-Vucht.pdf.

systems in Russia and in countries like the UK, particularly in terms of their connection with and uses for neoliberalism, while at the same time drawing some fine distinctions between them. Finally, the main subject of consideration—university education—is used to bring out some of the shared concerns but also the sharp distinctions between systems theory and critical theory.

Robert Ferguson deliberately steps back from any extended analysis of geographical regions or national cultures. Instead he seeks to explore the liberatory potential of education as such, which can, and as Ferguson suggests, must be applied to diverse local situations, particularly but not only within post-Communist universities dealing with the demands of state and business to put education to use. Drawing on Paulo Freire's ideas about the need to treat teachers and students as equally integral elements in the learning process, Ferguson argues for the centrality of pedagogical work that fosters critical thinking, especially when allied to the power and utility of digital technologies—the full implications of which have not yet been widely internalised. However, while new technology can certainly be an important tool for political improvement and emancipation, Ferguson harbours no illusions about how easily and swiftly it may be used for commercialisation and political control. There is always a choice about its use, however, and it is up to educators working with what is available to them in a particular place at a particular moment to decide what role to play. This applies as much to those working in Western Europe or North America, where the very idea of education as a tool for progressive change has been the subject of sustained attack, as it does to those inhabiting post-Communist states, now undergoing deep changes under the pressures of powerful commercial and institutional forces.

Strongly influenced by the ideas of Isaiah Berlin, Michel Foucault and Herbert Marcuse, Tom Driver explores the impact of commercialisation on Russian universities. Driver first places Russia's adoption of neoliberal policies since 1991 in a much broader political and historical context of global neoliberal politics and economics, before turning to the issue of reforms in university education in the country, and meditating on, among other things, the meaning of the shift from a publicly funded university system to a market-led and business-oriented one, the similarities and differences in the bureaucratic mechanisms governing academic work before and after 1991, and the implications of such developments for academic freedom and critical thought. What emerges is a new situation structurally and ideologically, albeit one close to the neoliberal regime with which academics in the UK and elsewhere are very familiar, which presents itself as a natural and moral system where students are transfigured as shoppers and consumers, and where universities are not expected to serve any purpose beyond academic training in career advancement. Coupled with performance targets, auditing and surveillance mechanisms — including some that are not dissimilar from the UK's Research Excellence Framework[22] — and the reduction of qualitative distinctions to quantitative ones, students' disconnection and a demoralised educational staff can directly result, while there is little space left for free expression, productive dialogue and participation or — and this is what is most dangerous for Driver — the fostering of critical faculties, very much of the kind described by Ferguson.

---

22 Here we may think of Russia's Project 5-100, also known as the Russian Academic Excellence Initiative, administered by the Council on Competitive Enhancement of Leading Russian Universities among Global Research and Education Centers. For further detail, see for example Enora Bennetot Pruvot and Thomas Estermann, "Excellence Schemes are Blooming in Europe's Universities", *European Universities Public Relations and Information Officers* (EUPRIO), 2 March 2015, http://www.euprio. eu/excellence-schemes-are-blooming-in-europes-universities/ (as of 1 September 2017). See also their "DEFINE Thematic Report: Funding for Excellence", European University Association Report, http://www.eua.be/Libraries/publication/DEFINE _Funding_for_Excellence.pdf?sfvrsn=4; and Ellie Bothwell, "Revision of Russia's Project 5-100 could be 'Step Backwards'", *Times Higher Education*, 17 October 2016, https://www.timeshighereducation.com/news/revision-russias-project-5-100-coul d-be-step-backwards (as of 1 September 2017).

Financing Higher Education: Policy Transformations in Lithuania

Olga Suprun

1. Introduction

The Lithuanian higher education system has undergone considerable transformation during the period since national independence in 1990. In that period rates of student participation have increased fourfold, while continuing low financial expenditure on educational institutions per student has signalled the pressing need for political action in order to rebalance the system in financial terms, and to resolve its other systemic defects. In order to so readjust the Lithuanian system of higher education finance there were a number of available models of reform to choose from, notwithstanding the prevailing need to ensure equal access to HE for all prospective students. Some other countries have chosen to increase public funding in order to keep higher education free for all, while others have instead opted to introduce tuition fees and have implemented various student loan systems in order to ease the 'burden' on the overall state budget which is imposed by their respective HE systems.

On 30 April 2009, the Lithuanian Parliament passed a new Law on Higher Education and Research which embodied the model of higher education reform which had been chosen by the government. This new law was framed in accordance with the rulings of the Constitutional Court of the Republic of Lithuania, which broadly interpreted the meaning of the 3rd part of article No. 41 of the Constitution of the Republic of Lithuania, declaring that "citizens who are good at their studies shall be guaranteed education at State schools of higher education free of charge".[1] As such, the Constitutional Court's rulings had a decisive influence upon the newly implemented model

---

1   As written in the Constitution of the Republic of Lithuania (1992), http://www3.lrs.lt/home/Konstitucija/Constitution.htm (as of 20 September 2017).

of higher education reform, since the Court had stated that free education cannot in fact be granted to *all* students who are 'good at their studies', but only to those students who opt to study within specific subject areas which were deemed likely to satisfy future employment demands, as determined by the government. Thus, in effect, the constitutionally sanctified academic criterion of the 'good student' became transformed into a political instrument which was utilised by the government in order to restrict the overall budgetary expense of higher education. However, even though the Constitutional Court had so narrowed the meaning of the 'good student', and, accordingly, restricted the overall level of entitlement to free HE, there was still sufficient financial and administrative flexibility remaining to enable politicians to reform the Lithuanian HE finance system so as to ensure quality, while ensuring equal access to HE for all qualified prospective students. Unfortunately, it very soon became evident that equal access to higher education was not among the priorities of the country's political elite.

Since the implementation of the Law on Higher Education and Research, approximately half of the prospective student cohort who have completed secondary education, exceeds the numerical targets for free HE which are set by the government each year. If these 'surplus students' wish to study in their home country they are required to pay for their tertiary education at full price, which varies significantly—from about EUR 1,250 to EUR 11,600 per academic year—depending on the study programme and the university in question. Thus, under the terms of the current Lithuanian HE funding policy framework, access to HE for those students who exceed the state-defined numerical quotas per subject area is no longer dependent purely upon their intrinsic academic aptitude or ability. Rather, in practice, access is circumscribed by their ability to pay tuition fees, or by their willingness to risk being indebted to a bank, since, following the reform, the state-owned student loan system has been reorganised into a state-supported commercial bank loan system.

This chapter aims to analyse the current model of Lithuanian Higher Education finance reform against the context of relevant Constitutional

Court rulings, and from the perspective of a concern with issues of equity and fair access to HE (at bachelor degree level). The chapter will compare the Lithuanian model against higher education finance models which have been implemented in other countries; it will also seek to recommend possible alternative mechanisms of further HE funding reform within Lithuania, ones which embody an overriding social concern for quality, equity and fair access to HE. The methodology combines a comparative analysis of scientific literature, empirical and statistical analysis, discourse analysis, and the critical analysis of legal documents.

2. A Review of Changes in the Lithuanian Higher Education System: Factors that Spurred the Need for Higher Education Reform

Changes in HEI Networks and Student Numbers

When Lithuania was incorporated into the Soviet Union, there was only one formal university in the country: Vilnius University. At that time the government strictly controlled the practice of higher education, and the numbers of students enrolling. As a result of the ending of Soviet rule, this degree of governmental control has lessened, and this has resulted in a period of spontaneous and chaotic development across the HE sector. Prior to the restoration of independence in 1990, Lithuania already had 12 schools of higher education.[2] After the restoration of the country's independence, the ambition of higher education schools to become free of government control was satisfied by means of enshrining their institutional autonomy in law. The granting of this autonomy, without retaining any direct leverage over this area by the state, has led to the chaotic expansion of the higher education system. Figures provided by the Lithuanian Department of Statistics[3] present clear evidence of the pace and scale of the expansion in the number of higher

---

2   Rimantas Želvys, "Aukštojo mokslo kaita ir problemos", *Acta Paedagogica Vilnensia* 14 (2005): 169–178, http://www.zurnalai.vu.lt/acta-paedagogica-vilnensia/article/viewFile/9765/7488 (as of 20 September 2017).

3   See http://osp.stat.gov.lt/ (as of 30 June 2015).

education institutions, and of the expansion in student numbers. Between 1995 and 1996 Lithuania had 15 state universities, with 54,000 students enrolled. According to the available data for 2008–2009, this had increased to 22 universities (15 state universities and 7 private), with 149,000 students enrolled, and 27 colleges (15 state colleges and 12 private), with 61,400 students enrolled. In sum, by 2009 Lithuania had a total of 49 institutions of higher education, with 201,400 students enrolled — which means that, from 1995 to 2009, the number of higher education institutions had significantly increased, while the total number of students enrolled had increased almost four-fold.[4] Based on the number of students enrolled, Lithuania has now become one of the most academically intensive countries not only in Europe, but throughout the world (see below).[5]

Gross enrolment ratio, tertiary, both sexes (%), 2008

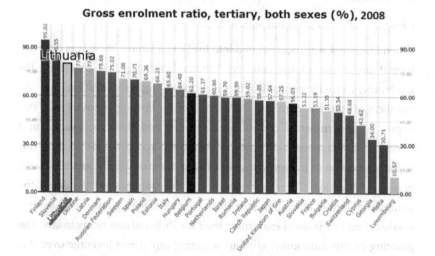

Given this rapid increase in the number of higher education institutions, and in overall student numbers, access to higher education as such has, of

---

4   This information is taken from my MA dissertation: Olga Suprun, "Higher Education Reform within the Context of Constitutional Court Decisions", (Vilnius University, 2010).

5   Based on UNESCO Institute for Statistics data, http://data.uis.unesco.org/index.aspx?queryid=142andlang=en (as of 30 June 2015).

course, increased — however this has in turn led to a lowering of academic requirements for students, and hence to a devaluation of higher education diplomas, as well as to a decrease in the overall quality of higher education.

Higher Education Funding Changes

With the rapid increase in student numbers, schools of higher education began to experience a shortage of public funding. In terms of annual expenditure on higher educational institutions per student, according to Eurostat data,[6] among 27 countries Lithuania was ranked 23rd in this respect. The shortage of funding for higher education was not the only problem. The model of funding being implemented was also faulty: only 30% of the students of any given study programme were fully funded by the state, which led to an expansion in the overall number of study programmes, rather than to any increase in academic quality.

The need for higher education reform within Lithuania has not been determined purely by the shortage of funding. There are other factors which have been identified within preparatory documents relating to reform.[7] Amongst these factors are the following: about 70% of graduates do not find work within their chosen profession; only about 12% of scientists in Lithuania are aged under 35 years; PhD graduates who travel abroad rarely return; and the overall citation index for Lithuanian scientists is the lowest amongst the new EU member states. Another factor which motivated the need for reform was undoubtedly that of global economic competition. The preamble to an agreement amongst Lithuanian parliamentary political

---

6   Eurostat, "Annual Expenditure on Public and Private Educational Institutions per Student in PPS, at Tertiary Level of Education", http://ec.europa.eu/eurostat/tgm/table.do?tab=tableandplugin=1andlanguage=enandpcode=tps00067 (as of 6 June 2015).

7   Mokslo ir studijų sistemos reformos metmenys (2006), http://www.lsas.lt/modules/document_publisher/documents/3/Mokslo%20ir%20studiju%20reformos%20metmenys.pdf (as of 20 September 2017).

parties regarding the reform of the science and education system[8] asserted that an effective and competitive Lithuanian science and study system would help to ensure competition with the best European and world universities, and moreover that adequate HE provision is an essential precondition for ensuring economic prosperity, and for the maintenance of a high quality of life for the country's citizens.

Section Summary

The higher education system in Lithuania has undergone considerable transformation since the state re-established its independence in 1990. Drastic increases in the number of schools of higher education, a four-fold increase in rates of student participation, and low expenditure on educational institutions per student, have signalled the need for reform. This would be in order to rebalance what has become an irrationally functioning higher education system, by rectifying its defects, and by ensuring the quality and competitiveness of Lithuanian higher education.

3. The Higher Education Funding Model: Choices and Alternatives

The need for reform was recognised by all Lithuanian political parties,[9] by the Lithuanian University Rectors' Conference, together with the Lithuanian Confederation of Industrialists,[10] as well as by national student unions.[11]

---

8   Lietuvos parlamentinių politinių partijų susitarimas dėl mokslo ir studijų sistemos pertvarkos principų, http://lms.lt/archyvas/?q=lt/node/556 (as of 4 June 2015).

9   Ibid.

10   Romualdas Ginevičius and Rimas Varkulevičius, "Lietuvos universitetų rektorių konferencijos ir Lietuvos pramonininkų konfederacijos pareiškimas dėl Lietuvos aukštojo mokslo reformos pagrindų", http://lzinios.lt/lzinios/Ekonomika/lietuvos -universitetu-rektoriu-konferencijos-ir-lietuvos-pramonininku-konfederacijos-pareis kimas-del-lietuvos-aukstojo-mokslo-reformos-pagrindu/113943 (as of 4 June 2015).

11   Rimantas Uknevičius, "Aukštojo mokslo reforma studentų atstovų akimis", http://naujienos.vu.lt/komentarai/aukstojo-mokslo-reforma-studentu-atstovu-ak imis/ (as of 4 June 2015).

However the question of which model of higher education finance to implement has resulted in widely differing opinions; hence this issue has become an object of sharp political and ideological debate within political and academic circles.

As this debate developed, the trends and challenges emerging within higher education globally came to the fore. It was acknowledged that higher education functions as an important growth factor in terms of the national economy, and that it contributes considerably to the personal well-being of the population and to public welfare.[12] The world-wide massification of higher education, as evidenced by statistics, was also recognised,[13] as was the fact that in many countries governments were unable to increase higher education funding in line with the increase in the number of participants within their resepective higher education systems. In global terms, participation in HE has increased across the board, from the traditional elite model (<15% of participants), to a mass (15–50%), or even universal (>50%) model (as defined by the M. Throw classification).[14]

Following the massification of higher education, the Committee of Ministers of the Council of Europe have drawn up recommendations for the governments of member states regarding access to higher education,[15] which

---

12　On the impact of higher education on economic growth, and its personal and public benefits see, for instance, Gary Becker, *Human Capital* (Chicago: University of Chicago Press, 1964); Mary Jean Bowman, "Schultz, Denison, and the Contribution of 'Eds' to National Income Growth", *Journal of Political Economy* 72:5 (1964), http://www.jstor.org/stable/1828479?seq=1#page_scan_tab_contents (as of 25 June 2015).

13　See http://epp.eurostat.ec.europa.eu/tgm/table.do?tab=tableandinit=1andlanguage=enandpcode=tps00062andplugin=1 (as of 4 June 2015).

14　Maureen Woodhall, "Funding Higher Education: The Contribution of Economic Thinking to Debate and Policy Development" (Washington, D.C.: World Bank, Education Working Paper Series, No. 8, 2007), http://siteresources.worldbank.org/EDUCATION/Resources/2782001099079877269/547664-1099079956815/Funding_HigherEd_wps8.pdf (as of 26 June 2005).

15　Council of Europe Recommendations R(98)3, http://www.coe.int/t/dg4/higher education/resources/access%20to%20higher%20education_recommendation.pdf (as of 7 June 2015).

outline the principles of fair and equal access to HE, as well as addressing the issue of the finance of higher education systems across the European Union. It is recommended that financial support per student should be differentiated according to need, and that fees in general should be reasonable in level, and uniform across the public system. Eventually different countries have implemented higher education funding systems in ways which reflect their respective broader socio-economic policy positions, not always complying with the Council of Europe Recommendations (e.g., Lithuania). Analysing the higher education policies of economically advanced countries, Ben Ansell[16] has identified three predominant types of higher education system and funding models: (1) *the Anglo-American model* — which results in a mass participation, partially privatised, and publicly inexpensive system (as in the United States, United Kingdom and South Korea); (2) *the Continental model* — which results in an elite, fully public, and inexpensive system (as in Germany or the Netherlands); (3) *the Scandinavian model* — which results in a mass participation, fully public, but highly expensive system (as in the Scandinavian countries, which have strong social democratic traditions). In his subsequent works, Ansell referred to the Anglo-American model as 'Partially Private', the Continental model as 'Elite', and the Scandinavian model as 'Mass Public'.[17]

Beyond Europe, countries that have followed the path of massification of higher education (i.e. moving from the Elite model to the Mass model) have faced the challenge of how to reform their respective systems of higher education funding, and have experienced a two-sided pressure — that of a growing number of participants within HE against a limited budget. In practice these countries have had two possible choices: (1) to apply the Scandinavian model of Mass Public higher education, which results in higher

16 Ben Ansell, "University Challenges: The Trilemma of Higher Education Policy in Advanced Industrial States" (2006), http://research.allacademic.com/meta/p_mla_apa_research_citation/1/4/0/5/3/p140531_index.html (as of 21 June 2015).
17 Ben Ansell, "University Challenges: Explaining Institutional Change in Higher Education", *World Politics* 60:2 (2008): 189–230, http://www.yale.edu/leitner/resources/docs/ansell.pdf (as of 21 June 2015).

budgetary expenditure on higher education, mostly at the expense of spending reductions in other areas; or (2) to apply the Anglo-American model of Partially Private higher education, which implies a partial privatisation of higher education and the direct collection of tuition fees from students. The decision as to which of these two funding models to apply — whether HE should be fully financed from the state budget, or whether it should be partially financed by students paying tuition fees, and only partially funded by the state — has been predicated in practice upon wider debates regarding the issue of who it is that benefits most from higher education: whether it is the student, the state, or partly the student and partly the state. It has been the resultant understanding of whom the principal beneficiary of higher education is that determines the eventual selection of a particular higher education funding model.

Who Should Pay for Higher Education and Why?

Personal benefits: that there is a correspondence between personal earning power, and the level of educational attainment, is unequivocally indicated by statistics, both within the United States[18] and the United Kingdom,[19] and is further attested to by numerous scientific papers.[20]

Non-personal benefits: the recent massification of higher education across the world has been premised upon claims by social scientists to the

---

18 US Department of Commerce, Economics and Statistics Administration, "The Big Payoff: Educational Attainment and Synthetic Estimates of Work-Life Earnings" (2002), http://www.census.gov/prod/2002pubs/p23-210.pdf (as of 30 June 2015).

19 The National Committee of Inquiry into UK Higher Education, "The Dearing Report" (1997), http://www.leeds.ac.uk/educol/ncihe/nr_001.htm (as of 28 June 2015).

20 E.g. Zvi Griliches, "Education, Human Capital and Growth: A Personal Perspective", *Journal of Labor Economics* 15:1 (1997): 330–344, http://www.jstor.org/stable/2535410 (as of 23 June 2015); Barbara Sianesi and John Van Reen, "The Returns to Education: A Review of the Empirical Macro-Economic Literature", The Institute for Fiscal Studies, WP02/05 (2002), http://www.ifs.org.uk/wps/wp0205.pdf (as of 23 June 2015); Barbara Sianesi, "Returns to Education: A Non-Technical Summary of CEE Work and Policy Discussion" (2003), http://www.ifs.org.uk/docs/cee_summ.pdf (as of 23 June 2015).

effect that higher education contributes to economic growth.[21] However, as Alison Wolf has noted, the fact that human capital is of critical importance to modern economies does not necessarily imply that all and any forms of educational 'input' will necessarily result in increased economic 'output'. The relationship between 'input' and 'output' as regards this area of educational policy is crucially dependent upon the way in which the links between education and economic growth have been measured and analysed.[22]

Measuring the impact of higher education upon the individual and the country solely by reference to economic indicators would imply a very narrow and pecuniary approach, one which would tend to neglect or overlook those wider personal or social benefits which might accrue from higher education. Thus, according to Andrew Weiss,[23] better-educated workers have lower propensities to quit work or to be absent, are less likely to smoke, drink or use illicit drugs, and are generally healthier. Jonathan Temple[24] notes that the wider benefits of higher education can include positive effects as regards public health, crime rates, the environment, parenting, and levels of political and community participation. Grant Johnston[25] argues that increases in overall levels of educational attainment result in reductions in cigarette smoking, and in a demonstrable lessening of

---

21 Ben Ansell, "University Challenges: The Trilemma of Higher Education Policy".

22 Alison Wolf, "Education and Economic Performance: Simplistic Theories and Their Policy Consequences", *Oxford Review of Economic Policy* 20:2 (2004): http://oxrep.oxfordjournals.org/content/20/2/315.full.pdf+html (as of 25 June 2015).

23 Andrew Weiss, "Human Capital vs. Signalling Explanations of Wages", *The Journal of Economic Perspective* 9:4 (1995): 133–154, http://people.terry.uga.edu/mustard/courses/e4850/R-Weiss.pdf (as of 25 June 2015).

24 Jonathan Temple, "Growth Effects of Education and Social Capital in the OECD Countries" (2001), http://www.oecd.org/edu/innovation-education/1825293.pdf (as of 15 June 2015).

25 Grant Johnston, "Healthy, Wealthy and Wise? A Review of the Wider Benefits of Education", New Zealand Treasury Working Paper (2004), http://unpan1.un.org/intradoc/groups/public/documents/APCITY/UNPAN017821.pdf (as of 15 June 2015).

psychological anxiety and anti-social disorders, and in measurable reductions in rates of suicide, crime, teenage pregnancies, unemployment, and reliance on welfare benefits. Nicholas Barr[26] offers an additional argument with respect to the wider social benefits of higher education. He argues that if education increases a person's future earnings, it also thereby increases the level of his or her future tax contributions. Thus investment in education in effect confers a 'dividend' upon future taxpayers. Further positive social effects of higher education are described by Barbara Wolfe and Robert Haveman.[27]

The above arguments make it clear that both the person and the state benefit from higher education: therefore the assertion that *both* students *and* the state should share the cost of higher education — as with the Anglo-American (Partially Private) model of higher education finance — would seem to gain traction. However in fact these arguments are not sufficient in themselves to favour the Anglo-American (Partially Private) model, since in the case of the Scandinavian model students and their relatives also participate in financing higher education through the tax system. Taxes are paid by working parents, and will be paid by graduates once they will start work; while, given that higher education increases a graduate's eventual earnings, it thereby also increases the eventual tax contributions of HE graduates. However, there are arguments which do favour the implementation of the Anglo-American model, for example:

---

26 Nicholas Barr, "The Benefits of Education: What We Know and What We Don't" (2001), http://www.researchgate.net/publication/242458843_The_benefits_of_edu cation_What_we_know_and_what_we_don't (as of 9 June 2015).

27 Barbara Wolfe and Robert Haveman, "Accounting for the Social and Non-Market Benefits of Education" (2000), http://www.oecd.org/innovation/research/18251 09.pdf (as of 15 June 2015).

Responsible selection of programmes of study. As noted by George Psacharopoulos,[28] student loans encourage students to make more prudent choices with respect to the subjects that they study.

Limited national budget. It is difficult to ensure free higher education in countries that experience a limited tax return due to a reduced tax rate, or the existence of a shadow economy. According to D. Bruce Johnstone,[29] low-income countries, and those in transition from command to market-driven economies, experience a diminution in available public (taxpayer-based) revenue. This diminution may, in turn, be a result either of inherent difficulties with regards to tax gathering, or of competition from other, oftentimes more politically compelling, public needs (or a combination of both).

Emigration. In each instance where a graduate emigrates from the country which has provided his or her free higher education, the public investment which has been made is, in effect, wasted given that the state does not receive any tangible return on that investment. This factor has been particularly important to Lithuania, in light of its considerable emigration flows.[30]

The above arguments would seem to speak in favour of higher education funding based upon the Anglo-American model: however it is important to

---

28 George Psacharopoulos, "Why Some University Systems are Collapsing: Realities from Europe" (paper presented at the ACA conference, "The Future of the University", Vienna, 30 November-December 2005), http://www.sci.ccny.cuny.edu /~themis/greekuniversityreform/psach.pdf (as of 15 June 2015).

29 D. Bruce Johnstone, "Cost Sharing in Higher Education: Tuition, Financial Assistance, and Accessibility in a Comparative Perspective", *Czech Sociological Review* 39:3 (2003): 351–374, http://sreview.soc.cas.cz/uploads/fb12ec3edf90cf183643fe7651da107f1d5 dfd11_288_34john32.pdf (as of 21 June 2015).

30 See Ona Gražina Rakauskienė and Olga Ranceva, "Strengths of Emigration from Lithuania: Demographic, Social and Economic Consequences", *Intellectual Economics* 6:2 (2012): 89–101, https://www.mruni.eu/upload/iblock/f14/008_rakauskiene_ ranceva.pdf (as on 6 June 2015).

note that this model can be applied in a number of very different ways—
some more, and some less, socially responsible.

Anglo-American Model, or English versus American?

As was mentioned above, the partial privatisation of higher education,
combined with the direct collection of tuition fees from students, was dubbed
by Ansell as the 'Anglo-American model', and was subsequently referred to
as the 'Partially Private' model. However, such a classification is
insufficiently precise, as the sole similarity between the English and
American models of higher education finance which is alluded to by these
characterisations—whereby the Anglo-American model implies a partially
privatised higher education system—cannot erase the fundamental and
conceptual differences between the English and American models: such that
it would be more objective to further sub-divide the Anglo-American model
into English and American models respectively.

According to Barr,[31] the American system of higher education finance
shows the ill-effects of under-regulated markets, and the consequences of
insufficient strategic planning; however this cannot in itself serve as an
argument against well-regulated markets implemented as part of an explicit
strategy. A successful example of a well-regulated market, according to
Barr,[32] is the English model of higher education finance. Since 1998, the UK
has implemented a system of income-contingent student loans, with
repayments collected by the income-tax authorities. In summary, the English
model functions as follows: individual universities each set their own fees,

31 Nicholas Barr, "Markets in Higher Education: The Good, the Bad and the Avoidably
Ugly", (paper resented at the conference on the "Operation of the Market in Higher
Education: Opportunities and Constraints, Experience and Ideology", London, 14
January 2008), http://www.hepi.ac.uk/wpcontent/uploads/2014/03/Marketsin
HigherEducation-NickBarr.pdf (as of 9 June 2015).
32 Nicholas Barr, "Financing Higher Education for Quality and Access" (paper
presented at the conference "White Paper and Beyond: Tertiary Education Reform"
(Prague, 16–17 October 2009), http://citeseerx.ist.psu.edu/viewdoc/download?doi
=10.1.1.175.8037andrep=rep1andtype=pdf (as of 9 June 2015).

but these cannot exceed a fee cap, which is decreed by government (before 2012 this was set at GBP 3,000 per year; after 2012 this cap rose to GBP 9,000 per year). So, in effect, a system of state loans guarantees free higher education during the period of undergraduate studies, with repayments being recouped subsequently, once each graduate exceeds a given earnings threshold. Thus, in practice, student loans are repaid as an additional 9% income tax levy only by those graduates whose earnings exceed an amount set by the government (before 2012 this earnings threshold was set at GBP 15,000 per year; after 2012 it rose to GBP 21,000 per year) – hence students do not in practice have to rely upon parental contributions in order to fund their studies. After a period of 25 years, any unpaid portion of the overall loan amount is written off. As Barr further notes,[33] there is a key distinction implicit within this model between upfront fees and deferred fees. The latter promote quality by bringing in additional resources, while the freedom of universities to set the former serves to increase competition and to promote quality by enhancing efficiency, diversity, and choice.

Within the terms of the English model of higher education finance, the higher the fees which are initially set by universities, the greater the funds that will eventually accrue to the state from those well-paid graduates who will have benefited the most from their higher education. Thus, the English higher education funding model might be said to essentially embody a consistently applied *progressive* taxation system, whereby higher earning graduates pay a higher rate of state income tax, which can then, potentially, be available for socially progressive redistribution. By linking student loans with future earnings, the British have, in effect adapted Milton Friedman's[34] ideas with respect to the notion of the state 'buying a share' in an individual's eventual earning prospects. While Friedman envisages this primarily as a

---

33 Ibid.
34 Milton Friedman, *Capitalism and Freedom* (Chicago: University of Chicago Press, 1961), 75–90, esp. 88–90, http://www.pdf-archive.com/2011/12/28/friedman-milton-capitalism-and-freedom/friedman-milton-capitalism-and-freedom.pdf (as of 3 June 2015).

means to do business and to make a profit, the British have not turned their higher education finance model into a profit-making enterprise as such; rather the English funding model was crafted according to the nostrums of a well regulated market, but with an overriding focus on issues concerning equity and fair access to higher education.

The incorporation of private funding into the costs of state-provided higher education has proven to be a very popular idea as far as Lithuanian reformers of higher education are concerned,[35] while, as argued above, such a process could potentially have been implemented in a variety of ways, some of which would have been more, and some less, socially responsible in nature.

Section Summary

An appreciation of who stands to be the principal beneficiary of higher education — the individual, the state, or both — helps in the selection of a particular higher education funding model. However, the eventual choice of a higher education funding model — Mass Public or Partially Private — largely depends upon a given country's prevailing political and economic ideologies, which have a direct impact upon the policy model which is chosen. Hence some instances of the application of the Partially Private model may prove to be more socially equitable (i.e. England), and some less (as in the US).

4. The Neoliberal Model of Higher Education Funding in Post-Communist Lithuania: Distinctive Features and Effects of Its Application

The developers of the Lithuanian policy with respect to higher education funding were engaged in a process of choosing not only which particular model to implement — Mass Public, Elite or Partially Private — but also the

---

35 Lietuvos parlamentinių politinių partijų susitarimas dėl mokslo ir studijų sistemos pertvarkos principų (2007), http://lms.lt/archyvas/?q=lt/node/556 (as of 4 June 2015).

actual means by which the selected model would be applied in practice. Since elections were won by the Conservative Party, which has since formed the ruling majority of the Seimas of the Republic of Lithuania (i.e. the unicameral Lithuanian parliament) together with the Liberal Parties,[36] these parties have acquired the legal authority to implement the reform of higher education funding on the basis of their own intrinsic—neoliberal—beliefs in a "free market" ideology. They have, accordingly, rejected alternative reform models, such as those which have been proposed by groups within the academic community,[37] or by oppositional parliamentarians.[38] On 30 April 2009 a new Law on Higher Education and Research[39] (LHER) was passed. It was framed according to the policymakers' understanding of the constitutional doctrine on higher education, which had previously been developed by the Constitutional Court of the Republic of Lithuania (CC) in its numerous rulings on this subject.

The Lithuanian Constitution, 'Good Students' and the Guarantee of a Free Education

As is stated in the 3rd part of the 41st article of Constitution of the Republic of Lithuania,[40] "Higher education shall be accessible to everyone according to his individual abilities. Citizens who are good at their studies shall be guaranteed education at State schools of higher education free of charge". As we see here, the first sentence defines the conditions of access to higher

---

36 Seimas of the Republic of Lithuania "X Seimas (2008–2012)", http://www3.lrs.lt/pls/inter/w5_show?p_r=6111andp_k=1 (as of 15 June 2015).
37 Lietuvos akademinės bendruomenės narių Kreipimasis dėl aukštojo mokslo reformos (2008), http://www.balsas.lt/naujiena/179149/lietuvos-akademines-bendruomenes-nariu-kreipimasis-del-aukstojo-mokslo-reformos (as of 15 June 2015).
38 Lietuvos Respublikos Švietimo ir Mokslo Ministerijos projektas "Lietuvos Respublikos Mokslo ir Studijų Įstatymas" (2008), http://www3.lrs.lt/pls/inter3/dokpaieska.showdoc_l?p_id=316047.
39 Republic of Lithuania: Law on Higher Education and Research (2009), http://www3.lrs.lt/pls/inter3/dokpaieska.showdoc_l?p_id=478933 (as of 15 June 2015).
40 Constitution of the Republic of Lithuania (1992), http://www3.lrs.lt/home/Konstitucija/Constitution.htm (as of 3 June 2015).

education—individual academic ability—which in turn must imply that no other factors—such as wealth or social status, race, ethnicity and so on—can be permitted to restrict such access. The second sentence defines the conditions under which a free higher education in the State schools is guaranteed: one must be good at one's studies. This particular provision of the Constitution has subsequently become the subject of controversy and of numerous debates since it explicitly links a free higher education in State schools to the condition of being a 'good student'. Free higher education as such is easy to define: it is an education funded from the State budget, which is drawn from taxpayers' money. However the practical definition of the term 'good student' is harder to establish. According to Bronislavas Genzelis and Vytenis Andriukaitis,[41] former members of a commission formed to prepare a draft of the Lithuanian Constitution, the term 'good students' was clearly understood by the members of that commission as meaning those students who passed all of their examinations on schedule.

At the time of the preparation of this draft of the Constitution, the prevailing higher education model within Lithuania was the Continental (or Elite) model, whereby only the very best applicants were admitted to the high schools. This in turn meant that, since the overall number of students was relatively small, such public funding as was provided was sufficient to cover the cost of the tuition of all HE students (while at this time the exact definition of the phrase 'good students' was not subject to question). However once the State had re-established its independence, the number of students enrolled in the high schools rapidly increased four-fold, and thus high schools began to experience shortages of state funding. This in turn led to attempts to re-interpret the (now contested) term 'good students', and to debates concerning the possibilities for the continued provision of free higher education. Higher education funding in Lithuania depends upon the implementation of higher education law as enacted by the Seimas. The Constitutional Court (CC) then rules as to whether or not the laws passed by

---

41 Bronislovas Genzelis and Vytenis Andriukaitis, private interview (2009).

the Seimas are in conflict with the Constitution. By means of its rulings in this respect, the CC thereby develops a body of constitutional doctrine with regard to the overall provision of higher education, which the Seimas is obliged to follow and to take into account whilst preparing draft laws.

The concept of the 'good student', and the guarantee of free higher education which had been related to that concept, had changed several times before the LHER was passed. It changed according to new rulings by the CC, which had added new meanings to the constitutional doctrine on higher education. Before 2008, 'good students' had been considered to be the most able 30% of each study programme cohort, on each semester, while, after 2008, 'good students' were defined as being those who had not failed any examinations or course credits, and whose overall average subject assessment across a given semester was at least 8 on a 10-point assessment scale. Henceforth those students whose academic performance did not comply with the new 'good student' criteria had to pay the HE institution in question a tuition fee equal to the amount of 4 minimum standards of living units fixed by legal acts (approximately EUR 150 per semester). Meanwhile, part-time students at state high schools had to pay the full price of their studies, as did those who were studying at private high schools.

Here follows a summary of higher education finance regulations in terms of the Constitutional Court's ruling, as established before the LHER:[42]

> State schools of higher education independently establish the price of particular programmes of study; meanwhile the State determines existing and future demands as regards the numbers of graduates from within respective disciplinary areas, as related to projected social trends and likely demands. The State then allocates funds from within the central State budget so as to meet its projected State order based on future requirements with respect to numbers of graduate specialists from within specified disciplinary fields. The State thus guarantees higher education free of charge in State schools only to those 'good students', who study on the basis of the State order.

42   The Constitutional Court of the Republic of Lithuania Ruling: On the Number of Students and Their Financing in State Schools of Higher Education (20 March 2008), http://www.lrkt.lt/en/court-acts/search/170/ta1368/content (as of 8 June 2015).

Meanwhile the criterion of 'good learning' must be defined in law, and it must be known in advance. It cannot contradict the ordinary definition of the word 'good' as is generally understood and recognised; it must be clear, transparent and reasonable; and it cannot be expressed as either an absolute or a relative measure (i.e. a quota). Those persons who do not meet the criteria for free HE as defined above may seek higher education according to their abilities—but *not* at the expense of the State—both in State and/or non-State higher education schools. Non-State higher education schools may receive State-funded student places only in cases where sufficient numbers of specialists in State-designated disciplinary areas, as defined above, cannot be taught in State schools of higher education due to extenuating circumstances. The system of student loans and student support should be efficient and reliable.

As we can see from the above, the CC has effectively divided HE students into two distinct categories: those students who satisfy the demands of projected disciplinary specialists as established by the state and who therefore have the right to receive free higher education (assuming that they also meet the 'good student' criteria), and those who exceed this demand (so called *surplus people*) and who therefore must pay for their higher education as set by the HE school in question. According to the CC, non-state higher education schools may receive state-funded student places only in cases when specialists of the state-designated areas of future disciplinary demand cannot be trained in state schools of higher education. Thus non-state higher education schools cannot compete directly with state schools of higher education on the same terms.

As a result of this CC ruling, various additional questions and doubts necessarily arise. Firstly, the mission and purpose of the higher education system as a whole is narrowed to the apparatus which serves the state in preparing professionals in specified fields which the state has itself defined as being of utilitarian value to its own future demands. Secondly, prescribing an exact demand number of future professionals was implicit in a planned economy; however, under the conditions of a market economy, and given the global movement of citizens, such an exact prescription is no longer possible. Any specialist so trained by means of a state-funded HE place may now go to live and work abroad if he or she so chooses; in such instances the state's investment in the training of that specialist would in effect be wasted.

Thirdly, in cases when a specialist trained by means of a state-funded student place chooses *not* to work according to that speciality after graduation, the argument for that state funding becomes moot. Conversely, a non-state-funded graduate who may subsequently come to work within an area defined by the state as meriting state funding might well resent the fact that he or she was initially required to fund his or her own undergraduate studies. Fourthly, all graduates—those whose studies were funded by the state, and those who had to pay fees—will eventually find themselves paying taxes to the state. This has clear implications with regard both to social, and indeed natural, justice given that tax-payers' money was used to fund the studies of some of those now tax-paying graduates, whereas others had no such recourse during their studies.

With regard to these issues, Dennis Farrington[43] has criticised the practice of new member states of the Council of Europe (the countries of the former Soviet Union and other central and Eastern European states, such as Lithuania) in selecting students for entry to higher education on the basis of what amounts to a form of manpower planning. Such planning—which Farrington has termed "state orders for specialists"—has led within these countries to a highly regulated, restrictive curriculum, and to a concentration on the obligations, rather than the rights, of students. In addition to this, Farrington has been critical with regard to the implementation of 'fees-only' student places in addition to those subsidised by the state. As he says: "the result [of this] is a two-tier system in which students compete for an arguably inadequate number of state-subsidised free places", and who, "failing to secure one of those, can then compete for entry at market-level fees to an additional quotas of places which the institution is licensed to offer".[44] As Farrington further notes, such a "procedure has been criticised as unfair and

---

43 Dennis Farrington, "A Study of Student-Institution Relationships in Selected Member States of the Council of Europe", *Responding to Student Expectations* (Paris: OECD, 2002): 115-131, http://www.edra.gr/pdf/8902041E-OECD.pdf (as of 7 June 2015).
44 Ibid.

inefficient by the Council of Europe and the OECD. In doing so, two principles have been formulated: that equal access requires financial support differentiated according to the need", and that, "any fees should be partial, reasonable in level, and uniform across the public system. These norms are explicit in Council of Europe Recommendations R(98)3".[45]

The draft of the LHER, which has been prepared by the ruling majority of the Lithuanian Seimas, has been crafted so as to not only bypass the above mentioned recommendations, but also to explicitly apply those rulings of the CC such as are in accordance with the prevailing ideological concepts and ideas of Conservative and Liberal parties. As Petras Ragauskas[46] notes, according to its institutional mission, the CC plays the role of guardian by supervising the compliance of the legislative process with the provisions of the Constitution. The formal participation of the CC in the legislative process is thereby expressed in its rulings, and the adoption of those rulings has a direct influence upon the legislative process. However, the CC evaluates only existing laws, as opposed to draft laws, and it thus does not perform any preventative control over the constitution.

After the LHER had been passed, new rulings of the CC were promulgated in 2011,[47] and in 2014,[48] which concluded that some LHER paragraphs are indeed in conflict with the Constitution of Lithuania. As a result of this, *some* paragraphs of the LHER have thus far been amended, and

45 Ibid.
46 Petras Ragauskas, "Konstitucinio Teismo vaidmuo įstatymų leidyboje", *Teisės problemos* 43 (2004): 8–54, ISSN 1392–1592.
47 The Constitutional Court of the Republic of Lithuania Ruling: On the Law on Science and Studies (22 December 2011), http://www.lrkt.lt/en/courtacts/search/170/ta1116/content (as of 3 June 2015).
48 The Constitutional Court of the Republic of Lithuania Ruling: On the Formation of the Council of a School of Higher Education and on Funding Studies (10 November 2014), http://www.lrkt.lt/en/court-acts/search/170/ta881/content (as of 3 June 2015).

the rest will need to be amended in the near future.[49] Here follows a summary of the higher education finance regulations within the LHER, based on the rulings of the Constitutional Court:

> The cost of a given programme of studies is fixed by the higher education institution concerned. The cost of higher education studies which are charged to persons who study in student places which are not funded by the State, may include additional expenses. The Ministry of Education calculates the normative cost of studies. The State pays the normative cost of studies of those students who study in State-funded student places, from central budget funds. In cases where the cost of studies fixed by a higher education institution is lower than the normative cost of those studies, the State pays the cost of the studies as set by the higher education institution. Each year the government determines the distribution of State funding between respective disciplinary areas, taking into account the requirements of national economic, social and cultural development, and the financial capacities of the State. The Ministry of Education and Science sets a preliminary number of State-funded student places within each disciplinary area. A ranking list of the persons who have completed a secondary education program with the best results is then drawn up. State-funded student places, within each selected disciplinary area, are then allocated to particular higher education institutions, in accordance with the overall preferences made by suitably qualified applicant students (those from the ranking list above), provided that the overall State funding which has been established for each study area is not exceeded. A person whose studies are funded by the State shall lose State funding for his or her studies if the mean of his or her overall study results falls to more than 20% below the mean of the study results of all students studying at the same study program, form, year and higher education institution during a given period[50] (the 20% formula). A person who thus loses State funding must then pay a tuition fee fixed by the higher education institution in question for his or her studies; while his or her State-funded HE place will then be taken up by a suitably qualified student who had hitherto been obliged to pay for his or her studies. A person whose studies are funded by the State has the right to change a study program *within the same disciplinary area*, without relinquishing the remaining portion of State funding. Students whose studies are not funded by the State must pay the full cost of their studies, as set by the higher

---

49 Notably, while new CC rulings have stated that some LHER paragraphs are in conflict with the Constitution of Lithuania, the HE finance model contained within LHER does not have to be changed by parliamentarians (even though this is desirable and possible from the viewpoint of equal and fair access to higher education for all prospective students); rather, it is enough for them to enact a few cosmetic changes, at least until a new ruling of CC is released.

50 Republic of Lithuania: Law on Higher Education and Research, par. 70.7 (2009), http://www3.lrs.lt/pls/inter3/dokpaieska.showdoc_l?p_id=478933 (as of 15 June 2015).

education institution at which they choose to study. Students may receive State-supported bank loans to pay their tuition fee, to cover living expenses, and to pay partial studies pursuant to international agreements.

Problematic Issues and Consequences of the Higher Education Funding Reform

The legislators of the LHER had hoped that the implementation of a new model of funding for HEIs, based on free market principles, would stimulate competition between institutions for the best students, would increase the quality of studies, and would eventually lead to the elimination of poor quality study programmes. Furthermore, they hoped that this would lead eventually to a reduction in the number of higher education institutions as such, i.e. as market forces took hold, and poorly performing institutions suffered reputational damage, with a consequent loss of enrolments. However, practice has shown that higher education institutions which do thus suffer a loss of enrolments have adapted to the market, and are in fact able to survive by reducing the cost price of their study programmes. Hence the model of higher education finance as implemented has not been effective in achieving its objectives. Without any relevant changes in terms of policy, the number of higher education institutions may in fact only decrease in the future as a consequence of the forthcoming demographic deficit in childbirth[51] and high rates of emigration.[52]

It is important to note that the chosen model of higher education finance within Lithuania was introduced to the public as being an innovative model based on free market principles, however, as implemented, it does not

---

51 Juris Krumins, "Demographic challenges for societies on the Eastern shore of Baltic Sea", http://www.sh.se/p3/ext/res.nsf/vRes/cbees_engelsk_1412582982411_juris _krumins_pdf/$File/juris_krumins.pdf (as of 7 June 2015).

52 Ona Gražina Rakauskienė and Olga Ranceva, "Strengths of Emigration from Lithuania: Demographic, Social and Economic Consequences", *Intellectual Economics* 6:2 (2012), https://www.mruni.eu/upload/iblock/f14/008_rakauskiene_ranceva. pdf (as on 6 June 2015).

comply with the ideas of Milton Friedman,[53] the progenitor of free-market economic theory. According to Friedman, it is intrinsically difficult to correctly calculate the optimum amount of state investment per individual, and any attempt to do so necessarily involves rationing, in an essentially arbitrary way, the restricted amount of available state finance amongst more claimants than can be adequately financed. Thus, those fortunate enough to receive state funding for their training receive all of the returns from the investment made by the state, whereas the costs are borne by taxpayers in general. This results in an entirely arbitrary, and almost surely perverse, redistribution of income. Hence Friedman's advice is rather "for government to engage in equity investment in human beings",[54] and to finance the training of any individual who meets minimum quality standards.[55]

Three main problematic issues arise as a result of the higher education finance model embodied within the LHER. First, students not funded by the state must pay the full cost of their studies as set by the higher education institution — which can be higher than the amount normally provided by the government for the studies of state-funded students. Since prices of different study programmes vary from about EUR 1,250[56] to EUR 11,600[57] per

53 Milton Friedman, *Capitalism and Freedom* (Chicago: University of Chicago Press, 1961), 88–89, http://www.pdf-archive.com/2011/12/28/friedman-milton-capita lism-and-freedom/friedman-milton-capitalism-and-freedom.pdf (as of 3 June 2015).
54 Ibid., 89.
55 Milton Freedman discusses these ideas in a chapter entitled "The Role of Government in Education" — and in the immediate context of a section called "Vocational and Professional Schooling" (which follows one called "Schooling at College and University Level"). His argument can be applied to colleges and universities alike, since he discusses ways of financing the training of individuals at post-secondary level generally, whether at the professional or at the higher education level.
56 See Vilnius University, "Tuition Fees for Undergraduate (Bachelor) Studies (2015)", http://www.vu.lt/kviecia/images/priemimas_2015/I_pakopos_studiju_programo s_VU_2015.pdf (as of 13 June 2015).
57 See Vilnius Gediminas Technical University, "Tuition Fees for Undergraduate (Bachelor) Studies (2015)", http://ti.vgtu.lt/fakultetai/studijos/bakalauro-studijos/ studiju-kaina/63295 (as of 13 June 2015).

academic year, access to higher education does not depend purely upon a given student's academic ability. Rather, access is conditioned by her or his ability either to incur the full cost of the study programme in question, or to incur the risk of being indebted to a bank. This does not comply with the Council of Europe Recommendations on the issue of fair and equal access to higher education.[58] Second, the 20% formula as set out in the LHER (see above) guarantees free education to state-funded students throughout their whole study period, even in cases where their study results may be significantly lower than the results of the best performing students amongst their non-state-funded counterparts. The consequences can be demonstrated by the following thought experiment. Let us assume that there are ten students enrolled in one study programme: five of them state-funded, and the other five paying the full cost of their studies. Assuming that, after assessment, the mean grades among the five state-funded students are 7, 7, 7, 7, 7, while the mean grades among the five paying for the full cost for their education are 10, 10, 9, 9, 9 — then the total mean of all the students' grades would be 8.2. If we now apply the 20% formula, we can see that — despite their poorer academic results (7 versus 9 and 10) — all of the state-funded students will retain their state-funded education, because their study results do not fall to more than 20% below the mean of the study results of all students enrolled on the same study programme. This thought experiment shows that fair and equal access to university education was not foremost amongst the priorities of the former Seimas; the priority was rather to secure state funding for the higher education of those completing their secondary

---

58 Council of Europe Recommendations, R(98)3, http://www.coe.int/t/dg4/higher education/resources/access%20to%20higher%20education_recommendation.pdf (as of 7 June 2015).

education with the best results.[59] Various studies[60] have shown that there has been a direct correlation between children's social background and their school performance; thus the allocation of state funding for HE exclusively to those who have completed secondary education with the best academic results will in practice mean that such funding will go disproportionately to the children of wealthy parents (who can afford to hire private tutors for their children). Therefore, in effect, the less well-off pay for the higher education of the more wealthy. Third, the state-supported student bank loan system is unfavourable to poorer students due to the inflexibility of loan repayments, which are taken out on purely commercial terms. On these terms, repayment begins immediately after graduation, can only be deferred in cases of low income, and may not be deferred at all if the student continues their studies at the same or at a higher level.[61]

According to a European Commission paper on national student fee and support systems in European higher education,[62] Lithuania is amongst those countries which have the highest fees. But this need not be the case. Even though the CC has narrowed the meaning of the term 'good students', and accordingly has restricted access to free higher education, there is still latitude remaining for Lithuanian politicians to further reform the

59 The 20% formula was recognised as being in conflict with the Constitution of Lithuania in a CC ruling announced on 10 November 2014 – and thus will have to be changed in the near future (hopefully in the Autumn of 2016).

60 See Rita Asplund et al., "An Equity Perspective on Access to, Enrolment in and Finance of Tertiary Education", http://www.etla.fi/wpcontent/uploads/2012/09/dp1098.pdf (as of 4 June 2015); George Psacharopoulos, "Why Some University Systems are Collapsing: Realities from Europe", http://www.sci.ccny.cuny.edu/~themis/greekuniversityreform/psach.pdf (as of 4 June 2015); Rimantas Želvys et al., Švietimo politika ir monitoringas (Vilnius: Garnelis, 2003).

61 National Audit Office of Lithuania: Public Audit Report on Study Loan Scheme (2014), https://www.vkontrole.lt/pranesimas_spaudai_en.aspx?id=18029 (as of 7 June 2015).

62 European Commission: National Student Fee and Support Systems in European Higher Education (2014/15), http://eacea.ec.europa.eu/education/eurydice/documents/facts_and_figures/fees_support.pdf (as of 12 June 2015).

Lithuanian higher education finance system so as to retain quality, whilst ensuring equal access to HE for all qualified prospective students – as will be shown with the recommendations presented below.

Recommendations Regarding Further Reform of Higher Education Finance in Lithuania

Whilst acknowledging that the State must guarantee higher education in state schools free of charge only to those 'good students' who are deemed to satisfy the established demand for specialists in selected academic areas, the CC has also stated that "the State [...] may choose and establish in laws various models of financing of higher education".[63] Thus, taking into account all CC rulings on higher education finance, Council of Europe Recommendations R(98)3, which outline the principles of fair and equal access to HE, and examples of higher education finance policies as implemented across economically advanced and socially responsible countries, it is recommended to reform the existing Lithuanian higher education funding model in accordance with one of two proposed scenarios: either to implement the English model of higher education finance, adapting it to Lithuania's particular circumstances, or else to apply flat, uniform, reasonable and partial tuition fees across the board within Lithuania.

In either of these scenarios it is envisaged that the current system, whereby the state, according to the rulings of the CC, is obliged to fund higher education only for those 'good students' who study on the basis of the state order, would only need to be applied where there is an identifiable shortfall of applicants, such that the state may ensure an adequate future supply of appropriately qualified professionals. In these cases, considering the high emigration rates that Lithuania experiences, in order to protect public investment from being wasted – as occurs in each case where a

---

63 The Constitutional Court of the Republic of Lithuania Ruling: On the Number of Students and Their Financing in State Schools of Higher Education, Ch. II, par. 21 (20 March 2008), http://www.lrkt.lt/en/court-acts/search/170/ta1368/content (as of 8 June 2015).

graduate emigrates – the state could provide free higher education by signing contracts with prospective students, obliging them to work in Lithuania for a set number of years after graduation, under mutually beneficial terms. Thus, state investments would not be wasted, and students would have a guaranteed job after their graduation. In addition to this, it is envisaged that all applicants (notwithstanding State order limits) would be free to choose whether to pursue their studies in state, or non-state, higher education establishments. Thus, a situation of genuinely fair competition between the two sectors would be established.

Section Summary

The rulings of the CC had a decisive influence upon the model of higher education finance which was embodied within the LHER, since it was stated that free higher education in state schools should be granted only to those 'good students' who satisfy a state-defined demand for future specialists within specific disciplinary areas, while all other HE students are required to pay for their education. However, there is still latitude remaining for Lithuanian politicians to reform the country's higher education finance system so as to ensure quality, while at the same time ensuring fair and equal access to HE for all qualified prospective students. Since elections were won by the Conservative Party, who have, together with the Liberal Parties, since formed the ruling majority of the Seimas of the Republic of Lithuania (the unicameral Lithuanian parliament), these parties have gained the legal authority to implement the reform of higher education funding on the basis of their own intrinsic – neoliberal – beliefs in a "free market" ideology, and they have accordingly rejected alternative reform models, such as those proposed by groups within the academic community or by oppositional parliamentarians – proposals which are predicated upon the recognition of the importance of equal and fair access to higher education.

The draft of the LHER was prepared by applying rulings of the CC in accordance with the ideological concepts and ideas of Conservative and Liberal parties. Following the implementation of the LHER in 2009, about half of applicants to HE have exceeded the state quota each year and so must pay the full cost for their higher education (ranging from approx. EUR 1,250 to EUR 11,600 per year, depending on the study programme and the university in question). Thus access to higher education is in practice becoming restricted according to students' ability to pay tuition fees, or their willingness to accept the risk of being indebted to a bank. New rulings of the CC released after 2010 have concluded that some paragraphs of the LHER are in conflict with the Constitution of Lithuania, which needs to be changed accordingly in the near future. In this chapter it is recommended to further reform the Lithuanian higher education funding model in one of two proposed directions: either to implement the English model of higher education finance, adapting it to Lithuania's conditions, or to apply flat, uniform, reasonable and partial tuition fees.

5. Conclusions

The reform of higher education finance in Lithuania was a necessary political action, undertaken in order to address the chaotic expansion of the higher education system as a whole, and to resolve its systemic defects. Reform was also necessary in order to reduce the number of high schools, to optimise existing resources, and to address the deficit of available higher education finance. The rulings of the CC had a decisive influence upon the particular model of higher education finance which was embodied within the LHER, since it was stated that the state will guarantee higher education, free of charge, in state schools only to those 'good students' who satisfy a state-defined demand for future specialists within specific disciplinary areas, while all other HE students will be required to pay for their higher education. Hence, the academic criterion of the 'good student' was transformed into a political instrument which was used by government to restrict the budgetary expense of higher education as such.

Following the implementation of the LHER in 2009, about half of prospective students who have completed secondary education have exceeded the state quota for free HE each year, and have therefore been obliged to pay the full cost of their higher education (varying from about EUR 1,250 to EUR 11,600 per year depending on the study programme and the university). Thus, access to higher education is in effect restricted according to students' ability to pay tuition fees, or to undertake the risk of being indebted to a bank. Since there is a known link between school performance and a child's social background, this de facto allocation of state-funded HE places only to those who have completed the secondary education programme with the best results, effectively means that in most cases state funding has gone to the children of rich parents – and that therefore taxpayers have subsidised the higher education of the rich.

The chosen model of higher education finance was introduced to the Lithuanian public as an innovative model based upon free market principles. However, as enacted, it does not comply either with Friedman's theories regarding the market economy, nor with the Council of Europe Recommendations R(98)3 on equal access. Neither does it accord with existing higher education finance policies as implemented across economically advanced and socially responsible countries. The state-supported student bank loan system is not favourable to students, as it necessarily applies stringent market conditions to the loans which are taken out. After the LHER had been passed into law, subsequent rulings of the CC were promulgated in 2011 and in 2014, which have explicitly stated that certain aspects of the LHER as enacted is in conflict with the Constitution of Lithuania. Some paragraphs of the Constitution will need to be amended in the light of these rulings in the near future. Thus, there is now an opportunity to change the current higher education finance model in order to achieve quality, equity and fair access for all students.

It is recommended to further reform the Lithuanian higher education funding model in the direction of one of the two following proposed scenarios: either to implement the English model of higher education finance, adapting it to Lithuania's conditions, or to apply flat, uniform, reasonable and partial tuition fees across the HE sector within Lithuania. In either instance, it is envisaged that the current practice whereby the State, according to rulings of the CC, is obliged to guarantee higher education free of charge in state schools to those 'good students' who satisfy the state-ordained demand for future specialists within specific disciplinary areas, will only need to be applied where there is an identifiable shortfall of applicants, such that the state may ensure an adequate future supply of appropriately qualified professionals.

Local Global:
Global Society and Higher Education in Hungary

Zoltán Ginelli, Attila Melegh, Sabina Csánova, Emese Baranyi and Rudolf Piroch

1. The Global Contexts of Higher Education

In the current phase of global capitalism, there is an increasing need to provide a global perspective for students in order to understand global mechanisms and the ways local societies are integrated into global processes and structures. Consequently, this has involved a shift in higher education in the midst of an intensifying fight for future employees, jobs and intellectual resources that are not produced in the relevant local community, either connected to a nation state or a bloc like the European Union.[1] In a related process, national educational systems have become more and more dependent on a global educational market, as they are increasingly underfunded, and thus constantly have to find global resources in financing their activities.[2] There has also been also a growing demand for international

---

1   See Ulrich Beck, *What is Globalisation?*, trans. Patrick Camiller (Malden, MA.: Polity, 2000); and Yoni Ryan, "Teaching and Learning in the Global Era", in *The University in the Global Age*, Roger King, ed. (Basingstoke: Palgrave Macmillan, 2004), 164–180.

2   See Stephen J. Ball, "Big Policies/Small World: An Introduction to International Perspectives in Education Policy", *Comparative Education* 34:2 (1998): 119–130; and Nicholas C. Burbules and Carlos Alberto Torres, eds., *Globalisation and Education* (New York: Routledge, 2002); and Malcolm Tight, *Researching Higher Education* (Maidenhead: SHRE and Open University Press, 2003); and Heather Munroe-Blum and Carlos Rueda, "Universities: Serving as, and Educating Global Citizens", in *Global Sustainability and the Responsibilities of Universities*, eds. Luc E. Weber and. James J. Duderstadt (Paris: Économica, 2012), 129–142. For an extensive and comparative overview, see Leo Goedegebuure et al., eds., *Higher Education Policy: An International Perspective* (London: Pergamon, 1993); and Jürgen Enders and Oliver Fulton, eds., *Higher Education in a Globalising World: International Trends and Mutual Observation* (Dordrecht: Kluwer Academic Publishers, 2002); and Carlos A. Torres and Daniel Schugurensky, "The Political Economy of Higher Education in the Era of Neoliberal Globalisation: Latin America in Comparative Perspective", *Higher Education* 43 (June

students as (owing to demographic factors) new cohorts of young people are shrinking. The younger cohorts in the relevant local communities are also more prone to look for opportunities abroad, which also means that higher education systems need to satisfy the learning and study objectives of these students in terms of global aspirations. Furthermore, even in the case of less mobile student populations, a knowledge of global society is increasingly relevant, as national economies have become more open to receiving foreign direct investment and more apt to localise global economic relations.[3] Thus there has been growing pressure on local faculties and academics to provide students with more 'competitive' knowledge concerning global societies.

In the light of these wider trends, the authors of this study assume that knowledge production is embedded in cognitive and non-cognitive historical structures and structural processes, which reduce the ability of higher education institutions to 'invent themselves' autonomously as global educators, leading to considerable path dependency. More specifically, in this study we aim to: (1) interpret higher education strategies and changes in Hungary in the context of global migration patterns and trends, and also the global hierarchy of knowledge production and implied cognitive hierarchies; (2) identify specific patterns of knowledge production concerning global issues and the representation of global societies and histories, specifically within undergraduate curricula at four Hungarian universities, in sociology, political science, international relations and human geography; (3) compare

2002): 429–455; and Heather Eggins, ed., *Globalisation and Reform in Higher Education* (Maidenhead: SHRE and Open University Press, 2003); and Michael W. Apple, Jane Kenway, and Michael Singh, eds., *Globalising Education: Policies, Pedagogies, and Politics* (New York: Peter Lang, 2005).

3   See Ball, "Big Policies/Small World"; and Graham Pike and David Selby, *Global Teacher, Global Learner* (London: Hodder & Stoughton, 1988); and Christopher Chase-Dunn, Yukio Kawano and Benjamin D. Brewer, "Trade Globalisation since 1795: Structures and Cycles in the Modern World-System", *American Sociological Review* 65:1 (February 2000): 77–95; and Attila Melegh, "Net Migration and Historical Development in Southeastern Europe since 1950", *Hungarian Historical Review* 1:3–4 (2012): 144–182; and Michael A. Peters, *Education, Science and Knowledge Capitalism: Creativity and the Promise of Openness* (New York: Peter Lang, 2012).

the curricula of these bachelors' degrees in the social sciences in terms of the representation of global societies and global social scientific knowledge.

2. Eurocentrism and Cognitive Maps of Global Society in Eastern Europe

A key concern of this study is to analyse to what extent Eurocentrism as a historically persistent system of thought determines cognitive structures in Hungarian higher education. Historically, Eurocentrism has been a dominant discourse throughout the region since the 18th century. According to this, all knowledge, innovation, wealth and culture predominantly emerged and subsequently diffused from the 'West', representing a unique, and the most progressive path of development. A complex set of cognitive hierarchies has determined the production of knowledge ever since.[4] This discourse appeared parallel to and as a consequence of colonisation and the expansion of West-centred world capitalism and imperialism, serving as a legitimating ideology for a rising European hegemony.[5] This process created

---

4   For critical reflections, see Larry Wolff, *Inventing Eastern Europe: The Map of Civilisation on the Mind of Enlightenment* (Stanford: Stanford University Press, 1994), 13–15, 356–374; and Maria Todorova, *Imagining the Balkans* (Oxford: Oxford University Press, 1997), 3–19, 42, 89–139, 140–160; and Immanuel Wallerstein, "Eurocentrism and Its Avatars: The Dilemmas of Social Science", *New Left Review* 226 (November/December 1997): 93–108; and Dipesh Chakrabarty, *Provincialising Europe: Postcolonial Thought and Historical Difference* (Princeton, NJ.: Princeton University Press, 2008), 3–16, 27–29, 42–46; and Arland Thornton, *Reading History Sideways: The Fallacy and Enduring Impact of the Developmental Paradigm on Family Life* (Chicago: University of Chicago Press, 2005), 13–46; and Attila Melegh, "Net Migration and Historical Development in Southeastern Europe since 1950"; and József Böröcz, *The European Union and Global Social Change: A Critical Geopolitical-Economic Analysis* (London: Routledge, 2009), 39–43; and Milica Bakić-Hayden, "Nesting Orientalisms: The Case of Former Yugoslavia", *Slavic Review* 54:4 (Winter 1995): 917–930.

5   See Samir Amin, *Eurocentrism* (London: Zed, 1989); and Immanuel Wallerstein, "The Modern World-System as a Civilisation", in Wallerstein, *Geopolitics and Geoculture: Essays on the Changing World-System* (Cambridge: Cambridge University Press, 1991), 215–230; and James Morris Blaut, *The Coloniser's Model of the World: Geographical Diffusionism and Eurocentric History* (New York: Guilford, 1993); and James Morris Blaut, *Eight Eurocentric Historians* (London: Guilford, 2000); and John M. Hobson, *The*

a 'civilisational slope' discourse—with the 'West' situated at the upper positions, and Eastern and Southern Europe, Asia, Africa, and Latin America placed at lower levels of development and civilisational 'achievement'.[6]

Such discourses determine, construct and disperse various concepts, taxonomies and fields of knowledge, naturalising dominant categories as universal,[7] which then form the basis of social epistemologies in formal and informal education. It has also been widely acknowledged that representational hierarchies serve as powerful tools for dominating and silencing marginalised groups: such hierarchies are therefore a key factor in power relations and structures, shaping future social development.[8]

Although the existence of this cognitive hierarchy is structurally stable and well documented, concrete hierarchical imaginations show variations. Certain elements might be of varying importance since, for example, various elites map the world and perceive it differently. Consequently, such mental maps require further empirical research.[9] Eastern Europe offers a very good test case for understanding how countries positioned in the middle of the hierarchy conceptualise global society — and consequently how development and global social experience is imagined within curricula. We can clearly identify in Eastern European perspectives a process of 'Westernisation': the

---

  Eastern Origins of Western Civilisation (Cambridge: Cambridge University Press, 2004); and Jack Goody, *The Theft of History* (Cambridge: Cambridge University Press, 2006).

6   See Wolff, *Inventing Eastern Europe*, 13.

7   See Michel Foucault, *The Archaeology of Knowledge*, trans. Sheridan Smith (New York: Routledge, 1972).

8   See Edward Said, *Orientalism* (New York: Vintage, 1978); and Gayatri Spivak, *The Post-Colonial Critic: Interviews, Strategies, Dialogues*, ed. Sarah Harasym (London: Routledge, 1990); and Chakrabarty, *Provincialising Europe*; and Eric R. Wolf, *Europe and the People Without History* (Berkeley: University of California Press, 2010).

9   See Arland Thornton et al., "Knowledge and Beliefs about National Development and Developmental Hierarchies: The Viewpoints of Ordinary People in Thirteen Countries", *Social Science Research* 41 (September 2012): 1053–1068; and Sorin Antohi, "Habits of Mind: Europe's Post-1989 Symbolic Geographies", in *Between Past and Future: The Revolutions of 1989 and Their Aftermath*, Sorin Antohi and Vladimir Tismenau, eds. (Budapest: Central Eastern University Press, 2000), 61–77.

conscious act of moving relevant societies upward along the 'civilisational slope' via continuous West-centric education. But there are other perspectives, among which we can find various nationalisms. They can turn their backs on 'Westernisation', while at the same time seeing themselves as part of the wider West—looking down on territories further East (from a Hungarian nationalist point of view, for instance, Romania, Moldavia, Russia and the wider 'Orient'). In addition, we can also find various 'ethnic ontologies', which aim at elevating the nation upwards in the hierarchy by imagining some kind of universally valid nationhood without any Western or Eastern reference points.[10]

The 'middling' group's civilisational frustration results from not being on the developmental level they believe they 'deserve', and so they invent various visions and strategies of advancement within the hierarchy. One such strategy is education itself. Such hierarchical understandings of global society can have a huge impact on individual and collective identities or orientations, and can also show how knowledge transferred to future elites through higher education is embedded in and reproduced by these hierarchically organised patterns and identities. Therefore, it is highly important to study how different social scientific courses reproduce the scaling of societies into developmental hierarchies, and what cognitive perspectives and patterns of representation they develop in relation to global societies.

3.   Higher Education Policies and Ideological Change: Nationalism and a Neoliberal Turn

When analysing the cognitive structures and perspectives apparent within Hungarian higher education, we need to take into account relevant political discussions. The country is currently experiencing a shift in its education policies. Overall, during the transformative changes of the 1980s and 1990s, the higher education system developed an almost unconditional West-

---

10   See Antohi, "Habits of Mind".

centrism, which implied that all political steps and reforms were seen as methods for advancing towards a more 'democratic' and 'developed European' status.[11] Efficiency, rationalisation, improved international competitiveness, and the reduction of 'overspending' were all key objectives during these reforms; practical measures arising from them included the introduction of competence measurements and the PISA,[12] which were further legitimised by contrasting these values against previous socialist-era ones. But despite these efforts, higher education has remained somewhat chaotic, even since the introduction of the Bologna system in 2005. During this system change, there was a dramatic increase in the proportion of students in the relevant age groups, from 12% to well over 40%. This expansion was not only the direct aim of national educational policy, but also an indirect reaction to the loss of jobs after the collapse of state socialism. Higher education was seen as a solution to high unemployment and a very low labour force participation rate.[13] Meanwhile, the local labour market discriminated against those having some kind of university degree.

In the name of competitiveness, there has recently been an interesting ideological shift towards a combination of neoliberal and nationalist ideals, coupled with a clear aim of centralisation and direct governmental interventions, these being identifiable characteristics of neo-nationalism.[14]

---

11   See Zoltan Báthory, "A Maratoni Reform", *Iskolakultúra* 10:11 (2001): 3–26; and Zoltan Báthory, *Maratoni Reform* (Budapest: Önkomet, 2001).

12   See Iván Bajomi et al., "The Reception of PISA in Hungary", https://www.researchgate.net/publication/265063839_The_Reception_of_PISA_in_Hungary; and Eszter Berényi and Eszter Neumann, "Grappling with PISA: Reception and Translation in the Hungarian Policy Discourse", Sisifo Educational Sciences Journal 10:9 (2009): 41–52; and Eszter Neumann, Adél Kiss and Ildikó Fejes, "The Hard Work of Interpretation: The National Politics of PISA Reception in Hungary and Romania", European Education Research Journal 11:2 (2012): 227–242.

13   For an overview see Eszter Berényi, Gábor Eröss, and Eszter Neumann, eds., *Tudás és politika: A közpolitika-alkotás gyakorlat* (Budapest: L'Harmattan, 2013).

14   See Eggins, *Globalisation and Reform in Higher Education*; and Margit Feischmidt and Peter Hervik, "Mainstreaming the Extreme: Intersecting Challenges from the Far Right in Europe", *Intersections* 1:1 (2015): 3–17.

This process is most tangible when it comes to reforming elementary and secondary schools, where there has been a dramatic effort to establish a dual educational model, separating humanities-oriented secondary and vocational schools. In fact, in line with the new national higher education strategy (see below), the government is reducing the role of secondary schools in favour of vocational education.[15] In 2011, the government reduced the compulsory age of schooling from 18 to 16 years, a move which was widely criticised by teachers and parents at the time. This particular action was paralleled by a change in the system of producing textbooks, from a market-oriented system to a completely centralised one, allowing only two versions of books for each subject. This was also paralleled by a 'nationalist turn' in curricula, emphasising the 'glorious past' of the nation and downplaying reflective critical perspectives.

Changes in higher education have been similarly radical. The new national higher education strategy bears a revealing title: "Gearshift in Higher Education".[16] This business-oriented document refers to the unconditional promotion of an "industrial structural policy" in education, which is expected to increase competitiveness by directly satisfying labour market needs and selectively developing only the "key fields" of education. According to the document, the new educational system will be able to keep up the accelerating tempo "dictated by the global world" with no room for "relaxation". Later, the document stresses that this can be achieved by clarifying "business relations" and identifying who gives the orders and who is the owner; this language clearly indicates a neoliberal or corporatist turn, underlined by the fact that the present strategy-makers hail from a group of

---

15 Recently, 80 secondary schools (primarily outside Budapest) which provide maturity exams have been targeted for closure and taken over by the Ministry of National Economy in order to transform them into vocational schools. See http://eduline.hu /kozoktatas/2015/6/9/Tobb_mint_80_iskolaban_szunik_meg_a_gimnazi_POW927 (as of 11 June 2015).

16 See http://www.kormany.hu/download/d/90/30000/fels%C5%91oktat%C3%A1 si%20koncepci%C3%B3.pdf (as of 11 June 2015).

industrially well-embedded natural scientists, promoting the education of "applied" and "useful knowledge". It will therefore come as no surprise that the strategic document focuses predominantly on medical education, informatics, engineering and the natural sciences as areas of special intervention, with no mention of the social sciences, with the exception of economics. Arguably, the government is using this strategic document to cover the reduction of public funds for the social sciences.[17] In the last few years, there have been various attacks on communication sciences, legal studies and economics, both in terms of quality and curricula.[18] State funds have been earmarked by the Hungarian National Bank to promote the education of "unorthodox" economics, while there has been a huge cut in public funding of economics at all other universities.

International studies programmes have been subjected to similar manoeuvres. The strategic document contains a short paragraph on further increasing Hungarian universities' international links (e.g. introducing more foreign language courses), but without specifying any real action. At the same time, the document refers to the Carpathian basin—including regions inhabited by Hungarian minorities in neighbouring countries—as a homogeneous cross-border national educational resource for Hungary, which is related to the fact that substantial Hungarian minorities live around the Hungarian borders. According to the document, these changes are expected to protect Hungarian minorities against assimilation and migration, the thinking being that providing higher education locally in the Hungarian language will reduce any need for these groups to move to Hungary for such services. However, Hungarian minorities from neighbouring countries—as we will see below—already constitute the

---

17 See Kemal Gürüz, *Higher Education and International Student Mobility in the Global Knowledge Economy* (New York: State University of New York Press, 2011), 83–84; and Ellen Schrecker, *The Lost Soul of Higher Education: Corporatisation, the Assault on Academic Freedom, and the End of the American University* (New York: New Press, 2010).
18 See http://eduline.hu/felsooktatas/2015/9/24/Szakok_megszunese_csak_2017ben_jon_a_valtoz_92IBWQ (as of 24 September 2015).

majority of 'foreign' students. In this light, we can claim that higher education policy has taken a clearly nationalist turn by trying to involve mainly Hungarian nationals from neighbouring countries as 'international students', and also that in some ways this trend conflicts with the neoliberal trend towards promoting the immediate economic exploitability of students.[19]

As part of these strategic actions, the government is constantly centralising not only primary and secondary education, but also higher education, by for instance enlisting state-elected chancellors as overseers of the financial management of universities, or by aggressively promoting the National Public Service University (NPSU), while providing programme monopolies to it. More specifically, this revivified institution, which hosts military, police and civil servant programmes, has been granted special privileges, money and physical resources, while other universities and colleges have been attacked for having 'too many' programmes, and for not being efficient enough. As part of these moves, the government is negotiating the complete banning or radical reduction of various programmes, including all international studies and public law bachelor degrees, having already reduced their state funding to zero.[20] This has been paralleled by a move to introduce a previously unknown "European and International Public Service" programme at the NPSU: this measure not only shows a complete distrust towards previous international studies programmes and the academics behind them, but also the will to increase centralised political control, and to offer further opportunities for academics openly loyal to the

---

19 A good example of this is the Stipendim Hungaricum Scholarship programme.
20 Beyond this, the government has decided to omit consultations originally planned to run until the end of August 2015; the registered list of programmes to be changed, created or terminated has already been published in the official government journal, *Magyar Közlöny*, with the new regulations coming into force from the start of September. See http://eduline.hu/felsooktatas/2015/6/10/alapszakok_megszun ese_felsooktatas_WUJ0ZN (as of 11 June 2015); http://eduline.hu/felsooktatas/ 2015/6/11/megszuno_mesterszakok_2016_O7IUSM (as of 11 June 2015).

government. This is further promoted by the fact that the NPSU has been granted a wide array of unparalleled benefits, including even the ability to bypass the official accreditation process of the Hungarian Accreditation Council (thus the NPSU can create educational programmes officially unchecked), which has only recently inspected the performance of all higher education institutions.[21] Based on this draft proposal, students interested in international studies will only be able to apply to this governmental university, if they wish to further their interest.

In our analysis, we can see an emerging nationalist vision in the new education strategy, in the sense that it subtly proposes that the country and the co-ethnic minorities of neighbouring countries should participate in a common and centralised educational system, one which would increase competiveness. On the other hand, the idea of creating a more global curriculum, potentially providing knowledge and linkages toward different regions of the world, does not even appear in the text.

4.   Student Migration and Migration Processes

In order to contextualise these cognitive structures, it is important to see how Hungary is embedded in migratory systems, and how it benefits from the international flow of migrants and students staying over a longer period of time. Immigrants themselves and their children create not only current but future 'demand' for a more global education in terms of subjects and curricula. Migrants, whether incoming or outgoing, have non-national educational needs, and therefore it is important to detect the main trends of immigration and emigration in Hungary. We also need to look at where we receive younger groups from, where we send them to, and what systems of migration they inhabit. Emigratory links can be instructive in terms of ideals about where Hungarians prefer to go, and which countries or societies they see as worth living in. These target societies also reveal something, on

---

21   See http://eduline.hu/felsooktatas/2015/6/10/Nemzeti_Kozszolgalati_Egyetem_ szakok_indita_3CXQTK (as of 11 June 2015).

various levels, about the sending countries, and as such they repay intellectual attention.

In line with the historical structural school of migration theory, Hungary has very stable migratory relationships in terms of immigration and emigration.[22] When analysing World Bank and United Nations migratory matrices, we can observe that since 1960, with only little variation in terms of country of birth, the top five sending countries have been Germany, (Czecho-)Slovakia, Ukraine, Serbia, Bulgaria and Greece (Melegh and Sárosi 2015). In general, we can claim that the sending areas have mainly been neighbouring countries, and that most of the immigrants concerned have been of Hungarian origin.[23] As we will see, these groups have been dominant among students with foreign citizenship, and the 'globalisation' of the Hungarian educational market has been very much limited to a co-ethnic space.

When looking at the internal composition of the immigrant groups (defined as having been born outside Hungary) we can see that they are younger in their age composition than the local population, and thus they constitute an additional group of students. Their level of education is also higher (with the exception of those from Austria); and we know from surveys that many of these students have had 'professional' and 'educational'

---

22 See Jozsef Borocz and Alejandro Portes, "Contemporary Immigration: Theoretical Perspectives on its Determinants and Modes of Incorporation", *International Migration Review* 23:3 (1989): 606–630; and Melegh, "Net Migration and Historical Development in Southeastern Europe since 1950"; and Attila Melegh and Annamária Sárosi, "Magyarország bekapcsolódása a migrációs folyamatokba: történeti-strukturális megközelítés", *Demográfia* 58:4 (2015): 221–264.

23 See Melegh and Sárosi, "Magyarország bekapcsolódása a migrációs folyamatokba"; and Irén Gödri, Béla Soltész and Boróka Bodacz-Nagy, "Immigration or Emigration Country? Migration Trends and Their Socio-Economic Background in Hungary: A Longer-Term Historical Perspective", *Demográfia Working Papers on Population, Family and Welfare* no. 19 (2014), http://demografia.hu/en/publicationsonline/index.php/workingpapers/article/view/318/571 (as of 11 June 2015).

interests.[24] Concerning integration mechanisms, migrants who come from China and Vietnam less frequently find jobs requiring higher education. This shows a de-skilling process at work within the migration process.

Out-migration can also have an impact on the higher education curriculum. It is quite clear that Hungary's key emigration targets — Germany, the United States, Canada and Austria — have remained the same for the last few decades, and only the United Kingdom has become a new key target in the last 15 years. This implies that 'emigrant' students are mainly looking for opportunities in these countries. Not surprisingly, out-migrant groups are an active population of significantly young age, especially with regard to the UK.[25] In terms of educational composition, it is clear that while the UK is predominantly the target for young, university-educated people, Germany and Austria attract larger number of skilled workers from slightly older age groups with lower levels of education.

When analysing the proportion of foreign students in the total student population, we can see that their share in higher education increased from 3% to 6% between 2001 and 2012 (this figure does not include those with dual citizenship). This increase applies only to higher education — at lower educational levels the total share is below 1% — which shows that immigrant

24 See Melegh and Sárosi, "Magyarország bekapcsolódása a migrációs folyamatokba"; and Irén Gödri and Pál Péter Tóth, *Bevándorlás és beilleszkedés A szomszédos országokból Magyarországra irányuló bevándorlás az ezredfordulón* (Budapest: KSH Népességtudományi Kutatóintézet), http://www.demografia.hu/kiadvanyok online/index.php/kutatasijelentesek/article/viewFile/389/147 (as of 11 June 2015).

25 See Zsuzsa Blaskó, "Surveying the Absentees—Surveying the Emigrants: A Methodological Paper on the SEEMIG Pilot Study to Survey Emigrants from Hungary and Serbia", *SEEMIG Working Papers* 4 (2014), Hungarian Demographic Research Institute, Budapest, https://www.researchgate.net/publication/270503279 _Surveying_the_Absentees_Surveying_the_Emigrants_A_methodological_paper_o n_the_SEEMIG_pilot_study_to_survey_emigrants_from_Hungary_and_Serbia (as at 17 September 2017); and Zsuzsa Blaskó and Irén Gödri, "Kivándorlás Magyarországról: szelekció és célország-választás az 'új migránsok' körében", *Demográfia* 57:4 (2014): 271–307; and Zsuzsa Blaskó, Zsolt Németh and Attila Melegh, SEEM IG press material, October 15, 2014, www.seemig.eu (as of 11 June 2015).

groups do not account for any meaningful demand for lower-level educational services in Hungary (Educational statistical database, HCSO).

Relevant educational statistics in terms of foreign-citizen students also reveal that there is a clear overlap with major immigrant communities; thus the educational 'market' seems to be closely tied to historical migratory links. In 2013, the majority of around 25,000 foreign students came from countries with already existing migratory links: Germany represents 12%, Slovakia 9%, Romania 8%, Serbia 6%, Ukraine 4%, China 3%, Israel 3%, and the US 2%. Over the last 12 years, the overall share of Hungarian-speaking students from neighbouring countries has declined (from above 60% in the first part of this period), the point being that there is an emerging trend for educating less closely linked groups. This is partly due to the country changing its citizenship law and providing external citizenship (without actual residency in Hungary) to those who can effectively claim links with the historical territory. These 'new' citizens can now enter higher education as Hungarian citizens: as such they are statistically inseparable from resident citizens. In addition, major universities have started English-language programmes running parallel to local-language ones. It is also worth mentioning that Budapest has some major postgraduate universities that attract a large number of students from regions well beyond neighbouring countries (i.e. the US-accredited Central European University and the German-speaking Andrássy University).

In addition, some sending countries not previously linked to Hungary, such as Brazil, Iran, Turkey and Nigeria, represent 17% of the total 25,000 students, amounting to a sizeable student population. The increase in these groups is related to the effects of cultural policies on the part of the sending countries. It is also important to note that these countries, together with some others like Vietnam, China, Mexico and South Korea, have huge foreign student populations that deserve more attention in terms of educational needs.

5. Curriculum Analysis Methodology

There is a large body of critical work aimed at understanding and deconstructing implicit or explicit ideologies reproduced through educational curricula, including Eurocentrism, race and nationalism.[26] Many of these studies offer narrative and discourse analysis of literature—a qualitative approach important in deepening our own research—but without combining such analysis with more standardised, quantitative and thus comparable data. Further, this literature, including a number of methodologically and theoretically grounded studies, has mainly been applied and developed in Anglo-Saxon and Western contexts, and is largely absent from the Eastern European region. Nevertheless, similar research work on the politics of representing or silencing different social groups has already been conducted in Hungary concerning the representation of Roma in textbooks for primary and secondary education,[27] though these studies are quite preliminary, and remain highly empirical. Despite its limitations, this strand of work is empowering, mobilising critique and opposition against establishment ideologies in education—for example by combining research with activism, by staging petitions, and by offering suggestions for

---

26 See Ivor Goodson, *School Subjects and Curriculum Change* (London: Croom Helm, 1983); and Rob Gilbert, *The Impotent Image, Reflections of Ideology in the Secondary School Curriculum* (Lewes: Falmer, 1984); and Rex Gibson, *Critical Theory and Education* (London: Hodder & Stoughton, 1986); and Pike and Selby, *Global Teacher, Global Learner*; and R. Young, *A Critical Theory of Education* (London: Harvester Wheatsheaf, 1989); and Stanley Aronowitz and Henry Giroux, *Postmodern Education: Politics, Culture and Social Criticism* (Minneapolis: University of Minneapolis Press, 1991); and Henry Giroux, *Border Crossings: Cultural Workers and the Politics of Education* (London: Routledge, 1992); and James Lynch, *Education for Citizenship in a Multi-Cultural Society* (London: Cassell, 1992); and Michael Peters, *Education and the Postmodern Condition* (Westport, CT.: Praeger, 1997); and Alicia de Alba et al., *Curriculum in the Postmodern Condition* (New York: Peter Lang, 2000).

27 See Sándor Hegedüs, "Cigányok a történelemkönyvekben", Lungo Drom (August–September 2002); Tamás Terestyéni, "Fekete pont", Beszélő, 9:5 (2004): 1–16; and Anna Balázs et al., "A cigányság reprezentációja az általános- és középiskolai tankönyvekben", Budapest: MONITOR Kritikai Platform és Nyitott Műhely (2014).

educational decision-makers.[28] A similar project involved students, artists and history teachers working together on the global mental map of Hungary to be found in international primary and secondary school textbooks.[29]

Curriculum analysis in educational sociology has various branches relying on qualitative or quantitative methods.[30] In our analysis, we have combined these approaches for two main reasons. While qualitative data helped us in highlighting specific patterns of knowledge production and in understanding underlying explanations, quantitative data enabled us to analyse and compare the syllabi of bachelor's degrees at our chosen universities. Our curriculum analysis includes the available syllabi in sociology, political science, international relations and (if applicable) geography found in the formal curricula of four major Hungarian universities. This sample includes universities playing a significant role in the Hungarian educational market, and those ranking among the most lucrative and attractive institutions in terms of student applications. Taken together they include: (1) Eötvös Loránd University (ELTE); (2) Corvinus University (BCE); (3) Pázmány Péter Catholic University (PPKE); (4) University of Szeged (SZTE). ELTE is the largest university in the country in terms of the number of students. Compared to this, BCE is a medium-sized university, but is the most important institution for the study of economics and certain other social science subjects; also, traditionally it has the highest entry requirements in the country. We have included SZTE as well, which has a good international reputation in the natural sciences, sits at the top of the national rankings for student experience, and has a major regional role in the southern borderland of Hungary, mainly due to the number of applicants from Serbia. In addition, we have analysed PPKE, a Catholic university offering social science education to a large segment of students.

---

28 For more about the project see https://monitorlive.wordpress.com/; for more on their suggestions and petitions see http://www.tte.hu/hirek/61/7951 (as of 11 June 2015).

29 See the work of the National Textbook Committee at: http://keserue.hu/index0.html (as of 11 June 2015).

30 See Tight, *Researching Higher Education*.

At the four universities, and on the above-mentioned programmes, we have collected 572 course data sheets, consisting of formal syllabi uploaded to the course databases of the universities. Table 1 contains the distribution of the data:

Table 1. Distribution of course data sheets by programmes and universities

	Human Geography	Sociology	Political Science	International Relations	Total
BCE	–	67	85	75	227
ELTE[31]	55	0	0	65	120
SZTE	38	14	26	52	130
PPKE	–	35	32	28	95
Total	93	116	143	220	572

An initial remark must be made on the special case of geography, as traditionally, and specifically in Hungary, the discipline institutionally unites both physical and human geographers. However, as only human geography was relevant for our study, we have selected only those courses directly relevant to global social issues. In addition, BCE and PPKE do not have such programmes, hence the empty cells in Table 1.[32] The above table contains all data sheets regardless of whether they include any valid data. It is important to note that our database consists of a large number of documents that have not been revised for several years, or which often include partially incomplete or empty data sheets. In sociology, there were 27 such data sheets, in international relations 22, and in political science twelve. These issues have been taken into account in assessing and

---

31 No data was provided by ELTE for the disciplines of sociology and political science.

32 BCE hosts an independent department related to human geography (Department of Economic Geography and Future Studies or "Gazdaságföldrajz és Jövokutatás Tanszék") which offers 16 courses of study; however this institution does not offer a separate geography degree as such.

comparing our data, and this is why we did not attempt to provide a more general and systematic statistical evaluation and comparison of university programmes. Although the records with missing data had to be taken out of consideration when looking at more detailed aspects (see below), we have still decided to use them for various reasons.

Most importantly – and this point was also reinforced by various personal communications – the data sheets gathered serve mostly as reference points: the syllabi actually used for educational purposes are different. Nonetheless, the ones in our sample are the publicly available syllabi accessible by current and prospective students. Moreover, the collection of actually used materials has proven to be very difficult, due to the fact that a large number of educators tend not to reveal publicly their syllabi beyond the group of students they are teaching. This inattention in terms of maintaining revised, up-to-date syllabi that could be used to inform students and other university teachers is a finding in itself, bearing as it does on the issue of the academic transparency of higher education in Hungary. We have, at any rate, nevertheless decided to use the syllabi concerned, firstly because they have been used to gain accreditation, and secondly because they can be systematically compared. We have also assumed that cognitive structures (including Eurocentrism) are resilient to change in such a short period of time.[33]

We examined the datasheets by closed coding, pre-defining a set of variables concerning the representation of global societies and global knowledge, together with various other related aspects of the representation of social and historical experiences. We defined the categories of gender, ethnic, racial, religious, geographical, developmental, international political, and historical categories in order to map and compare the representations of

---

33 Beyond this, gathering the actual syllabi used would have required enormous resources, as well as the time needed to overcome an atmosphere of deep distrust; in some cases our requests for information were regarded as an attempt to review 'private' data with 'dubious' motivations. To emphasise the severity of this problem we should note, for example, that we were informally but blatantly rejected at another targeted university.

global societies. Some variables were two-valued (true/false), but most were coded by several values, while there were also some nominal variables. In these latter instances, multiple-value scales have sometimes been given. We also analysed course titles, course descriptions, and compulsory readings for each course.

Table 2. Distribution of readings by programmes and universities

	Human Geography	Sociology	Political Science	International Relations	Total
BCE	–	209	223	212	**664**
ELTE[34]	237	0	0	127	**364**
SZTE	111	78	122	139	**450**
PPKE	–	171	157	68	**396**
Total	**348**	**458**	**502**	**546**	**1854**

We scrutinised compulsory reading lists using most of the analytical categories mentioned above (Table 2). Also, we supplemented this analysis by collecting information on the ways in which global social scientific knowledge is represented via authors. Here we considered which authors are featured in teaching programmes, their respective regional focus in terms of research interests, and where they have actually spent most of their academic career, based on their biographies on the Internet.

6.   The Representation of Global Society in Course Descriptions

In thinking about the representation of global society in curricula, we have coded the course titles and descriptions to see whether they claim universal validity when relating the main concerns of their academic fields. Many of the core subjects in the curricula analysed claim in their course titles and descriptions a 'universality', such as economic history, cultural

---

34   No data was provided by ELTE for the disciplines of sociology and political science.

anthropology, media studies etc., while proportionately few courses cover specific matters within more general subjects, such as "Hungarian-Austrian Foreign Policy" or "The Secret Services in the 20th Century". However, claiming universal validity does not mean that the knowledge included is free from geographical particularity.

Universality

If we look at the distribution of universal and non-universal themes in the four undergraduate degrees (Table 3), geography appears to provide the largest share of the former (84%), while political science takes in courses based on more particular topics (53%). The relatively high number of universalist courses (62%) is partly due to syllabi focusing on methodology, management studies or economics; in geography this aspect is supplemented by a large body of compulsory courses with very general themes – e.g. world history and regional geography. However, non-universalist instances in geography consist of courses exclusively concerned with either Hungary or the European Union (see our discussion of geographical categories below).

Table 3. Distribution of themes

	Human Geography	Sociology	Political Science	International Relations	Total
Universal	84%	57%	53%	59%	62%
Non-Universal	16%	43%	47%	41%	38%

With the other three social sciences, it was often the case that a seemingly universal presentation contained very visible contradictions when compared to actual content. To take a telling example, a course entitled "The History of Everyday Life from 1500 to 2000" claims universal validity in its description, but focuses solely on European history, using only texts authored by classical Western scholars about the development of European societies. More importantly, general introductory social science courses, like "The Foundations of Sociology" or "Social Inequalities", tend to present an international perspective or a more general introduction, but still mainly focus on examples or case studies drawn exclusively from Europe or the West, or Hungary. Even in courses such as "Environmental Sociology", case studies mainly refer to Europe and Hungary. In geography, courses on spatial and settlement planning and infrastructure are solely based on Europe, especially European Union planning objectives.

Geographical Categories

To offer further detail concerning universality, the distribution of geographic units in the course descriptions show us the spatial concepts and perspectives used in them and, most importantly, the extent of their focus on geographic categories, spanning: globe, continent (Asia, Africa etc.), supra-national macro-region (Central Asia, South East Asia etc.), country or sub-national spatial units (Bretagne, Golan etc.), city (huge metropoles like Lagos, Mexico City etc.), settlement (below the size of metropoles), smaller geographical units (local governments, districts etc.), and non-territorial spaces (suburbs, tropics etc.) (Diagram 1).[35] Due to the complexity of geographical categories, we applied multiple coding, sometimes assigning several variables to a record. Almost half of the courses (45%) do not contain any reference to geographical units; thus they do not specify the geographic relevance of their knowledge content during teaching. This may point to a 'hidden universalism' but, as we will see below, it could also mean that the courses concerned claim universal relevance while applying a national or regional focus.

---

35   The term 'city' refers here to capital cities, or large cities with at least a regional hierarchical rank and catchment area; the term 'settlement' denotes all other forms of urban entity. The term 'smaller geographical units' refers to territorial entities, usually either local governments on a micro-regional or district level, or specific landscapes or urban areas. The more abstract category of 'non-territorial spaces' covers spatial phenomena and processes that have a distinct spatiality, but which are not specifically linked to a bounded territorial entity or scale (e.g. brownfield sites, suburbs, tropics, networks).

Diagram 1. Geographical categories in course descriptions

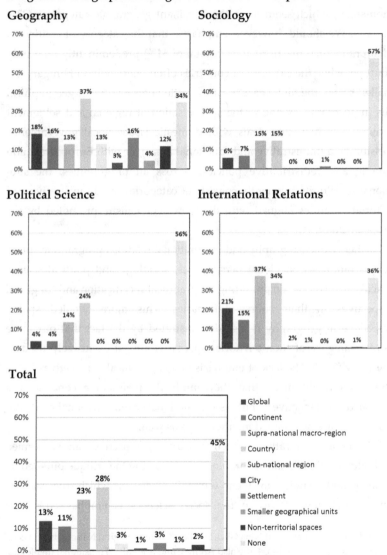

Courses containing references to either a global perspective or a continent are quite common (around 13% and 11% respectively), but a good deal less common than the ones containing references to supranational blocs or nation-states, which seem to be the dominant geographic categories (23% and 28%). We should, however, emphasise that the category of continents and supranational macro-regions (a total of 34%) predominantly refer only to Europe, while the category of countries often refers only to Hungary. At 'smaller' scales, the high share of cities, settlements or smaller geographical units in geography is due to the specialisation of regional and settlement planning, which mainly deals with domestic issues (local governments, accessibility, administrative and functional areas), or with European Union planning and redistributive policies. Across all programmes, the sub-national level quite frequently consists of categories of administrative and territorial identities aligned with the 'new regionalism' promoted by the European Union.

Further, while geography and international relations programmes place stronger emphasis on global perspectives, sociology and political science curricula are less keen on providing geographical specification and/or global perspectives in their course summaries. This more detailed spatial perspective in geography is also demonstrated by the fact that our more abstract category of 'non-territorial spaces' is almost exclusively used in geography (20%). The lack of emphasis on geographical perspectives in the latter cases might mean that they implicitly maintain a concrete and positioned perspective, but supra-national and national-container perspectives are maintained in other ways as well.

In general, this rather reductive spatial perspective can be termed 'methodological nationalism' or 'blocism', following the critique pursued by Wimmer and Schiller in their seminal article in which the lack of transnational perspectives in the social sciences is emphasised.[36] This

<hr/>

36   See Andreas Wimmer and Nina Glick Schiller, "Methodological Nationalism", *Global Networks* 2:4 (2002): 301–334; see also Andre Gunder Frank, "Transitional Ideological Modes: Feudalism, Capitalism, Socialism", *Critique of Anthropology* 11:2 (June 1991): 171–188; and Sabina Csánóova, "Rank-Ordering Modernity: Perceptions of Global Hierarchies and Development in Hungary" (MA dissertation, Central European University, Budapest, 2013); and Thornton, *Reading History Sideways*.

inherent nationalism, in many cases, is present even in courses with a global perspective—especially in geography and international relations programmes where the units of analysis and historical agency are traditionally nation-states, and where there is little critical reflection on globalisation, little comparative analysis in global terms (even between nation-states), and little questioning of value-laden cognitive structures and spatial preconceptions.[37] Critical international studies identify this interpretative framework as Westphalianism, where the foundation of global history and politics is the competitive, sovereign nation-state. This conception is determined by European ideals of territoriality, enlightenment, modernity, democracy, sovereignty and human rights, while internationality is based on European values and "standards of civilisation".[38]

Developmental Categories

It is also very important to analyse spatial perspectives in terms of global developmental hierarchies, as the former are closely related to the presence and reproduction of the latter. In such cases, global society is seen as a composition of unequally developed regions, labelled as, for instance: either the First, Second or Third World; as undeveloped or developed regions; or as traditional or modern societies.[39] The vast majority of course descriptions omit any explicit link to developmental categories (Diagram 2). Only a quarter of the courses analysed refer to a concrete category, but even when

---

37 See Martin W. Lewis and Kären Wigen, *The Myth of Continents: A Critique of Metageography* (Berkeley: University of California Press, 1997).

38 See Hedley Bull and Adam Watson, eds., *The Expansion of International Society* (New York: Oxford University Press, 1984); and Turan Kayaoglu, "Westphalian Eurocentrism in International Relations Theory", *International Studies Review* 12 (June 2010): 193–217.

39 See Csánóova, "Rank-ordering Modernity". The term 'developed world' refers specifically to the First World, i.e. 'developed' countries, centre states, OECD countries etc. The term 'developing world' refers to the direct peripheries of these centres, i.e. the 'Second World', 'semi-developed', or semi-periphery states etc. The term 'undeveloped world' refers to the 'Third World': the absolute peripheries of the world economy, peripheral or undeveloped countries etc.

they do, they overwhelmingly refer to what they call the "developed" part of the world, with little attention paid to other regions. In terms of developmental hierarchies, this can be interpreted as reflecting an implicit need to 'catch up', or a view that the task of Hungarian social science is to promote national advancement in terms of a developmental hierarchy.[40] This mental map may also suggest that the academics involved thoroughly identify themselves with those regions seen as the most 'developed'.

Diagram 2. Developmental categories in course descriptions

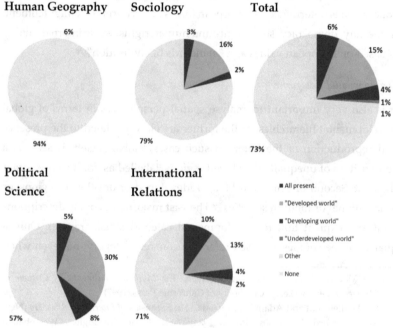

It seems that only political science programmes show some interest in all developmental categories, while sociology is less representative in this respect, and geography shows no such explicit interest in its course

---

40   See József Böröcz and Mahua Sarkar, "What is the EU?", *International Sociology* 20:2 (June 2005): 153–173.

descriptions. Although not explicitly stated through concrete developmental categories, the geography course descriptions indicate a marked modernisation discourse, as "development" itself appears as a common but all-too general term, while the descriptions refer to "differences in development and modernisation", "economic performance", "competitiveness", "innovation", "knowledge society" etc., without offering any critical reflection on these developmental processes and agendas. The only critical concept present is "sustainability" or "sustainable development", but this concept also often shows a technical conformity with mainstream Western or European Union policy agendas, leaving out any differentiated critique of e.g. modernisation, capital interests, social inequalities and/or uneven relations in technology transfer.[41]

In terms of representing developmental categories in course descriptions, international relations programmes seem the most balanced in terms of utilising all developmental categories, while political science seems the most West-centric, with over 30% of records referring exclusively to the "developed world". In sociology, political science and international relations, even basic courses like "Modern Social History", "The Social History of Consumption" or "The Roots of European Civilisation" focus exclusively on the "developed world", or the development of "modern society", mobilising a civilisational discourse loaded with Eurocentric and colonialist meanings; this tendency is also present in geography, but surfaces explicitly only in reading lists. In all four programmes there are a great many categories regularly associated with the "First World" or the "developed world", with little consideration of other contexts, though one international relations course (on the political and economic history of Latin America) does consider the "periphery".

---

41 The minimal proportion of development categories in the geography course summaries is also due to the fact that these are rather sketchy or even deficient; a more revealing picture is provided by reference to the course reading lists.

International Political Organisations

The representation of international blocs is also Eurocentric in that most courses explicitly refer mainly to the political organisations of the Western world. Around 21% of the courses analysed were found to show this characteristic, in part indicating that in the syllabi there is only somewhat limited interest in such subjects. On the other hand, where these topics are covered the world is mainly reduced to Europe and the European Union. Nearly three-quarters of international political organisations mentioned in course descriptions referred to the European Union; in contrast, ASEAN was referred to four times, BRICs three times, and Mercosur, the Andean Community or the African Union once; no explicit reference was made to Eurasia. In many cases, international political blocs were referred to only in very general terms, while there were also a few exceptional cases mentioning various other existing or historical organisations, such as the Austro-Hungarian Monarchy, the Soviet Union, the Arab League, or the more economic category of Newly Industrialised Countries (NICs). Further, we rarely found any courses comparing two or more political blocs, and thus offering a more global comparative perspective to students. While these tendencies are only apparent at the level of course descriptions, there is nevertheless the suggestion of the operation of a mental map which, through direct references in terms of topics, grants 'real' validity to the West and the European Union, while other regions—if they appear at all—can only be an 'aspect' or epiphenomenon of these two, lacking any symmetrical value.[42]

At the level of coverage of international political blocs, the four programmes differ significantly, since such blocs are not generally discussed in sociology courses, while they are fairly prominent in geography and political science course descriptions—though in both these cases the dominant focus is on the European Union. In the case of international relations, there are courses combining coverage of a wide variety of international organisations and blocs, but they often remain rather

---

42   See Said, *Orientalism*; and Chakrabarty, *Provincialising Europe*.

superficial and formal in their descriptions. If we combine these findings with other types of macro-regions appearing in our sample, then the representation becomes slightly more balanced, as frameworks of "Eastern and Central Europe" appear in larger numbers, and quite a number of courses discuss such themes as "The Political Systems of Central and Eastern Europe". These two results together do not contradict each other, as many scholars have shown that the category of Central and Eastern Europe relies on the concept of the West, to the extent that 'Central' and 'Eastern' are regarded as an intra-European inferior other of the 'West' and 'Europe'.[43]

If we compare this data with the geographic categories discussed previously, certain connections can be identified. First of all, nation-states or countries appear to be the most significant categories in geographical references. All the programmes analysed maintained this perspective, serving to underline the importance of 'methodological nationalism' beyond the disproportionate stress on the European Union.[44] Geography and political science courses are keen to embrace this type of geographic specialisation, which can be related to the fact that nation-states are key political actors, amounting to foundational methodological units within these academic disciplines. Yet the countries mentioned are predominantly from the West: a great number of cases are, for example, about the constitutional systems of the US or the UK, or cover political developments in France or Italy. Aside from these Western countries, only one or two other countries appear – namely Russia or China – both of which are major geopolitical players. Thus the mental map consists of mainly European nations and the European Union, which all have some interaction with non-European major powers, while other areas, such as Latin America, Africa and large parts of Asia receive very little or no attention at all in themselves.

Crucially, this positioning leaves out the possibility of exploring the comparative historical experiences of countries in a similar position in the global hierarchy (i.e. competing for global resources and markets on the same

---

43 See Todorova, *Imagining the Balkans*.
44 See Wimmer and Schiller, "Methodological Nationalism".

hierarchical level and with similar strategies in the world economy), for example in Latin America. In general, this shows how even a provisional and limited symmetrical and comparative global perspective basically does not exist in Hungarian social science programmes.

Historical Perspectives

Concerning constructed hierarchies, an important aspect is the way that historical time is represented in courses descriptions. When we look at whether a historical approach − and thus alternative socio-historical experience − is presented to students, we can see quite a variable pattern in terms of time-frames (Diagram 3).

Diagram 3. Historical perspectives in course descriptions

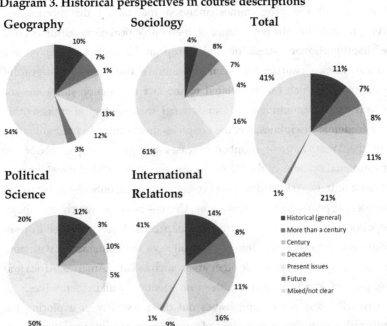

Overall, most courses do not refer to historical issues at all, or else use a 'mixed' approach (41%), such that even if historical cases are covered, it is in a highly selective manner, and without any attempt to provide a systematic overview or approach in terms of historical analysis. A clear example of this is a course on the US government, which to a limited extent covers the history of the federal government, but effectively concentrates only on current governmental mechanisms. The other dominant form of historical perspective is when the focus is on the present (21%); in many cases, however, it is difficult to distinguish these courses from those lacking any specific historical perspective.

General historical accounts with no concrete time-frame are evident in introductory or general courses (11%) with titles such as "The History of International Relations" or "The Social History of Consumption". Courses spanning a few decades or a century (11% and 8%) usually refer to the "modernity" of the 19th or most often the 20th century, or the social history of Europe, or Western "modern" approaches in social science ("Urbanisation", "Approaches in Social Theory"). This was especially the case in geography and international relations, where courses in the main look at the history of the European Union and at European political and legal history. A typical narrative of "Economic History", for example, will commence with the (European) "Industrial Revolution", before turning to globalising phases of economic development and technological innovation, along a markedly Western path—leaving out Asian, African and Latin American histories, along with the history of Eastern Europe. Similarly, general courses presenting subjects over a long time-frame—like "The History of Geography" or even the mentioned introductory courses in social science—also follow a Eurocentric narrative, and actually cover solely Western themes and concerns, while in geography there is a further concentration on Hungarian subject matter. Indeed in geography, nationalist narratives manifest themselves not only in ethnic and historical geography, but also in settlement planning—in one telling case, emphasis is given to "the historical origins and organic development of the Hungarian settlement system from the Árpád era to present times" (Árpád was the founder of the first royal dynasty in mediaeval Hungary).

Comparing the various programmes in this respect, it seems that sociology and political science curricula show relatively little interest in history: their focus is more on synchronic knowledge (in political science there is a high emphasis on political issues of the near present, mainly on issues of state politics). In geography and international relations programmes, courses offer deeper historical accounts, which more than the other programmes vary according to geographical contexts. However, West-centrism is not counter-balanced in these cases, since not only the present but also the history of particular regions is over-represented when compared to other areas.

Socio-Cultural Categories

The use of various other social categories, such as ethnicity, religion, and gender, provide insights into the representation of global societies. As we shall see, while most of these categories appear only as a general subject in the course data sheets, their operation tends to follow a consistent pattern.

In the data sheets gender issues are very much neglected or unregarded, strongly suggesting that such issues are felt to be unworthy of exposition and analysis in the universities' social science programmes. In a very small percentage of course descriptions, generally in sociology and international relations, and hardly at all in geography, there were some general references to gender categories: the statistical distribution of phenomena along classical male/female dichotomies was one such example, alongside only three cases dealing with genders other than masculinity and femininity. Further, beyond the neglect of gender in general, the issues actually raised still usually focused on Western culture and history, without any insight into globally varying contexts and globally structured differences.

During the coding process, we paid special attention to whether or not course titles and descriptions made any direct references to ethnic categories. Although most cases were not explicitly ethnic, they could still refer to a country or a definite geographical entity, and the mentioning of e.g. "French" or "Russian" showed us the preferred source of academic knowledge. In around 67% of cases there were no direct references to ethnic categories, and where such references occurred, "Hungarian" was the dominant category. To some extent, this is understandable, since the social science courses concerned aim to teach students about their local context (which also explains the occurrence of the "Roma" category in the data sheets). However, aside from these references, "English" or "French" were the most common ethnic categories appearing in the descriptions, in another sign of West-centrism in the programmes.

In 4% of the geography courses, 6% of political science courses, 6% of sociology courses and 13% of international relations ones, ethnic elements only appeared either very generally or, if a concrete ethnic category was mentioned, it was usually embedded in the context of a more general enumeration. Concrete ethnic categories are almost non-existent in the geography course data sheets, since only a sixth of the courses refer to ethnic groups at all, either in general terms, or (predominantly) to Hungarians (one course is about Roma). However, we should note that ethnicities are widely discussed in the actual content of some geography courses (see the section below on the reading lists), but only in rather general and enumerative terms, without providing any specialised analysis of the relevant phenomena. Ethnic categories are comparatively frequent (comprising a third of all cases) in sociology, political science, and especially international relations. The Hungarian ethnic category is over-represented throughout, in around 11% of cases across all four programmes: the lowest percentage was in international relations at 9%, and the highest was in political science at 17%. Other ethnic groups were scarcely mentioned. Roma and Jewish categories are present to some extent, but mainly in sociology degrees, and only referring to Europeans; while other course descriptions mainly refer to ethnicities in those countries neighbouring Hungary (Slovak, Romanian etc.).

Religion appears to be the least significant topic in the social science courses analysed: only 6% of all data sheets contained any religious category. In addition, where it is mentioned, religion is for the most part discussed only in general terms. It appears as a concrete issue primarily in international relations programmes (where 9% of the data sheets refer to religious categories), but even then the references usually include only three religions, namely Catholic, Protestant and Muslim. All other major religions are simply invisible in the social science course descriptions analysed, including e.g. Buddhism and Hinduism. This is an important finding, one well worth researching further, as it shows a Christian versus Muslim division appearing in terms of religion, which may indicate an intrinsic Orientalist vision.

7. The Representation of Global Knowledge in Compulsory Reading Lists

Besides course titles and descriptions, we decided to analyse the compulsory readings accompanying courses as well, since these may offer a more detailed picture of the actual content of knowledge as distributed in social science degrees. In this respect, we found it important to compare the course summaries and respective reading materials offered to students. Although we accept that this data provides only a very general picture of the knowledge disseminated, and does not directly represent actual course content, such material does indicate something of the sources used in courses, and remains an important tool for shaping students' orientation and coursework. Here we made use of similar categories as we did with the course descriptions, but the reading lists also provided us with a good deal of supplementary data — including for example useful information about authors' attributes.

Analysis of Authors

Concerning the authors' country of origin, we found a very clear predominance of Hungarian scholars across all programmes (Diagram 4). This implies that most of the social science teaching materials consist of textbooks and works by Hungarian authors: hence they are the primary source of academic knowledge for students. The preponderance of Hungarian-born authors (60%) is followed by a significant proportion of

Anglo-Saxons (24% altogether, with 16% from the US and 8% from the UK), coupled with scholars from Germany (6%) and France (4%). The proportion of Germans and French is particularly high in sociology (8% and 7%) and political science (7% and 4%), but also in international relations (6% and 4%). These cases usually consist of classic books from Weber, Durkheim and the like. Surprisingly, concerning the birth of authors, geography is the most inward-looking and provincial with an 85% share of Hungarian authors, with others being predominantly of Anglo-Saxon origin (USA: 6%, UK: 4%). The case of geography is contextually quite specific, as there is a historically strong focus on the national tradition of geography and on Hungarian geographers,[45] while much of the relevant international literature in the field is not included in the syllabi.

To summarise this data, about 84% of the social science readings analysed can be linked to authors coming either from Hungary or from the Anglo-Saxon world, rising to 94% when books by German and French scholars are included; when the handful of authors originating from other European or more broadly Western countries (e.g. Italy, Greece, Netherlands, Austria, Poland, Canada or Norway) are included, the figure becomes 97%. Interestingly, neighbouring countries that have a clear link to Hungary are also rarely represented: in sociology programmes we can find authors from Romania in only two instances, and from Slovakia in just one case. But even here the authors are from local Hungarian minorities, and their books address ethnic issues. Very few listed authors are from China, Brazil, Argentina or Egypt (generally a single author from each country). There is little deviation from this pattern even when we take into account the authors' countries of residence (as against their countries of origin) — in other words where they have spent most of their working lives — since in this case the predominance of the US only increases at the expense of other countries. What is indicated here is that for the most part authors coming from non-

---

45 For more detail on this point, see Zoltán Gyimesi, "The Contested Post-Socialist Rehabilitation of the Past: Dual Narratives in the Republishing of Tibor Mendöl's Introduction to Geography", *Hungarian Cultural Studies* 7 (2014): 242–273.

European areas are literally invisible: for example not one scholar from India is active in Hungarian higher education.

Diagram 4. Authors' country of origin in reading lists

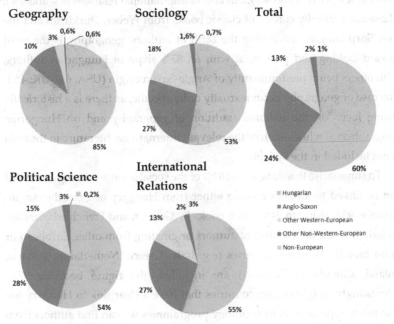

The charts above imply that the four degrees refer predominantly to local authors or to scholars from the Western part of the world. This has many implications, of which two are worth mentioning here. First, it shows a lack of global knowledge and references, omitting e.g. Asian, Latin American, African or other authors. Second, social science students read about the world mainly through the eyes of Hungarian scholars, in another indication of a withdrawal into national perspectives and frameworks of explanation, the operation of which does not favour non-nationalist responses to global social and political change.

When looking at the gender composition of authors, we can see a huge male majority across all four disciplines, with 81% of titles authored by men against 12% by women, while co-authored works have a 4% share (Diagram

5). In geography, especially, there were cases where gender was irrelevant as there were no specified authors – since policy documents, reports, laws or regulations made up a good part (14%) of the compulsory reading. The relatively high number of non-academic materials here is related to geography's applied focus, which distinguishes it from the other three social science programmes. In all, this picture shows a dramatic male dominance, implying that mainly male Hungarian and Anglo-Saxon authors are taught in Hungary. This dominance is greatly reinforced by the fact that gender and linked critical issues play such a minor role in all the course data sheets.

Diagram 5. Gender of authors in reading lists

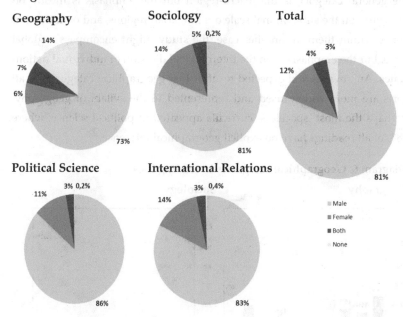

Beyond the matter of authors, as with the course descriptions we also analysed in the content of texts accompanying the courses occurrences of geographical, developmental, historical and social topics, categories or perspectives; due to the very high number of readings, this process was based on information gathered from abstracts, tables of contents and brief surveys of the literature.

Geographical Categories in Reading Lists

If we look at the specific geographical categories used (Diagram 6), smaller scales feature more often in readings compared to course descriptions, and there is a greater difference between geography and other social sciences (geographical categories are present in over 74% of the total records). Again as with the course descriptions, we applied multiple coding quite frequently. For example, in a study on the economic geography of East Central Europe, the general category is the macro-region but the emphasis is mostly on Hungary, on the sub-national scale of Hungarian regions, and on industrial zones within them. In another case, the study might encompass a global scale, but the emphasis is on the international division of individual nation-states. An obvious and expected result is that geographical categories of all sorts are more widely used and represented in the syllabi of geography. Perhaps the most 'spaceless' curricula appeared in political science, where 68% of all readings have no explicit geographical reference.

Diagram 6. Geographical categories in reading lists
Geography   Sociology

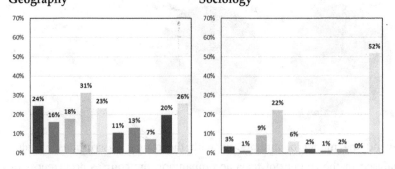

Political Science

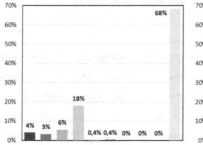

International Relations

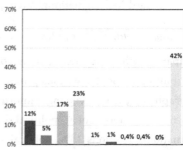

Total

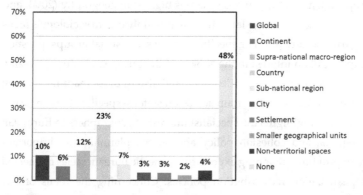

However, as in the course descriptions, the key perspective remains one of methodological nationalism and blocism. The predominant geographical category in all four social science programmes is the country (geography: 31%, sociology: 22%, political science 18%, international relations: 23%), which is mainly due to the prevalence of domestic, Hungarian topics. We can thus see that in general readings mainly limited in scope to the nation-state are provided for Hungarian students (23%), while macro-regions are the second-most important category (12%), though usually referring to Hungary and the European Union. In fact, the large percentage of sub-national regions in geography is also due to the specialisms of European Union regional policy and planning, and to the study of Hungarian administrative territories (local governments, micro-regions, planning regions). This not only shows geography's role in connecting European Union and domestic issues, but also its inward-looking nationalism in knowledge production.

International Political Blocs in Reading Lists

Compared with course descriptions, compulsory readings also show similar distributions across the various programmes. The data on the distribution of geographical scales is even more informative, mapping quite closely onto the presence of international political blocs in the texts (geography 35%, international relations 15%, political science 7%, sociology 2%). The most important category of international political entities is—not surprisingly— the European Union (10%), whose share is highest in geography (20%), and lowest in sociology (1%). The latter finding is mainly due to sociology's focus on Hungarian society or other specific countries and social groups, pursued at the expense of an interest in the subject of the European Union generally. A definite pattern can be identified here, and also in those readings relating to the European Union and certain accession states—specifically Hungary.

This picture highlights the specialist interest of geographers in European Union regional and cohesion policy and spatial planning—an important element in providing planning experts for domestic bureaucracies connected to European Union redistribution policies. Concerning the focus of our study, and leaving aside the internationality of European Union discourse prevalent in all syllabi, it is certainly possible to pick out a rather Eurocentric bias throughout, as the most dominant and interlocked categories are Hungary and the European Union, with no meaningful global contextualisation of domestic Union policies.[46] In total, the European Union is represented in 11% of readings, while other bodies such as ASEAN, Mercosur and the African Union are represented in just 0.3% of readings, and the BRICs and the Andean Community in just 0.1%. Other organisations, such as the UN, or more economic ones like OECD, or commercial and

---

46 See József Böröcz and Melinda Kovács, eds., *Empire's New Clothes: Unveiling EU Enlargement* (Shropshire: Central Europe Review, 2001); and Böröcz and Sarkar, "What is the EU?".

financial organisations such as GATT, the IMF or the World Bank also featured frequently alongside the European Union and NAFTA occurrences, especially in international relations, which was actually more oriented to the Western world. Surprisingly international political organisations featured mainly in the geography and international relations programmes. However, it must be emphasised that international relations courses did deal with other regional organisations, such as the African Union, the Andean Community or even the Maghreb Union; but many readings were pitched towards cultural and historical aspects, and there was still a greatly disproportionate predominance of readings on the European Union. This suggests that non-Westerners are not being represented or seen as real actors geopolitically, but rather as geographical or cultural (ethnic and religious) entities, reflecting a clear Orientalist perspective.[47]

Developmental Categories in Reading Lists

Specific references to developmental categories were found in around 37% of readings, showing that course descriptions and readings reinforce each other in these respects. Concerning development categories, the literature often uses only general terms, like "development", "growth" or "sustainability" — this is especially so in geography (25%), where in many cases there is a rather simplistic presentation of developmental terms in the compulsory literature (mainly due to the central presence of planning and policy-making issues), while development as a discourse is very common (50%). Nevertheless, like the course descriptions, there is a clear focus in all four programmes and across all reading lists on the "developed" world (Diagram 7). This is especially the case in political science, where almost half of the literature (48%) touches principally on the "developed" or industrialised "First World" (usually disregarding the "undeveloped" or "Third World"), though development categories are also represented in this field more than the others, in contrast to sociology (20%). The geography and

---

47 See Said, *Orientalism.*

international relations readings seem to be more balanced in terms of representing all globally perceived levels of development; in fact in these disciplines development categories of all kinds are usually present (geography 19%, international relations 8%).

The relative frequency of global developmental categories in geography readings is notable, in contrast to the field's course descriptions. International relations programmes, on the other hand, follow the same strategy as in its course descriptions, and the fairly frequent use of such categories is mainly due to a more global focus and scope of interest; in sociology, the comparative under-representation of these categories is due to an emphasis on general or domestic social issues, and on the dearth of readings on wider geographical categorisations. The strong presence of the "developing world" here can also be attributed to the preoccupation with the European Union, but in political science this pattern follows a more Anglo-Saxon and West-centric focus on case studies and political theory, observations which underscore a teleological West-centric focus.[48]

Diagram 7. Developmental categories in reading lists

Geography   Sociology

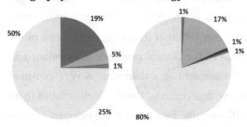

---

48   See Thornton, *Reading History Sideways*.

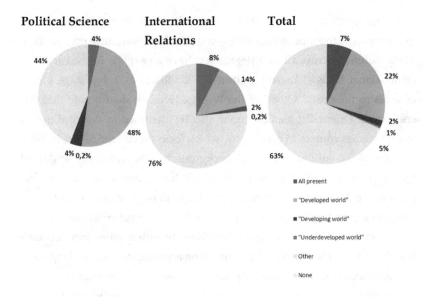

Historical Perspectives

With a few notable differences, the historical perspectives identified in the course descriptions are generally reinforced by the intellectual structures appearing in the reading lists.[49] Historical approaches were less prevalent in reading lists compared to course descriptions, but international relations and geography maintained their high proportion of historical perspectives. Geography has the highest proportion of studies with explicitly long-term historical analyses (22%), often closely linked to general textbook readings on regional geography, political geography, and the world economy (Diagram 8). The historical perspectives of the summaries of these readings are accordingly rather simplified and enumerative, with few comparative analyses and no concrete connection to or elaboration of certain

---

49   In the reading lists it was much harder to determine the concrete historical approach used by specific works as there were varying emphases. Nevertheless, in difficult cases, the dominant temporal framework was selected.

historiographic approaches (but rather often inherently connected to modernisation theories, which follow a typically West-centric perspective). Many volumes across all four degree sets have an explicit Eurocentric and civilisational focus ("Ancient Cultures", "Civilisations") that stage global cultures as the exotic 'Other' of the West[50] . Here we should note that this specifically Orientalist leaning could also be identified in the readings of tourist studies courses in geography, which focus on current issues, but still rely on mono-cultural historical backgrounds. The category "historical (general)" was applied to readings which have some kind of historical perspective, but only in very general terms, with no precise social historical categories (such as introductory texts on the discipline concerned and its evolution of ideas)—these could be based on either long-term accounts (going back to "the ancients"), century-long accounts or decades-long ones, but the focus is not on historical analysis *per se*. Again, as with the course descriptions, geography (at 5%) has by far the largest proportion of studies focusing on future aspects, due to the prevalence of planning, future studies, environmental science and issues of sustainability.

Diagram 8. Historical perspectives in reading lists

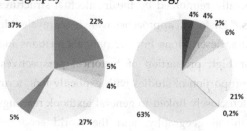

Geography   Sociology

50 See Said, *Orientalism.*

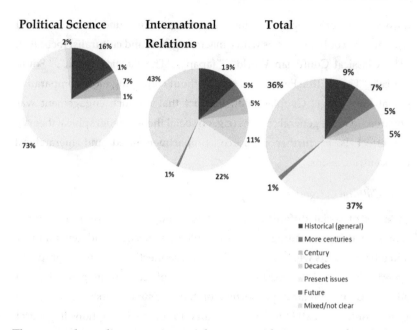

Political Science

2%   16%
1%
7%
1%
73%

International Relations

43%   13%
5%
5%
11%
1%   22%

Total

9%
36%   7%
5%
5%
1%
37%

■ Historical (general)
■ More centuries
▨ Century
▨ Decades
  Present issues
■ Future
▨ Mixed/not clear

The compulsory literature in sociology, as with its course descriptions, maintains a focus on current issues, and is the least historical in its presented selection of readings, since more than half of the records have no temporal foci at all (63%). However, the reason for the higher share of current issues in political science (73%) compared to its course descriptions is due to discussions of contemporary politics, which are largely about political issues and contexts in the West. Here we must also note—this being especially true of political science programmes—that many classical works, while being historical texts, are in part embedded in reading lists and readings that specifically stage them as contemporary or relevant to present issues, thus we had to code them accordingly.

Connecting to our concerns about Eurocentric perspectives, even where geographical categories were referred to widely (in geography and international relations), in all the programmes we still found a general lack of readings discussing the indigenous experiences of non-Western and non-European cultures, and there was a total absence of works mentioning non-

European historiography.[51] A few exceptions were found in international relations, but only in courses with a macro-regional and culturalist focus (e.g. "The Classical Confucian World", "Japan", "The Pacific Region", "South Africa", "The Middle East"), and then without conveying more comparative global knowledge. Coupled with the fact that no such engagement was apparent in more general courses (e.g. on social theory, geographical theory), the effect is to further reinforce compartmentalised and hierarchical Eurocentric visions.

Socio-Cultural Categories

In terms of social differences and ethnic groups, these were also under-represented in the reading lists (6%), while non-specified and general racial and ethnic aspects were common. However, connecting back to geographical aspects, it must be stressed that where ethnicity was in general terms addressed, the greatest proportion of these instances focused on either Europe or (historical) Hungary. Compared to course descriptions in general, Hungarian ethnocentrism shows an increase, and is most striking in political science. This might suggest that political science education reinforces ethnocentrism via its readings, which could also be related to the political changes and migratory contexts discussed above.

In geography programmes, the general reference to ethnic categories was much more common than in the other three disciplines, due to textbook readings of regional geography, yet even here such categories were discussed in very general, non-specific and descriptive terms. In fact, racist categories were represented in geography programmes, and were wedded to some dubious and uncritical categories. One reason was the presence of general (and sometimes old) textbooks on world history and mainly regional

---

51 See Goody, *The Theft of History*; and Daniel Woolf, "Of Nations, Nationalism, and National Identity: Reflections on the Historiographic Organisation of the Past", in *The Many Faces of Clio: Cross-Cultural Approaches to Historiography*, Edward Wang and Franz L. Fillafer, eds., (New York: Berghahn, 2006), 71–103; and Eric R. Wolf, *Europe and the People Without History* (Berkeley: University of California Press, 2010).

geography (where specific religions are dealt with in a somewhat statistical manner); another reason was the popularity of ethnic geography as a traditionally strong sub-discipline (many geographers reverted to this originally nationalist tradition after 1989, by rehabilitating works by pre-1949 geographers who pursued an overtly nationalist ideology).[52] There still seems to be a continuity in racist language, due to geography's imperial heritage, especially in the texts of geographers active before World War II, or in texts discussing geography and geographers before the war. Another peculiarity, linked to geographical categories, is that ethnic geographers' focus is predominantly on the ethnicities of the Carpathian basin, with books that explicitly lay emphasis on Hungarians outside Hungary (e.g. "Hungarians Beyond Our Borders – in the Carpathian Basin", "Hungarians in the Carpathian Basin", "The Geography of the Carpathian Basin"), though the geography of Eastern or East-Central Europe does feature in the geography reading lists. Ethnic relations are also highly popular among historical geographers, whose attention similarly falls exclusively on the Carpathian region or, with a smaller segment of geographers, on historical Europe. This is very much in line with the migratory contexts discussed above, fully reflecting a clear 'petty imperialist' attitude, and thus reinforcing the nationalist turn.

Roma figure only in geography and sociology (six cases in each field), while British (and North American) peoples were disproportionately represented in political science, in line with its more West-centric focus. The discussion of Roma and Jews here again remains only within the geographical boundaries of Hungary. While an explicit focus on Latin American and Arabian ethnic categories only featured in two cases, Eastern Asian categories were more common (in sociology and international relations programmes), but were still very under-represented, while e.g. African categories were totally absent from the readings. In the case of ethnic categories, we can say that a structure similar to that the course descriptions

---

52   See Gyimesi, "The Contested Post-Socialist Rehabilitation of the Past".

is at work here, to the extent that there is no major difference between the various programmes in this respect.

In the readings there is not much interest (10%) in religious categories and references overall. As in the course descriptions, there are some references mainly to Christianity and Islam, and these appear almost exclusively in sociology and international relations programmes. Our "other/general" category here refers to a non-specific or general use of religious categories, without any emphasis on particular religions. Geography's very widespread use of this category is due to a great concentration of descriptive and general materials (consistent with the distribution of ethnic and racial categories). These materials either introduce many religions at once but in rather descriptive historical or statistical terms, with no specific focus or academic elaboration, or else form only a small and very secondary part of a whole topic (e.g. World Factbook, statistical yearbooks, regional geography books, regional monographs, books on world history, atlases). This suggests that even if it is broadly present, the discussion of various religions is in no sense the focus of attention in the readings accompanying the course descriptions. In the readings of sociology and international relations programmes, we can clearly detect a thoroughgoing and consistent interest in Jewish experiences and topics, but with the qualification that this interest is connected to nothing other than European and Western historical experiences. In terms of geographical and spatial perspectives, the relevant course readings are aligned with the picture found in the course descriptions: Hinduism and Buddhism do appear in one or two cases, but only in the presumably Orientalist context of representing Christian and Muslim religions above other global religions.

Concerning the representation of gender issues in the readings' abstracts and tables of contents, we can clearly see that—as with the course descriptions—gender is conspicuously absent even at the more detailed level of literature content, with only 2% of readings dealing with gender issues at all. The field of geography is most striking in this respect, as it touches on gender issues in particularly minimal terms (e.g. the distribution of different sexes), and as we have seen excludes such issues from course descriptions or compulsory readings altogether. In sociology, four texts (for instance by Pierre Bourdieu) deal with masculinity, and two with homosexuality; the situation is quite similar in political science and international relations. However, these texts form an extremely small proportion of the literature as a whole, and this deficiency is exacerbated by the unequal gender ratio of authors. As already suggested in the context of the course descriptions, this also holds true for readings that almost exclusively represent West European gender experiences.

8.   Conclusions

Our aim was to decipher in the undergraduate social science degrees of four Hungarian universities the mental maps and cognitive hierarchies concerning the representation of global society; we have also shown that educational strategies and educational migratory links in Hungarian higher education are somewhat consistent with these mental maps, inherent attitudes and values. We suggest that these dynamics not only condition the social mental maps of global societies, but they can also consequently further influence other related social processes.

Understanding the cognitive content of current Hungarian higher education strategies is a key issue, especially in light of newly proposed educational plans. Higher-educational curricula are influenced to a large extent by the prevailing government. The social sciences are especially at risk, as the natural sciences and technical studies are officially sanctioned and promoted, while social science undergraduate degrees are shrinking and fundamentally changing. In international relations this is a particularly critical issue: as our analysis has shown, international relations is a traditionally important, indeed key programme in conveying knowledge about global history and society, yet the government is planning to undercut all university degrees in the subject with the exception of the one offered by Central Governmental Public Service University.

Although we are aware of the fact that these recent changes in Hungarian higher education cannot be directly captured through social science curricula, we have still managed to develop some relevant findings, since cognitive structures in higher education alter only in the long-term. Although the documents analysed are mainly from the period just prior to the implementation of these changes, it should be clear that the publicly available content of social science curricula already shows a significant Eurocentrism, with knowledge production and education effectively turning a blind eye toward other parts of the world. Further, the knowledge promoted here is mostly based on national elements, while the knowledge transmitted comes predominantly from Hungarian and to a lesser extent Western (mainly Anglo-Saxon) scholars. While we can argue over how far undergraduate study can encompass knowledge of global societies, and over what form this knowledge should take, few would deny the growing necessity for such knowledge — especially under already globalised education systems.

Our research shows various elements of nationalist and Eurocentric cognitive structures. First of all, it is striking that the scope of the curricula analysed is largely restricted to nation states and supranational blocs, while regional analysis and data sources are usually absent. Further, these geographical units are predominantly Western, with a particular focus on Anglo-Saxon regions and, in rare cases, on some Eastern geopolitical players (e.g. Russia or China). Besides this, the single most dominant geopolitical bloc appearing throughout is unsurprisingly the European Union, at the expense of an engagement with other major international political blocs. In line with this, comparative classes or sources are also missing from the curricula, indicating the lack of a critical perspective, but also a reluctance to convey global knowledge to students in a more open, coherent and systematic manner.

Eurocentrism is also indicated by the fact that the historical knowledge included in the programmes comes only from this region, and mainly from Hungary. It is interesting that while Western social structures and knowledge are widely covered, information about even the regions neighbouring Hungary is often missing. The resulting cognitive structure is very narrow in its focus: not only is the overall global context missing, but even an understanding of the local embeddedness of Hungary is absent. This tendency is exacerbated by the previous finding: that the remaining educational material comes predominantly from Hungarian sources, and the rest from Western scholars. This points to a significant provincial inwardness, as even knowledge of Western countries is to a great extent transmitted by Hungarian scholars, and through their quite particular understanding of these regions.

In terms of the use of ethnic categories or religion, further signs of Orientalism and related ethnocentrism can be detected. Knowledge is produced mainly by white male authors, and thus a particular understanding of prevailing power relations is disseminated through the texts, conditioning students' perceptions of their surrounding — as we have seen, artificially limited — world. Thus we can identify in the curricula analysed what seems to be a deeply conservative and ethnocentric mental map.

But how can these aspects of knowledge production be related to migratory and ideological changes? First of all, it is clear that through its migratory links Hungarian higher education mainly attracts students from Hungarian ethnicities living in neighbouring Romania, Ukraine, Slovakia and Serbia, and that these incoming groups are in turn provided with a conservative, ethnocentric and more generally highly Eurocentric education. They also do not receive adequate knowledge about Hungary's political or social relationships with the countries they came from. Consequently, future emigrants among the younger generations of social science graduates will have little knowledge of themes and concerns beyond the European Union and the West, which will make them most comfortable with destinations like the United Kingdom and the United States. There is therefore a real possibility that, beyond other factors, Hungarian social science degrees as they exist and develop are contributing to the rise of young graduates emigrating to these primary destinations—not only as students but also as deskilled service industry workers. The cognitive hierarchies inherent in higher education might therefore reproduce pre-existing social inequalities through migratory links.

If we turn towards the relation between ideological changes and the mental map of social science programmes, we can see that although there are great tensions (including those accruing from the closing down of programmes and other related conflicts), the basic ideological assumptions of these programmes, and of the current neoliberal, conservative and neo-nationalist turn, do not contradict each other. The country's higher education system imagines itself to be in a European space, and is dramatically focused on the European Union and on Hungary itself, while providing little education or knowledge of what lies beyond. In fact, this system provides inadequate knowledge even of emerging international political blocs outside Europe, and of social experiences that are likely to be of service in an increasingly globalised world. In this respect, the neo-nationalist turn emphasises more and more the 'Hungarianness' of compulsory curricula, making for even more parochial mental maps and geographical representations. All this implies that once the currently planned changes in higher education come into effect, they will reduce an already small cognitive circle of reference points, and will further enhance the apparent neo-nationalist turn.

The Role of Civic Education at University: Lessons from Azerbaijan

Piers von Berg

1. Civic Education at University

In this chapter civic education is understood as a means to empower young citizens, one that involves personal and social awareness, agency and skills, and that entails: (1) cultivating students' awareness of social norms and socialisation, and introducing them to the idea of prosocial behaviour; (2) challenging them to identify issues that they care about, affect them and they could change; and (3) developing their academic, professional and life skills.[1] The chapter first describes how the author developed a civic education programme in Azerbaijan to achieve these three aims. It then proceeds to reflect on this experience, and to ask whether it could apply to a British university before finding, in a brief survey of educational, scientific and legal literature, strong reasons to say that it could apply. In that sense the chapter traces out an example of how experiences in post-Soviet universities can inform approaches in Western universities.

I taught an experimental programme on civic education as a Civic Education Project (CEP) Visiting Faculty Fellow (Baku, Azerbaijan 2001–2003).[2] This section will discuss how the programme concentrated on students gaining academic and professional skills while studying themes that had direct meaning and relevance to their everyday lives. The discussion is in four parts. First I describe how the difficulties intrinsic to the teaching

---

1   A shorter version of this chapter was originally published in Evangelia Papoutsaki and Tinatin Zurabishvili, eds., *Caucasus Higher Education in Transition* (Tbilisi: CEP, 2004): 95–105. I am grateful to Ruth Deakin-Crick, Geof Giacomini, Annie Hughes, Gerison Lansdown and Tristan McCowan for their comments on the study.

2   The course was the brainchild of myself and Geof Giacomini. He taught some of the classes and we organised the "Youth Forum" conference together. I am very indebted to him for his ideas and encouragement.

of regular Western undergraduate courses led to experimentation with civic education. The next two parts discuss a civic-education programme that was taught, along with the results. Lastly, I analyse these results in detail. Throughout, in different ways, I seek to draw out some of the implications for our own use today.

Teaching with CEP and the Youth Forum

In my first year with the Civic Education Project (CEP), I taught undergraduate courses in International Relations which were broadly similar in content and method to a course which one might expect to find in a Western university. I found teaching this course to be very hard because my students did not know how to take notes, to write essays, or to conduct independent research or make presentations. This was compounded by the teaching material, which was not directly relevant to the Caucasus. For example, we studied the Kosovo conflict and the 1993 Asian financial crisis. By the end of the year, I felt that my students had learned little that was practical or relevant to their everyday lives, especially when they had recently become citizens of a country experiencing dramatic change after the collapse of Communism and independence. They had learnt about things which did not affect them, and yet had learnt nothing with regard to the practical skills required to understand, or to constructively engage with and change the world around them.

The courses which I taught probably had a greater impact through the method of their tuition, than through their academic content, similar to the experience of other CEP Fellows.[3] For example, I tried to generate discussions whereby students felt comfortable to express their own views, and to question the teacher. This was an entirely novel experience for most of my students, who were accustomed to Soviet-era methods where there was little debate in the classroom, and certainly no questioning of the teacher. Although this approach was interesting and popular among students, it

---

3   See A. Salem, ed., *A Question of Method: Teaching in the Social Sciences at Post-Soviet Universities* (Budapest: Civic Education Project, 2002), 157.

could not in itself teach them how to write or to conduct their own research. I realised after my first year with CEP that my courses may have been a liberating and fun experience, but that they were inappropriate to the students' needs.

This idea was reinforced by my experience of a student conference, which I organised at the end of the first year. The conference was called the "Youth Forum", and was close to a discussion-based approach to civic education. This approach holds that the core part of civic education is learning to talk and to listen with others about public problems. It was similar in design to a Model United Nations or youth parliament. At the "Youth Forum", the students represented in teams different groups in Azerbaijani society. The goal of each team was to put forward proposals to forward the interests of their group in three areas of the economy, politics and social reform. The goal of the conference was for the students to produce a manifesto for the future on each area. The object of each team was to include their proposals in the final manifesto. In order to do so, they had to obtain support from other teams, who were in turn vying for support for their own proposals.

Observing the Forum, it was clear that the students thoroughly enjoyed being 'in role', arguing, listening (sometimes) and working together to find common ground. None seemed bored, disinterested or in need of encouragement. We observed that the skills required by the Forum such as how to negotiate, work in teams, give a presentation or write a proposal, for example, were not well developed. We also noticed that the proposals on paper had no practical repercussions beyond the Forum.

I decided that it was more valuable for my students to learn about themselves and issues they could connect with and interact with in their lives, particularly as they were going through an important period of personal change as adolescents and young adults. Looking at the ideas and experiences of other CEP Fellows, I agree with Etibar Najafov's understanding of democratic education,[4] which entails an active engagement

---

4   Ibid., 28–34.

in personal development, and a commitment to social reform. I also find Daniel Moses's use of C. Wright Mills's concept of the 'sociological imagination' highly relevant.[5] I wanted my students to awake the "sense of their own powers to think, make sense of the world, and take steps towards changing it".[6] This being so, during the second year of my teaching I designed and taught a year-long programme in civic education.[7]

A Civic Education Programme

Civic education is traditionally understood as entailing the preparation of democratic citizens, while democratic education is understood as comprising the democratic control of educational policy in general terms[8] or the democratisation of decision making in schools. It is beyond the scope of this piece to provide a review of the substantial literature on civic education.[9] Our approach is closest to the ideas of 'service learning' and civic education through discussion, and these ideas are explained in the essay—see above and below. Fundamentally, it understands civic education as a means by which to empower citizens through education. My students were already adult citizens and not children who were 'citizens in waiting'. As such, I focused on: (1) themes that were connected to everyday life, and (2) skills which would enable students to better acquire and deploy this knowledge outside the classroom. Our programme sought to achieve these aims in practice through the following means:

5   Ibid., 143.
6   Ibid., 143.
7   This programme was taught at Khazar University in Baku, and at the Ganja Education Information Center, Ganja. 39 students from eleven different universities volunteered for and finished the course in June 2003; the same students participated in "Youth Forum" conferences in both locations in early May.
8   See Amy Gutmann, *Democratic Education* (Princeton, N.J.: Princeton University Press, 1999).
9   For a useful introductory overview of the area, see Jack Crittenden and Peter Levine, "Civic Education", https://plato.stanford.edu/archives/sum2013/entries/civic-education/ (as of May 30 2013).

The first course, "Civic and Cultural Change in Azerbaijan" (Autumn semester), broadly covered the issue of how we as individuals and communities create and experience personal and cultural values in a time of change. This course focused on personal development themes, such as learning to understand yourself — i.e. one's own beliefs and inhibitions. This entailed the study of students' immediate environment, e.g., their families and their values, and of how they interrelated through processes of socialisation.

The subject matter of the second course, "Personal and Social Change in Azerbaijan" (Spring semester), covered how personal attitudes and experiences create identity in a time of change. The course focused on themes of social activism, e.g. prosocial behaviour and attitudinal change — with field research conducted on the needs of social minorities, e.g. drug addicts and homeless children, and an examination of the help provided by the State. The students then each chose a problem/issue to research from their own lives, which fulfilled this criteria: 1) that it was important to them, 2) that it affected them directly, and 3) something they could in some way influence. They were allowed to either work individually or in teams of no more than three. They used the research skills learned in semester one to put together a research report that described their chosen problem and explained the reasons for it. They then used the skills learned in semester two to construct a project proposal to address the problem over the summer holidays. Both pieces of work were then presented at a second Youth Forum conference at the end of the year.

Each week, discussion classes were followed by skills workshops that covered basic academic skills, with a particular focus on writing and research skills. Some professional skills such as teamwork and problem solving were also introduced. The methods used in these workshops included team debates, competitive and cooperative group exercises, and research exercises undertaken on the streets of Baku and in students' own homes. One of the first research assignments was to interview young people on the streets of Baku about their aspirations for the future, and for the students to interview their own parents and grandparents about their aspirations when they left university during the Soviet Union period. Reflecting on this experience helped us to examine social norms as distinct from laws and morals.

The Forum was a four-day conference held in May 2003, which was designed to exercise skills and knowledge derived from the course. Students assessed each other's research on a specific problem in their community, e.g., the lack of student activism at their university, or pollution in their local river. They also worked in teams to constructively criticise others' plans for voluntary community projects. These were designed to address the specific problems which they had researched—e.g, a student summer club, or a neighbourhood clean-up campaign. After the conference, the students were expected to do their own fundraising, if needed, and to implement their projects during the summer holidays.

Results

The results of these experimental courses and of the conference were difficult to measure because they were by nature provisional and developmental. The following checklist includes indicators of the programme's success drawn from sources including student feedback after the "Youth Forum", course grades, students' research, and progress on student projects as well as my observations.

Self-organisation: "Apart from [learning] skills I became active, independent and organised. Now I can't live a day without planning it ahead and it helps a lot when you know what you've got to do and know how to distribute 24 hours among all the things you have to do".[10]

Writing and presentation: in the Autumn semester 24 out of 29 students passed the essay component, 13 improved their grades by 25% or more, and 10 students achieved an A grade. Half the students achieved an A grade for their presentations.

---

10   This is from an essay by one of the students which was written in response to the question "Do you think personal change is different to social change?".

Research: a number of students identified significant gaps in the available student support services. These shortcomings included: the virtual absence of educational extra-curricular activities during the summer break at Baku's largest university; the lack of girls' sports activities or facilities at Baku's most modern private university; and the lack of information about universities for school-leavers in the districts of Baku (and the possible connection of this to bribery at universities).[11]

Problem-solving: the students learned and applied a rigorous problem-solving methodology, which took the following schematic form: what is the problem; is it important to me; does it affect me; can I solve it; how do I describe the problem; how do I explain the problem; how do I establish goals; establish action-goals (objectives); and, a logical framework for the project. The logical frameworks included goals, objectives, methods, results, indicators of results and monitoring, resources and risks. All students completed this process successfully: none dropped out or failed any of the stages of it. One student remarked: "If before I used to say that I can do something, now I say that first I should go into details, then say that yes, I can do [it]".[12]

Teamwork: the Youth Forum encouraged the students to express themselves as individuals, and yet to cooperate with each other in order to achieve their aims collectively. They worked without adult direction for four days, and then planned to continue their work during the summer holidays. Some students expressed their appreciation of the challenge of doing this: "Working in a group, in a team is REALLY difficult! That's what I understand. A team should know what its goals [are], what interests each team member".[13]

Personal development: the experience of the course and the Youth Forum encouraged students to understand more about themselves: "I was

---

11   These findings were drawn from unpublished research reports by several students.
12   Anonymous "Youth Forum" student feedback #8.
13   Anonymous Forum student feedback #15.

motivated by [the] wish to learn new skills, associate with new people and try and understand my own wishes, abilities, opportunities".[14] One student even remarked: "This course has changed me in great ways. I have learned many new things. I have learned to be independent, to make projects. This course has changed my life'.[15]

Social awareness and activism: in their questionnaires, interviews and experiments from the Autumn semester, students gathered evidence which suggested a lack of independent decision-making on the part of other students, especially girls, studying in the Azerbaijani sector at university. One female student expressed surprise at how conservative she felt her culture had become. Other students argued that there was a lack of opportunities for students to hold real positions of responsibility at university, e.g., in organising extracurricular clubs and activities.[16] In addition, the Youth Forum (Spring semester) gave the students the opportunity to think about a social issue/problem that they were concerned about, to research it, and then to try to change it. Students enjoyed this because it gave them "more independence, i.e. working, deciding what's important to me, affects me and that [I] can affect; putting forward the ways and means of solving it".[17]

Volunteerism, motivation and interest: of the 36 students who completed the course in June 2003, all had volunteered for the course, and had undertaken the extra classes and workload, although this did not earn them any additional academic credit. They also took responsibility for all aspects of their respective projects. Some students were required to undertake substantial time commitments of 7–8 hours a day for 10 days,

---

14 Anonymous Forum student feedback # 4.
15 Anonymous Forum student feedback #17.
16 The Pioneer and Komsomol organisations of the Soviet era had disappeared by this time. In their place was a handful of youth activities (e.g., Summer camps), which were mostly restricted to the English-speaking elite in Azerbaijan; civics as a subject was not taught at secondary level at the time.
17 Anonymous Forum student feedback #7.

or drawn out commitments of 15 hours a week for 6 weeks of the summer holidays.

Student autonomy: the most frequently used word in the student feedback from the Youth Forum was "independence" (this was not a mantra from the course). Students expressed this in different ways, for example, "I liked hard working students in Azerbaijan and now I definitely believe that we can change and solve problems in Azerbaijan by ourselves".[18] They related this either to "acquiring new skills, new views, being more independent and organised",[19] or to the projects themselves: "projects are symbols of [our] ability to work independently".[20]

Community projects: 20 different community service projects were designed, including a model United Nations-style conference, neighbourhood ecology campaigns, summer schools for orphans and refugee children, and skills and conversation clubs for students and schoolchildren. Almost all of the projects involved an endeavour to transmit skills and knowledge derived from the course to other students and schoolchildren. Many of these projects, especially in Ganja, had no budget and simply required access to a supply of paper and a photocopier.[21]

Analysis and Implications

First of all, it can be confidently argued that 36 students attained varying levels of skills and social awareness which they did not possess previously. These volunteers from different faculties, universities, and regions, had never attempted to apply any of these skills before; nor had they seriously

---

18 Anonymous Forum student feedback #3.
19 Anonymous Forum student feedback #15.
20 Anonymous Forum student feedback #23.
21 At the time of writing (2003) the students had received USD 935.00 from foreign embassies and oil companies in Baku for projects that required funding. The students elected to make the applications themselves.

investigated the behaviour, expectations and motivations either of themselves, or of the society and culture around them.

To the extent that we may take students' responses as being reliable, it could be said that the course was successful in empowering students: "I could never imagine that some day I would make my own project and also I would write reports, make presentations, negotiations etc".[22] Students subsequently believed that they could change their society, with minimum help and assistance, and they hoped that they would actually be able to effect such change during the summer.

The actual subjects of the course were the students themselves, the changes they experienced in their personal lives, and what could be observed in society. Discussing the ability and capacity for change was a fascinating theme for post-Soviet adolescents and young adults who have seen ideology turned upside down. The students could actually witness what we were discussing, and more importantly could test these ideas against prevailing social reality (which made teaching theory commensurately easier). Our subject-matter—e.g., the students' own beliefs and values—emanated from the students themselves, and from their experiences of the world outside the classroom. In this way, the teacher can learn with the students, and the students can learn through trying to teach others and this was a particularly effective teaching method. Therefore, our subject-matter was visible, was connected to post-Soviet reality, and was directly accessible to the students.

The course helped the students to develop skills through consistent guidance, practice and repetition, especially as many of these skills were new.[23] For all of the skills taught we used clear criteria, and categories that conformed to what was taught. In practice, these criteria and categories became forms of assessment which could be used to help to diagnose the teacher's assessment, and by means of which the students could assess each other's work. This responsibility to assess each other's progress in turn

---

22   Anonymous Forum student feedback #23.

23   For valuable teaching materials on all the skills mentioned in this article, see Sue Drew and Rosie Bingham, *The Student Skills Guide* (Aldershot: Gower, 1999).

helped students to understand how to constructively criticise one another, something which was also useful in developing teamwork skills. It was these life skills, which included prioritising, compromising, saying "no", which could be said to be the most beneficial once the course was finished.

The teaching methodology used was participant-led and experiential. I learned with the students about them and their society around them by engaging with it through introspection, discussion, and real world research. This approach can be found in the writings on learning citizenship. As Storrie argues:

> Citizenship is at best learned by engagement in relevant contexts where the everyday codes of social, cultural and political behaviour can be observed, rehearsed, experimentally used and developed. Apprentice citizens are in effect invited, in the best traditions of action research, to use intervention into social processes to gain knowledge about those same processes.[24]

This approach (above) formed a circular process of experiencing, sharing, theorising, applying, and testing.[25] In all aspects, we encouraged the students to decide for themselves how to proceed, given the initial structure, interactive environment, and theoretical information which we had provided. As one student observed: "the Forum—conference was free, I mean, there wasn't [sic] official manners, lectures in this Forum, it gave independence to participants to think clearly and without any force".[26] In simpler terms, it meant us being 'hands-off', so as to allow the students to be 'hands-on'.

Although critical thinking, debating and even rote-learning were used in the course, we placed greater emphasis on collective decision-making and discussion skills. I have found it more rewarding to have discussions rather

---

24 Tom Storrie, "Citizens or What?", in Jeremy Roche and Stanley Tucker, eds., *Youth in Society* (London: Sage, 1997), 65.
25 James A. McCaffrey, "Independent Effectiveness: A Re-consideration of Cross-Cultural Orientation and Training", *The International Journal of Intercultural Relations* 10:2 (1986): 159–179.
26 Anonymous Youth Forum student feedback #6.

than debates in my classes.[27] I consider it a more valuable civic skill because it is indispensable to working with others.[28] Working with others to exercise your rights and responsibilities for, with, and in your community, helps form the basis of civic competence. This concept is drawn from Benjamin Barber's well-known theory of 'strong democracy' that emphasises democracy as civic duty and participation, not merely the defence of private interests and representative politics.[29]

The social context for these activities was youth as a disenfranchised group. The course showed that a low skills base and few opportunities for extra-curricular activities amongst young people (especially if organised by them), served to disenfranchise them as a social group.[30] The results showed that students could act independently for their own benefit when they have the skills and opportunities to research their own problems, and those of the education system within which they live and learn.

In order to identify any long-term impact of the programme, a questionnaire was sent to 14 contactable former students. It asked them to comment upon the perceived benefits of the courses, as they understood them, some twelve years after completion. Of the 14 sent, ten replied. It is significant that the response rate was over 70% twelve years after the students completed the courses. They were not provided with any incentive or benefit to reply, or given information to recap and summarise what they had studied.

---

27 For possible strategies used by CEP Fellows see Anush Shahverdyan, "Cooperative Learning in Undergraduate Education", in Salem, ed., *A Question of Method: Teaching in the Social Sciences*, 97–106.

28 For the importance of collective reasoning for civics see Gutmann, *Democratic Education*, 106–107.

29 See Benjamin Barber, *A Passion for Democracy* (Princeton, NJ.: Princeton University Press, 1998), 95–110.

30 As an example of this disenfranchisement, a 2001 UNICEF survey of young people in Azerbaijan recorded that of 20% of those who regularly participate in clubs in their free time, only 16% believe they have a voice in municipal decisions affecting young people, while 51% did not know of any their rights.

Three of the respondents were able to provide a list of five to seven skills as examples of what they had learned on the course. One said: "The base of my writing skills was founded then during the courses. Now in my professional life this helps me to write high quality proposals, reports, concept papers, training materials, prepare clear presentations to the point".[31] Another commented: "From the specific examples—15 years later I remember our discussions in groups—that was a great practice of team working skills. I remember the survey we had to conduct at the Universities we studied at—that was great experience of project planning (and managing) skills".[32] One respondent later said that she valued the research skills the "most".[33] Six of the respondents were able to identify skills that had proved useful in later life. One went so far as to say: "I believe the skills we obtained there were so fundamental for any citizen that all other knowledge and skills we got later have been built on them".[34]

In terms of civic participation, most of the respondents agreed that the courses have affected the decisions which they have subsequently taken as citizens. The specific examples they cited related variously to voluntary activities; to the expression of one's own opinions; and to working with others. Three respondents said that the courses were not helpful for civic participation because they were cynical about politics and wished to stay out of it.

Every respondent agreed that students should be encouraged to talk about their personal values. They said that this helped break down barriers, and to build self-confidence and self-knowledge. One former student said: "Many concepts were interesting to learn about yourself and ask yourself simple but important questions (i.e. personal and social values, norms which

---

31 Author Questionnaire, 2 February 2015.
32 Author Questionnaire, 6 February 2015.
33 Author Questionnaire, 29 January 2015.
34 Ibid.

were important) [...]. Eventually, both the courses and projects helped me to strengthen my self-confidence too and desire to help others".[35]

The respondents were asked whether the courses had contributed to any major decisions which they had subsequently taken in their lives. Three said yes. One gave a specific example of an experience when she was offered a job with an NGO. Her parents objected as the job entailed a long journey, and they did not understand or take seriously the work involved. She said:

> Those days I remembered our courses and topics on decision making and a person's own accountability for his own actions and his future. I spoke a lot with [my] parents, we had quite intensive discussions and in the end they couldn't resist more letting me start the work I was striving for that much [...]. I think it was a really important decision I took. And it was because I was thinking of the topics of self-realisation, independence, decision making that we all covered during the course.[36]

She said that in the end she worked there for five years, progressed her career, made new friends, felt very satisfied and had access to new training opportunities.

Two students mentioned people they met on the prosocial part of the course and expressed sympathy for their plight and a willingness to help. One said: "He was alcoholic. Up to [to]day, me and my friends remember him, wondering what has become of him".[37] Another said one of the things she liked about the course was that "unintentionally I could help a man. He stopped drinking [..,] restored relationships with his child and changed his life. He moved to Russia and started publishing".[38]

In terms of reasons for initially volunteering, six students wanted to practice their English. Three of them said they were attracted to the course in part because there was a lack of extracurricular opportunities. Six of the students felt that they were not learning in their normal classes, and that our class provided more interesting and relevant topics. When it came to reasons for attending throughout, five said they enjoyed the experience of the class

---

35   Author Questionnaire, 13 February 2015.
36   Author Questionnaire, 12 February 2015.
37   Author Questionnaire, 29 January 2015.
38   Author Questionnaire, 9 February 2015.

in terms of making new friends, getting on with their teachers, and getting out of the classroom for activities. One said that the course seemed of value with regards to their future and "our professional life". Two others simply stated that they were learning.[39] Only one respondent mentioned her improved English as a reason for continuing with the course.

It is clear that 15 years later, a small sample (10) was able to identify specific skills which they had learned on the programme and, remembered quite clearly the experiences which they had had. In particular, they were able to give examples of how they have subsequently used what was learned to the benefit of their personal or professional lives.

Of course these courses also involved limitations and obstacles. The most obvious drawback as a civic education programme was that they taught students very little about their rights and duties as Azerbaijani citizens. It appears that three of them were not more encouraged by the courses to engage in politics. This was a deliberate omission. We focused on creating opportunities for students to learn about the possibilities for and limits of meaningful action in their lives. The courses were about them. One cannot deny the importance of learning about the law, the power structures in their polity and relevant contemporary issues. The argument here is that through our programme, students can – and do – pursue prosocial projects that they care about. In other words, they start to become active citizens.

Importantly, the students volunteered for the course. They gave up their own free time and received no credit. On this basis, they were highly motivated and interested. Not all teachers are so lucky. Also, I was a foreigner, teaching in a foreign language to students excited at the prospect of doing something new.

Consequently, I need to bear in mind the Azerbaijani context in which I was teaching, and my own status as a Western lecturer. At the time there was evidence of a culture among young people in the post-Soviet republics, including Azerbaijan, of a rejection of forced compliance with normative

---

39 "I was learning! I learned how to research, how to write, how to argue!". Ibid.

standards.[40] I benefited from this by offering something different to the prevailing educational norm. In 2003, Azerbaijan was starting to witness and be subject to the forces of globalisation, not only through the substantial investment and construction activities of international oil companies, but also in the visible presence of mostly American funded NGOs such as my own in schools and universities. Blum's field research supports the idea that the reaction to Western cultural influences by the education authorities was accommodating and, if anything, supportive of greater exposure of young people to ideas from the West, which did not undermine Azerbaijani national identity.[41] It could be said that my status as a Westerner and part of an American-funded international NGO gave me a standing with which I could negotiate with my university in order to introduce the programme.

Therefore, there was inevitably a cultural dimension to our activities and there were unequal power relations going beyond those of the teacher-student relationship. However, the argument here is that the key components of the programme, as described in this subsection and summarised below, can have applications in another context, such as a British university. Of course, it remains to be seen in practice whether such a programme could be as effective and engender such positive responses from students, who are not as similarly motivated or interested, or with teachers whose identity and approach does not arouse curiosity, and who have less freedom to innovate. This is understood as a call for more research and is discussed below.

Fundamentally, it is argued that the opportunities to learn more about oneself, to work in groups and to effect change, is of itself attractive to this age group. The newness and difference was indeed an initial attraction but no more than that. It is significant that no students dropped out of this

---

40 See Douglas W. Blum, *National Identity and Globalization: Youth, State, and Society in Post-Soviet Eurasia* (Cambridge: Cambridge University Press, 2007), 156–158. This work is based partly on field research done in Azerbaijan, including focus groups at Khazar University where I taught this civic education programme. I met with the author and discussed his research when he visited Baku.

41 Blum, *National Identity and Globalization*, 159.

voluntary programme. The responses in questionnaires suggest that this was mostly because they made friends and enjoyed interacting with them. The education experience is of course a social one. They also said they were learning something of value.

A disadvantage of this approach was the dependence on foreign donors. At the end of the year CEP had a new donor, the US State Department, which required CEP Visiting Fellows to be US nationals. As a British national, my contract came to an end. I was not able to support myself in Azerbaijan and had to find alternative work. Efforts to monitor the students and to develop the programme the next academic year did not come to fruition.

Turning to my students' subsequent progression after university, for the most part they have subsequently gone on to obtain good positions in skilled professions — suggesting on their part aspiration, motivation, intelligence and, of course, opportunities. They could be said to have a predisposition to look back upon my courses favourably, as their lives have progressed well since the time of the courses.

2. Looking Back: Reflections 15 Years On

What is the relevance of this course today? I will henceforth refer mostly to the UK context. For British students, citizenship studies are compulsory from ages 11–16. Many of the academic skills that we taught in Azerbaijan will be found either within the content of courses, or as part of stand-alone classes, in a British university, e.g. as part of a personal tutorial system.[42] At some UK institutions this forms part of what is called 'Personal Development Planning'. This idea stems from the concept of a 'Progress File', which was endorsed by the Dearing Report as the "means by which students can monitor, build and reflect upon their personal development".[43] Courses on citizenship *per se* are also taught in some UK universities, albeit such courses

---

42 I am grateful to Dr Annie Hughes of Kingston University for showing me the system they have put in place at Kingston as an example.

43 The Dearing Report comprised the findings of the 1997 UK National Committee of Inquiry into Higher Education, entitled *Higher Education in the Learning Society*.

are about citizenship, not for citizenship.[44] Courses on developing citizenship skills are less common.[45]

It is not my aim to comprehensively examine the provision of civic education within the higher education system in the UK. Instead, as points of reference for the ensuing discussion, there are several features of the above courses that make them distinct and arguably led to their success:

> The personal: students examined their own values and norms, and asked how these were formed. To a great extent the course centred upon such self-examination.[46]
> The interpersonal: students learned how to deal with conflict and criticism in a safe environment, how to work in teams, and how to evaluate each other's progress and many made lasting friendships.
> The social: students investigated the values, norms and culture of their family, friends (and peers), and that of their university.
> The practical: students spent a lot of time learning how to do things by actually doing them. Ultimately, some did tackle a real life problem.

Justifications for such an enterprise are now explored below. These can be found in current thinking on higher education, especially the role of civic education at university, the emerging evidence of the development of young adults, and the new field of adolescent rights.

---

44 Tristan McCowan, "Opening Spaces for Citizenship in Higher Education: Three Initiatives in English Universities", Studies in Higher Education 37:1 (February 2012): 51–67.

45 An example of the courses available on citizenship skills is the HEFCE-funded project POLIS (Politics Online Learning and Citizenship Skills), which commenced in 2005. See McCowan, "Opening Spaces for Citizenship in Higher Education", 53.

46 Two-thirds of the respondents in 2015 affirmed, for different reasons, that this specific part of the course was worth repeating.

Does Civic Education have a Place at Universities?

British and European thinking on higher education accepts and advocates a role for universities in the development of citizenship, and acknowledges personal development as being one of the core purposes of higher education. The Council of Europe Steering Committee on Higher Education and Research identifies four broadly interlinked purposes: (1) preparation for the labour market; (2) preparation for life as active citizens in democratic societies; (3) personal development; (4) development and maintenance of an advanced knowledge base in a broad area of academic disciplines.[47] In the UK, the Dearing Report provided a broadly liberal understanding of higher education, in which civic education is directly relevant to the second of the 'four main purposes', this being "to play a major role in shaping a democratic, civilised, inclusive society" (para. 5.11).

Today, many universities subscribe to the idea of 'graduate attributes', to the extent that they form a central piece of their strategy.[48] Such attributes also envisage a prosocial role for students, and may include:

> the qualities, skills and understandings a university community agrees its students should develop during their time with the institution. These attributes include but go beyond the disciplinary expertise or technical knowledge that has traditionally formed the core of most university courses. They are qualities that also prepare graduates as *agents of social good in an unknown future* [emphasis added].[49]

---

47 See http://www.coe.int/t/dg4/highereducation/Activities_en.asp (as of 5 September 2017).

48 See John Bowden et al., "Generic Capabilities of ATN University Graduates", http://www.missouristate.edu/fctl/89072.htm (as of 5 September 2017). For example, in the University of Birmingham's "Education Strategy 2015-2020" it is written that: "students will acquire and be able to demonstrate a common set of attributes that together characterise the 'Birmingham Graduate'". These include "responsible and ethical citizens" as well as "effective problem solvers and communicators" who are "globally and locally culturally aware". See https://intranet.birmingham.ac.uk/staff/teaching-academy/documents/public/education-strategy2015.pdf (as of 31 July 2016).

49 Bowden et al., "Generic Capabilities of ATN University Graduates" (as of 5 September 2017).

Academic thinking also displays a multilayered understanding of higher education, in which the fostering of civic and personal virtues plays a part. Liberal theory stresses aspects of self-realisation and social transformation while professional formation theory regards universities as providers of expertise — and both suggest some civic and community engagement on the part of universities.[50]

In an important recent book, Sir David Watson argued that: "At its heart the university is a reservoir of intellectual capital: its most fundamental purpose is about the creation, testing and application of knowledge".[51] He saw a "traditional battle" between an economic focus on human capital, i.e. the production of qualified manpower essential for economic growth, and a community focus on the creation of social capital, as a means of fostering socially cohesive norms of collective behaviour (Watson 2014: 11).

Among these divergent claims on the role of university, there are new ideas about different forms of what is termed 'capital'. One is of real relevance to civic education. The concept of 'identity capital' includes the fostering of individual self-reliance, self-confidence and self-efficacy — "the goal is a personal story based upon sound and informed decision-making and an ultimate trust in the individual to get it right eventually".[52] As Watson points out, these different notions of capital inevitably overlap. As I shall explain below, identity capital is relevant because of our increasingly complex societies and fast pace of change.

Overlaid upon these different ideas are varieties of pedagogic style. We employed what might be termed 'service learning', that is to say the utilisation of life experiences and experiential learning techniques (see above). We also sought to involve the students in assessing their own work, and encouraged them to choose which topics they wished to focus upon

---

50 See Martin Watson, *The Question of Conscience: Higher Education and Personal Responsibility* (London: Institute of Education Press, 2014), 10–11.

51 Watson, *Higher Education and Personal Responsibility*, 11.

52 James Côté, "The Role of Identity Capital in the Transition to Adulthood: the Individualization Thesis Examined", *Journal of Youth Studies* 5:2 (June 2002): 117–134.

within the wider parameters of the course syllabus. This pedagogical concept of 'co-creation' and 'co-design' is now receiving some acceptance as a technique for more effective teaching.[53]

The theme of change highlights the civic role of the university:

> As the world becomes ever more complex and fast-changing, the role of higher education as a guardian or transmitter of culture and citizenship needs to be protected. Higher education needs to help individuals and society to understand and adapt to the implications of change, while maintaining the values which make for a civilised society.[54]

One should note there also are others who question the 'resilience' of higher education with respect to the need to prepare graduates for a world of complex change;[55] or, more radically, who suggest that the globalised world of the 21st century requires a wholesale rethinking of conventional university education.[56]

Following from this focus on social change and on the roles of graduates within a changing society, there is a progressive argument that the role of universities is to contribute to the public good. For example, some argue that universities should ideally be engines of reform directed towards social change, particularly towards the reduction of poverty and the enhancement of human development, and in terms of improving lives and expanding

---

53 Watson, *Higher Education and Personal Responsibility*, 18.
54 See para. 21 of the 1997 Dearing Report, "Higher Education in the Learning Society: Main Report", http://www.educationengland.org.uk/documents/dearing1997/de aring1997.html (as of 5 September 2017).
55 Ronald Barnett and Susan Hallam, "Teaching for Supercomplexity: a Pedagogy for Higher Education", in Peter Mortimore, ed., *Understanding Pedagogy and Its Impact on Learning* (London: Sage, 1999).
56 Jay Hays, "Chaos to Capability, Educating Professionals for the 21st Century", *Unitec ePress Monograph Series* 1 (2015), http://www.unitec.ac.nz/epress/wp-content/ uploads/2015/10/Chaos-to-Capability_Educating-Professionals-for-the-21st-Centu ry.pdf (as of 5 September 2017).

choices and opportunities.⁵⁷ They therefore advocate the creation of 'public professionals' by universities — persons who have the necessary values, knowledge and skills required to provide services to the public which will expand opportunities, and so lead to better lives and enhanced achievements across society.⁵⁸

The above idea is a way to reinvigorate universities. This is particularly important in the era of globalisation, when our attention is so easily drawn to events happening further afield. This is best expressed by Moglen:

> Some will say that, in the era of globalisation, focusing research and teaching energies on local problems is an invitation to provincialism. I disagree. Globalisation does not happen elsewhere. The movement of capital and its attendant social, political, and cultural effects are as evident in our own communities as anywhere on earth [...]. Elite research universities must ask themselves why [...] so many of our institutions contain experts on clean water technology, the history of feminism, and the rise of religious intolerance in the West who have never asked their students to consider how we might address tainted water supplies, sexual violence, or religious conflict in their own communities.⁵⁹

Why Teach University Students about Citizenship?

Watson argues that universities are the "natural seed bed" of what he calls "soft citizenship".⁶⁰ Such a conception entails self-awareness on the part of academics, along with an awareness of the needs and identities of others, and "deeper senses of sympathy and connection than civic conformity will ever bring about"; this conception of the university also contributes to the sense of personal responsibility, and to a capacity for "public reasoning".⁶¹

57   Melanie Walker and Monica McClean, *Professional Education, Capabilities and the Public Good: the Role of Universities in Promoting Human Development* (London: Routledge, 2013).
58   Ibid.
59   Seth Moglen, "Sharing Knowledge, Practicing Democracy: A Vision for the Twenty-First-Century University", in *Education, Justice and Democracy*, eds. Danielle Allen and Rob Reich (Chicago: University of Chicago Press, 2013), 282–283.
60   Watson, *Higher Education and Personal Responsibility*, 58.
61   Ibid., 59. Some of these arguments can find empirical support from a 2003 study by the Higher Education Funding Council for England (HEFCE), which found that

According to Watson, academic communities ideally provide models for practical action in the real world, as well as a commitment to progressive engagement with intractable problems, and a presumption that knowledge can actively inform responsible social activity. He writes that university attendance is likely to improve a person's capacity to make sound moral as well as technical judgments. Ultimately, Watson contends that the purpose of the university is to engage students in self-creation and authentic life, to develop the habit of thinking deeply, and to foster the capacity to connect with others empathetically.

It might be said that university is less about academic study and more about the experience of learning, sometimes living, and studying somewhere new. This can change the way you think and alters your self-perception. It gives young people space to 'find themselves'. A typical British university provides a host of extracurricular activities, organised by students. There is also a wealth of information provided with regard to future career opportunities and work placements.

While I agree with Watson's notion of 'soft citizenship', the means and methods which he attributes to the university are poorly equipped to achieve this. He is right that university study challenges students to tackle hard questions, to meet deadlines and to communicate what is learned. Also student clubs and societies, and simply socialising, does allow them some space to experiment with ideas, behaviour and, ultimately, identities. But the typical student's spectrum of activities in terms of lectures, tutorials, library research and essay-writing, and extracurricular pursuits, does not give as much scope to build self-awareness, social awareness, or to model practice in the real world as a civic education programme does. Such a programme has a more systematic approach, as explained above, and can arguably

---

graduates have higher rates of 'race tolerance', are less likely to show unqualified support for authority, have less political cynicism and have higher rates of membership of voluntary organisations. See McCowan, "Opening Spaces for Citizenship in Higher Education", 53.

achieve more, cover more and challenge them more. Therefore, the current broad shape of university education can be greatly improved particularly if one focuses on enabling active citizenship, as distinct from detached critical reflection upon citizenship.[62] There is insufficient space here to look at empirical evidence from UK universities; rather the contention is that civic education in the form tried in Azerbaijan in principle promises greater impact than the current practices for instilling 'soft citizenship'.

Citizenship is a complex and disputed concept.[63] I shall here adopt a 'capability' approach to this concept. The core focus of this approach is what people are able to do. I shall adopt Amartya Sen's ideas on capability where capability can be defined as a person's capacity to achieve well-being.[64] It is the freedom to do something. The capability approach talks of the development of a person's functionings, and functionings are what people are and do in practice. Capabilities are the reflection of the ability to achieve valuable functionings. This requires an awareness of one's own needs and values, as well as those of the community in which one lives. As Sen writes, each person should be free to make reflective, informed choices about ways of living that they regard as important and valuable.[65] For example, a curriculum framework that is designed to enhance citizens' capabilities is one that aims at "giving people control over their lives".[66]

---

62   Ibid., 65–66.
63   Arguments centre on both the rights and responsibilities accorded to those entitled to the status of citizen under the laws of any given state, and the preferred normative attitudes, habits and values of any given person. McCowan provides a useful set of categories, covering rights/duties, universality/difference, the local, national and global, and criticality/conformity. See ibid., 53.
64   Amartya Sen, *The Idea of Justice* (Cambridge, MA.: Harvard University Press, 2009), 199.
65   Ibid., 18–19.
66   David Watson and Tom Schuller, *Learning Through Life Inquiry into the Future for Lifelong Learning* (Leicester: National Institute of Adult Continuing Education, 2009), 68.

From my experience in Azerbaijan, the key ingredients to a person's capability are their self-awareness, efficacy and confidence. These enable a person to feel that they can take control of the things that matter. This is also reflected in the ideas of public professionalism as discussed above: "In the absence of a strong sense of personal efficacy and confidence, it is unlikely that professionals will be able to position themselves or sustain their positioning over time as public good professionals".[67] Self-awareness, personal efficacy and confidence are essential for agency. Sen's concept of agency is the ability to act according to one's own values: "what a person is free to do and achieve in pursuit of whatever goals or values he or she regards as important".[68] In the first semester of our course we encouraged the students to identify and assess the prevailing norms present within their own lives; and, in the second semester we asked them to choose what they felt to be of greatest importance in their own lives – and what they believed that they could actually change. If students are so supported in such activities, this contributes to their sense of personal efficacy and confidence. I repeat the words of the students: "now I definitely believe that we can change and solve problems in Azerbaijan by ourselves".[69] As was explained above, this included problems selected by the students from their own lives such as bribery and the lack of girls' sports at university.

Our classes coincided with the period of our students' lives when they were discovering and choosing their own values: late adolescence and young adulthood.[70] Similar to UK students, my students were still like adolescents in that most, if not all, lived with their families; none had children, neither

---

67 Walker and McClean, *Professional Education, Capabilities and the Public Good*, 30.
68 Ibid., 30, quoting Amartya Sen, *Commodities and Capabilities* (New Delhi: Oxford University Press, 1999), 206.
69 Anonymous "Youth Forum" student feedback #3.
70 There are several definitions of adolescence. The definition used here is the period of growth and development in the latter half of childhood and before adulthood from 10-19 years (World Health Organisation, 2014). Young adulthood overlaps to some degree at approximately 18-25.

were they married (with one exception); nor were they earning or expected to support themselves financially. They were becoming whom they now are as personal identity emerges through a process of identifying what you care about, what matters to you, and in discovering where you choose to invest your time and energy.[71] University is not always a 'natural seed bed' for such a process. Indeed some commentators are highly critical of the impact which universities have upon this process: it has been asserted that universities do much to alienate students as a consequence of such factors as assessments, examinations, overloaded curricula, unrealistic time frames, and impersonal institutional and social relationships.[72] According to the testimony of my students, one of the chief advantages of my courses was that they provided something which was attractive, and which was notably different to other courses. I entirely agree with Mann who argues:

> Students can be provided with varied opportunities to express and try out their capabilities. Such opportunities include structured, meaningful activities which require cooperative engagement between students who would not normally work together and which provide students with opportunities to investigate and work things out for themselves. Crucially these activities are given enough time and space for students to feel in control over and responsible for their learning.[73]

It is only if we help students to have such educational experiences at university, such as in a civic education programme, that we can better aspire to the 'soft citizenship' that Watson describes.

What Does Teaching Citizenship have to do with Personal Development?

Since the time when I taught my courses, the level of knowledge regarding the ways in which adolescents and young adults mature and develop has

---

71   Margaret S. Archer, *Being Human: the Problem of Agency* (Cambridge: Cambridge University Press, 2000), 58.

72   Sarah Mann, *Study, Power and the University* (Milton Keynes: Open University Press, 2007), 146.

73   Ibid., 137.

mushroomed.[74] There is a new consensus amongst neuroscientists that mid-to-late adolescence and early adulthood is a period of significant development in brain structure and function.[75] This period is approximately between the ages of 15–22 years.[76] Therefore, an important caveat to the discussion below, where the literature uses the term "adolescent", is that many of these changes continue into a person's twenties.[77] Neurological changes are known to occur in mid-to-late adolescence which affect the areas of the brain which govern activities such as forward planning, risk assessment, and complex decision-making.[78] Also, neural connections strengthen between the regions of the brain that deal with the processing of emotional information, and with emotional self-control.[79] The way in which the brain functions also changes. There is a strengthening of activity in neural systems which govern self-regulation. There is a heightened sensitivity with respect to anticipated rewards (especially pronounced when adolescents are with friends); and, there is increased simultaneous involvement of different regions of the brain in response to stimuli, which helps to control impulses.[80]

---

74 The adolescent brain has been studied systematically only in the last 15 years. See Laurence Steinberg, "The Science of Adolescent Brain Development and Its Implications for Adolescent Rights and Responsibilities", in *Human Rights and Adolescence*, ed. Jacqueline Bhabra (Philadelphia: University of Pennsylvania Press, 2014), 59–76.

75 See ibid., 63; and Louis Cozolino, *The Social Neuroscience of Education* (New York: W.W. Norton, 2013), 33–35.

76 Steinberg, "The Science of Adolescent Brain Development", 71; Sara B. Johnson et al., "Adolescent Maturity and the Brain: the Promise and Pitfalls of Neuroscience Research in Adolescent Health Policy", *Journal of Adolescent Health* 45:3 (Sept 2009): 8–9. This represents the minimum and maximum ages at which it is likely that any given individual has developed the brain structures and functions referred to in this section. See Steinberg, "Adolescent Maturity and the Brain", 71.

77 Ibid.

78 Cozolino, *The Social Neuroscience of Education*, 35; Johnson et al., "Adolescent Maturity and the Brain", 71.

79 Steinberg, "The Science of Adolescent Brain Development", 64.

80 Ibid., 64–65; Linda Spear, *The Behavioural Neuroscience of Adolescence* (New York: W.W. Norton, 2010).

It is important to add some qualifications to these findings. First, these changes are not uniform with respect to individual adolescents or across social groups: i.e. some students may have matured in some respects, but not others, by the time they arrive at university. An important area for future research is the degree to which neuro-behavioural function is influenced by genetics and experiences.[81] Secondly, some researchers are reluctant to conclude that brain development necessarily correlates with or directly determines, behaviour.[82] As mentioned, little is known about how the brain influences the expression of individual differences, or about the role of environmental influences.[83] The adolescent brain can be shaped by environmental stimuli, due to heightened neuroplasticity during adolescence.[84] The areas of the brain which deal with socio-emotional processing are those most affected by environmental influences[85] but the extent of this is unknown.[86] Thirdly, we are dealing with late adolescents and young adults for whom many of these processes are nearly complete and therefore careful distinctions must be made.[87]

How should we assess this evidence? At first glance it could be said merely to confirm what we already know experientially. Adolescence is a time of discovery, turbulence, existential angst, impulsivity: they are known to be especially vulnerable to road accidents, sexual diseases, suicidal

---

81 See Linda Spear, "Adolescents and Alcohol", *Current Directions in Psychological Science* 22:2 (2013).

82 See Steinberg, "The Science of Adolescent Brain Development".

83 See Spear, "Adolescents and Alcohol".

84 Neuroplasticity or neural plasticity refers to the ability of neurons and neural networks to be born, and to grow and change the way they relate to one another in the response to experience. See Cozolino, *The Social Neuroscience of Education*, 159.

85 Clea McNeely and Krishna Bose, "Adolescent Social and Emotional Development: A Developmental Science Perspective on Adolescent Human Rights" in Bhabra, ed., *Human Rights and Adolescence*, 108.

86 See Spear, "Adolescents and Alcohol".

87 See Steinberg, "The Science of Adolescent Brain Development".

behaviour and addiction.[88] Neuroscience should not be accorded privileged status with respect to other forms of evidence due to its novelty. Although if neurological evidence does appear to corroborate findings from other fields, such as behavioural science, then it can lend increased credence to those findings.[89] Lastly, neurological observations are very general in nature, and cannot readily be applied in individual cases: for example, there is as yet no agreed measure of neurobiological maturity.

It is worth inquiring into what other disciplines tell us about late adolescence and early adulthood. Developmental science sees adolescence as a period during which social and emotional competence is learned. Emotional and social competence is understood as a skill which is developed from "acquired experience derived from both modeled behaviour and direct nurturance".[90] Emotional competence is defined as "the ability to perceive, assess, and manage one's own emotions",[91] while social competence is "the capacity to be sensitive and effective relating to other people".[92]

McNeely and Bose posit four skills as being necessary in order to develop these competencies: self-awareness, social awareness, self-management and the ability to get along with others. This is very similar to the concept of emotional intelligence.[93] These are explained respectively as the ability to recognise one own emotions; the capacity to develop empathy; and the

---

88 See World Health Organisation (WHO), *Health for the World's Adolescents* (Geneva: WHO Document Production Services, 2014), 46.

89 See Steinberg, "The Science of Adolescent Brain Development".

90 McNeely and Bose, "Adolescent Social and Emotional Development", 102.

91 Ibid.

92 Ibid.

93 This is a disputed and controversial concept: see Jane McCleskey, "Emotional Intelligence and Leadership: a Review of the Progress, Controversy and Criticism", *International Journal of Organizational Analysis* 22:1 (2014): 76–93. Suffice to say here that McNeely and Bose use the terms of competence, which aligns with Goleman and Boyatzis's approach to emotional intelligence. See Daniel Goleman, *Working with Emotional Intelligence* (London: Bloomsbury, 1998); Richard E. Boyatzis et al., "Emotional Contagion and Proto-Organizing in Human Interaction Dynamics", *Frontiers in Psychology* 6:806 (June 2015).

monitoring and regulating of one's own emotions. Of central importance is the relationship with peers. It is recognised that peers can be both a positive and a negative influence with respect to social support, and with respect to risk taking. It is these environmental factors that most concern developmental scientists. They argue that, as a transition period toward adulthood, adolescence embodies many potential opportunities and risks, so that greater attention should be paid to the provision of environmental support measures and mechanisms. I agree but extend to some degree the transition period to young adulthood as explained above by findings from neuroscience. McNeely and Bose do identify two environmental supports and these have particular relevance with regard to civic education at universities. These are: respect for individuality, and autonomy in problem-solving. There is evidence that these support higher academic motivation and self-confidence.[94]

Support for efficacy and competence resonates with classic conceptions of civic education, and with Mann's argument above: "Healthy social and emotional development is supported when young people have opportunities to make a difference in their society in ways that are meaningful for them".[95] An alternative approach to teaching that allows for such opportunities, alongside orthodox study, can positively impact upon academic studies, as it gives students a sense of confidence in their own broader social competence.[96] Interestingly, as McNeely and Bose point out, all of these environmental supports correspond with key principles of the broader human rights agenda.

What Rights Do Students have to Civic Education?

Adolescents and young adults are not recognised as a distinct group in international human rights' conventions. The United Nations Convention on

---

94 McNeely and Bose, "Adolescent Social and Emotional Development", 112.
95 Ibid., 113.
96 Ibid.

the Rights of the Child (UNCRC) protects younger adolescents (i.e. those under 18), while the Committee on the Rights of the Child (CRC) considers that the UNCRC applies to children under 18.[97] More particularly, the UNCRC stipulates a universal right to education (Article 29). The significant sections of the UNCRC are as follows: "1. State parties agree that the education of the child shall be directed to: (a) The development of the child's personality, talents and mental and physical abilities to their fullest potential; [...] (d) The preparation of the child for responsible life in a free society". The CRC states that this is of "far-reaching importance". Three passages are of interest:

> 'Education' in this context goes far beyond formal schooling to embrace the broad range of life experiences and learning processes which enable children, individually and collectively, to develop their personalities, talents and abilities and to live a full and satisfying life within society [...].
> Thus, the curriculum must be of direct relevance to the child's social, cultural, environmental and economic context and to his or her present and future needs and take full account of the child's evolving capacities [...].
> Basic skills include not only literacy and numeracy but also life skills such as the ability to make well-balanced decisions; to resolve conflicts in a non-violent manner; and to develop a healthy lifestyle, good social relationships and responsibility, critical thinking, creative talents, and other abilities which give children the tools needed to pursue their options in life.[98]

The UNCRC also embodies important principles with regard to adolescents and young adults which further reinforce the concepts of agency and maturity as stated above. Firstly, the UNCRC stipulates that children should be fully able to participate in, and to influence decisions which directly affect them.[99] Secondly, the UNCRC recognises that children have capacities which

---

97 Jean Zermatten, "Protecting and Promoting Adolescent Rights: The Contribution of International Law and Policy", in Bhabra, ed., *Human Rights and Adolescence*, 27. Jean Zermatten was a member of the Committee on the Rights of the Child from 2005, Vice Chair from 2007–2011 and Chairperson from 2011–13. At the time of writing, the CRC was preparing a General Comment on Adolescence.

98 See UNCRC, https://www.unicef.org.uk/what-we-do/un-convention-child-rights/ (as of 6 September 2017).

99 Zermatten, "Protecting and Promoting Adolescent Rights", 27.

are still developing: which means in practice that children and, I argue by extension adolescents and young adults, must be allowed to achieve progressive autonomy in line with their age and maturity.[100] I contend that young adults must be included because the transition from childhood to adulthood is not always completed at 19.

In a new work focusing on the rights of adolescents, Bhabha and others argue that adolescents constitute a distinct interest group, which is neglected in current human rights discourse.[101] They justify this argument by emphasising the social importance of ensuring a successful transition from childhood to adulthood.[102] This transition process is itself becoming increasingly challenging, they argue, because of the growing sophistication of prevailing social structures, which require confident individuals capable of autonomous decision-making. Moreover, young people are coming into increasing contact with different ethnicities, sexualities, disabilities and socioeconomic divides. These trends together present young people with the challenge of making their own choices within information saturated environments and to negotiate differences amongst a myriad of conflicting norms and identities.

These commentators accept that the challenge of adolescence is not a uniform one.[103] The tensions and the need for balance between "relative independence and qualified dependence" may manifest in different ways. This may result in an adolescence which continues for too long, whereby someone remains unable to establish themselves independently; or else it may necessitate reclaiming a person's adolescence, in circumstances where a teenager has become a parent and/or earner at a very young age. In either scenario, Bhabha argues that they will need a voice, and a focus on their particular rights and needs. In my view, those include educational

---

100 See Article 5 UNCRC; and Gerison Lansdown, *The Evolving Capacities of the Child* (Florence: UNICEF Innocenti Research Centre, 2005).
101 Bhabra, ed., *Human Rights and Adolescence*.
102 Bhabra, ed., *Human Rights and Adolescence*, 4.
103 Ibid., 4.

opportunities to develop their emotional and social competences, as well as the UNCRC's emphasis on participation in decision-making and progressive autonomy.

For these reasons, one can argue that adolescents and young adults are entitled to receive an education that not only prepares them for the social roles which they will take on in a changing society, but also one that is sensitive to, and helps them understand, the transitions which they are undergoing.

How Does Civic Education Work in Universities?

It can be asked whether a programme, such as the one I taught, does properly address students' needs to develop their capabilities and agency, at a point in their lives when they are developing their social and emotional competences. More broadly, we can ask whether universities could and should take on such a task. Some specific questions might include, for example, what particular social and emotional competences can and should be developed, and at what ages?[104] What relevance do such competences have to our conceptions of citizenship? What other competences are required? Do these fit in with the notions of agency and capabilities, and the idea of 'soft citizenship'? What is the current potential of universities, bearing in mind the secondary education system, the prevailing socioeconomic and cultural context and the wider context of higher education? This is a preliminary list, and a closer and more systematic review is required.

I do not dispute Watson's view, above, that the fundamental purpose of the university is to create, test and apply knowledge so as to provide a reservoir of intellectual capital. But I contend that a particular form of civic education designed for late adolescents and young adults, to aid the transition to adulthood, and with a focus on building capabilities, personal agency, and developing social and emotional competences, does have a place

---

104 See the Guidelines for Emotional Competence Training. See Goleman, *Working with Emotional Intelligence*, 251–252.

at university.[105] This then begs the question of how universities should change.

Some argue that change involves universities asserting their own vision of the purposes of education more strongly.[106] Consequently, a university may see its primary mission to teach academic doctrine and technical expertise. Others point to cautionary tales of how 'top-down' experiments have failed.[107] What little documented evidence we have of civic education attempted at UK universities suggests that suitably motivated and committed staff are needed, especially with 'service learning'.[108]

My own experience may be helpful, if understood in context, as a response to a particular set of circumstances, and with the benefit of certain favourable and special factors as considered above. It fits with those approaches that say that higher education reform should not be an attempt to fix something that is 'wrong with students', but rather to put skills in the hands of students which will enable them to explore their own personal projects.[109] The case provides an enticing goal for higher education that encompasses much of what civic education is trying to achieve: "a graduate who has developed sufficiently personally to have something to care about but who has also through an engagement with knowledge made themselves able to take on a social role that is in concert with their ultimate concerns".[110]

---

105 It is beyond the scope of this article to examine how civic education can be incorporated into higher education curricula. The reader is referred to the sources cited in Tristan McCowan, "Opening Spaces for Citizenship in Higher Education: Three Initiatives in English Universities", *Studies in Higher Education* 37:1 (February 2012): 51–67.

106 Jennifer M. Case, 2013. *Researching Student Learning in Higher Education: a Social Realist Approach* (London: Routledge, 2013), 143–144.

107 See McCowan, "Opening Spaces for Citizenship in Higher Education".

108 Ibid., 65.

109 Jennifer M. Case, *Researching Student Learning in Higher Education*, 145; citing Tamsin Haggis, "Pedagogies for Diversity: Retaining Critical Challenge Amidst Fears of 'Dumbing Down'", *Studies in Higher Education* 31 (2006): 521–535.

110 Case, *Researching Student Learning in Higher Education*, 63.

3. Conclusions

There is a compelling story of personal and social change to be told from Azerbaijan. When a student tells a teacher that their "course has changed my life",[111] we should sit up and take notice. Despite all the advantages I had, something in my courses got my students' attention and persuaded them to take a year's worth of study for no university credit. 15 years later, ten of these students were able to remember what they had learned.

Interestingly, in Europe and the UK, the idea of the civic purpose of universities is embraced on paper in policy statements and strategy documents, such as those on 'graduate attributes'. The concept of 'soft citizenship' goes to the heart of some thinking of what a university is for.[112] Yet when we consider in reality university life and study, its opportunities seem haphazard and incidental when compared to an organised civic education programme. For the vast majority of undergraduates, their experience is of sitting in lectures and possibly taking part in extracurricular activities. This is not without value, but the lessons of Azerbaijan suggest that is a superficial approach. It can be taken much further by posing challenging personal questions, providing training on a range of skills, encouraging critical examination of immediate environments, and most of all, supporting students to actively influence and change those environments for their own chosen ends. If we are serious about empowering university students as young citizens, these avenues compel investigation.

The justifications for introducing civic education are powerful. The world our students are entering is one of fast paced change. Cultivating self-reliant, effective and confident students who are able to interact autonomously with the world outside the classroom should be every university's foremost priority. That entails the students understanding the world immediately around them and how it impacts on their own values and priorities. It means students learning how to effect change in their lives to further those values.

---

111 Anonymous "Youth Forum" student feedback #17.
112 See Martin Watson, *The Question of Conscience: Higher Education and Personal Responsibility* (London: Institute of Education Press, 2014).

There is an inherent prosocial agenda here and it conforms to our growing understanding of how the students are maturing. Learning how to negotiate your way through social interactions, how to control your impulses and how to make realistic long term plans are all abilities that a late adolescent and young adult should be getting to grips with. This is not a debate about educational politics but an emerging biological fact.

What we learn from neuroscience and developmental sciences should not surprise us. The United Nations has been saying for years that a child's education must embrace the broad range of life experiences and learning processes. This is not a preference but a right. As university teachers, we must pay attention to the vital transition period to adulthood during which we can intervene with civic education to help students make that transition to informed, effective and confident adult citizens. To do nothing is to neglect the needs, and arguably, the rights of our students.

An undergraduate's experience confined to lectures, seminars, exams, and possibly some extracurricular activities, is an outdated straitjacket. Whether it is for individual staff, particular departments or the university as a whole to intervene is an argument for another day. Ultimately, we need further research into whether the lessons of Azerbaijan can apply in another context, such as a British university.

Teaching Social Science at Post-Soviet Universities: Challenges for Visiting Lecturers in the Former USSR

Andreas Umland

1. Introduction and Caveats

This chapter combines some previous findings, personal impressions, and a number of general observations on the teaching of the social sciences in post-Communist universities. It does so by examining the particular problems that Western-educated lecturers with little experience of post-Soviet higher education may encounter when taking up appointments at post-Soviet universities. Most of the information was gathered during visiting lectureships at two Russian and three Ukrainian higher education institutions.

Quite a number of similar reports on visiting appointments in Eastern Europe and the newly independent states have been published.[1] Here, an

---

1   John Donald Ball, "Russian Students and History", *Contemporary Review* 278:1632 (2001): 225–229; Anne Clift Boris, "Teaching History in Belarus: Differences in Teaching and Learning Strategies", *American Studies International* 36:2 (1998): 44–57; Elinor Burkett, "In Central Asia, an American Professor Finds Hostility Spiked with Cynicism", *The Chronicle of Higher Education* (23 April 2004); Civic Education Project, *Education for Transition Part II: Social Science Teaching at Central and East European Universities. A Needs Assessment* (Budapest: Civic Education Project with the Institut für die Wissenschaften vom Menschen, 1997); Katja Ezel, "Der Einsatz von Planspielen im fremdsprachlichen Unterricht: Ein Erfahrungsbericht aus Polen", in Andreas Umland, ed., *Geistes- und Sozialwissenschaftliche Hochschullehre in Osteuropa I: Eindrücke, Erfahrungen und Analysen deutscher Gastlektoren* (Berlin: Peter Lang, 2005); Andreas Goldthau and Oliver Schütt, "Ursachen, Mechanismen und Auswirkungen von Korruption an russischen Hochschulen: Ein Fallbeispiel aus Sibirien", in ibid.; Susan M. Gorga and Jeffrey J. Mondak, "Taking the Show on the Road: Teaching Political Science in English at Foreign Universities", *PS: Political Science and Politics* 34:1 (2001): 125–131; Hans Gutbrod, "Wie vermittelt man Urteilskraft?", in Umland, ed., *Geistes- und Sozialwissenschaftliche Hochschullehre in Osteuropa I*; Helge Hellberg, "Neue Markierungen und alte Fahrwasser", in ibid.; Nancy Hirschmann, Julie

attempt is made to review this literature and summarise the various challenges that visiting faculty from Western countries face when joining a post-Soviet social science department for a longer period. Unlike other analyses that deal with the generic problems of teaching social sciences in a language that is foreign to students,[2] this chapter focuses on the specific issues associated with teaching in a former Communist country that is undergoing a process of deep transformation.[3]

Mostov and Michael Mosher, "Political Theory in Albania: An Exercise in Democratic Culture", *PS: Political Science and Politics* 28:1 (1995): 146–149; Patrick C Jobes, Andra Aldea, Constantin Cernat, Ioana-Minerva Icolisan, Gabriel Iordache, Sabastian Lazeru, Catalin Stoica, Gheorghe Tibil, Eugenia Udangiu, "Using the Constant Comparative Method in the Foreign Classroom: Shopping as a Social Problem in Romania", *Teaching Sociology* 25:4 (1997): 292–303; Guido Müntel and Stefan Gänzle, "'Feind vor dem Tor?' Europastudien und Internationale Beziehungen in Kaliningrad", in Umland, ed., *Geistes- und Sozialwissenschaftliche Hochschullehre in Osteuropa I*; Tom Murphy, "The Intraclassroom Dynamic in Teaching Non-Native English Speakers", in Reuben Fowkes, ed., *Teaching Strategies in Higher Education: Effective Teaching, Effective Learning. Proceedings of the Third Regional Workshop* (Budapest: Civic Education Project, 2000), http://www.civiceducationproject.org/legacy/teachandlearn/doc/szeged99.pdf; Bruno Naarden, "'I am a Genius, but no more than that': Lev Gumilev (1912–1992), Ethnogenesis, the Russian Past and World History", *Jahrbücher für Geschichte Osteuropas* 44:1 (1996): 54–82; Tim Peters, "Wahlbeobachtung in Tatarstan: Möglichkeiten und Grenzen politischer Projektarbeit im heutigen Rußland", in Umland, ed., *Geistes- und Sozialwissenschaftliche Hochschullehre in Osteuropa I*; Christopher Phelps, "Prepare for Departure", *The Chronicle of Higher Education* (16 September 2004); Christopher Phelps, "Polish Autumn", ibid. (4 November 2004); Cyrus Salimi-Asl, "Strukturelle und kulturelle Rahmenbedingungen sozialwissenschaftlicher Hochschullehre in Kasachstan", in Umland, ed., *Geistes- und Sozialwissenschaftliche Hochschullehre in Osteuropa I*; Barbara Ann Stolz, "Teaching Democratic Principles in a Traditional Russian University: Fomenting a Quiet Revolution", *PS: Political Science and Politics* 29:3 (1996): 592–597.

2   Gorga and Mondak, "Taking the Show on the Road"; Mark Hallerberg and Bettina Cothran, "German Politics *auf Deutsch*: Teaching Comparative Politics in a Language Across the Curriculum Format", *PS: Political Science and Politics* 32:4 (1999): 739–742; Murphy, "The Intraclassroom Dynamic in Teaching Non-Native English Speakers".

3   Marek Kwiek, "Social and Cultural Dimensions of the Transformation of Higher Education in Central and Eastern Europe", *Higher Education in Europe* 26:2 (2001): 165–

In 1999–2001, I was a visiting lecturer for the Civic Education Project (www.civiceducationproject.org/legacy/) and the Robert Bosch Foundation (www.boschlektoren.de) in the Department of International Relations and the Faculty of Political Science and Sociology of The Urals State University, as well as at the Institute of Foreign Economic Relations and International Law of The Urals State Academy of Law, all located in the large, industrial city of Yekaterinburg. In 2002–2003, I was a Bosch Lecturer in the Faculty of History and the Institute of International Relations at the National Taras Shevchenko University; in the Department of Political Science at the Kyiv-Mohyla Academy National University, and in the Department of German at the National University of Linguistics, all in Kiev, the capital of Ukraine. The following, often critical, remarks on the state of social science higher education in Russia and Ukraine are neither expressions of Russo- or Ukrainophobia (I am half-Russian and have Ukrainian relatives), nor reflections of my particular experiences of the universities at which I taught. Though some of the following criticism does, for instance, apply to the three Yekaterinburg departments to which I belonged in 1999–2001, these faculties are probably among the more advanced and reform-minded institutions in provincial Russia.[4] In addition, it has to be said that the Kiev-Mohyla Academy, a newly founded university, stands out among the above listed as being particularly industrious in trying to attain Western standards. There are similar projects to be found in Russia, with the European Humanities University in St. Petersburg perhaps being the most successful one so far.

While my own experiences are limited to Russia and Ukraine, they seem to be similar to those of lecturers in other republics of the former Soviet

169; Peter Scott, "Reflections on the Reform of Higher Education in Central and Eastern Europe", *Higher Education in Europe* 25:1 (2000): 111–114; Umland, ed., *Geistes- und Sozialwissenschaftliche Hochschullehre in Osteuropa I.*

4   Andreas   Umland,   "Menschenrechtsschutz,   Provinzpolitik   und   westliche Institutionen im heutigen Rußland: Beobachtungen am Rande einer Konferenz in Jekaterinburg im April 2001", *Osteuropa-Recht* 48:1 (2002): 4–8.

Union.[5] This is why I feel justified in making here general statements about post-Soviet universities, keeping in mind that I am referring to those higher education institutions that belong to the countries of the former Soviet *inner* – and not outer – empire. Whereas the situation in the Baltic states is, by Western standards, apparently better than in Russia and Ukraine,[6] higher education in the social sciences in Belarus,[7] Central Asia,[8] and the Caucasus,[9] seems to be even more problem-ridden than in Russia and Ukraine. Here again, it needs to be said that such evaluations do not apply to some outstanding reform universities such as the former European Humanities University in Minsk and later Vilnius,[10] the new OSCE-Academy in Bishkek, or the small German-Kazakh University of Almaty.[11] Finally, I do not incorporate here relevant scholarly literature on the subject in question, i.e. academic papers and books on post-Soviet higher education reform. I have listed some of the relevant German-language academic literature on higher education reform in the former Soviet bloc in another survey.[12]

2. Higher Social Science Education in the Former USSR

Compared to similar faculties elsewhere, contemporary social science departments in the post-Communist and especially post-Soviet world seem to exist in a context that is peculiar in at least three ways.

---

5 Umland, ed., *Geistes- und Sozialwissenschaftliche Hochschullehre in Osteuropa I.*

6 Hellberg, "Neue Markierungen und alte Fahrwasser", in Umland, ed., *Geistes- und Sozialwissenschaftliche Hochschullehre in Osteuropa I.*

7 Sergej Laboda, "Die Entwicklung des Hochschulwesens in Belarus in den 90er Jahren: 'Back to the Future?'", in T. Coignard et al., eds., *Ost-West Perspektiven: Eine Schriftenreihe des Promotionskollegs Ost-West 1* (Bochum: Lotman-Institut, 2002), 85–94.

8 Salimi-Asl, "Strukturelle und kulturelle Rahmenbedingungen", in Umland, ed., *Geistes- und Sozialwissenschaftliche Hochschullehre in Osteuropa I.*

9 Gutbrod, "Wie vermittelt man Urteilskraft?", in ibid.

10 Boris, "Teaching History in Belarus: Differences in Teaching and Learning Strategies".

11 Salimi-Asl, "Strukturelle und kulturelle Rahmenbedingungen", in Umland, ed., *Geistes- und Sozialwissenschaftliche Hochschullehre in Osteuropa I.*

12 Ibid.

The Isolation Problem

First, until the late 1980s, social science faculties in the former Soviet bloc and, especially, the Soviet Union were, to a greater degree than faculties of the natural and technical sciences, isolated from their international disciplinary communities. In some fields, moreover, isolation was fostered by rather different methodologies and, indeed, definitions of the disciplines in question. Whereas Soviet sociology or jurisprudence developed, from the 1960s at least, in some ways similar to their Western counterparts, economics and political science were, until the late 1980s, academic disciplines rather different from those to be found in the West.[13] To be sure, a number of individual researchers, even in political science, did generate research — sometimes unpublished — that would be regarded as valuable in the West too.[14] Moreover, in the name of 'a critique of bourgeois approaches', some Soviet social scientists did engage in the systematic study of Western social sciences and history. Most of the literature published in these areas up until the late 1980s was, however, not very incisive and is now out of date. Thus, since the late 1980s, post-Soviet social sciences have been busy catching up with Western developments, and, in some sub-disciplines, engaged in building up from scratch entirely new research and teaching agendas.[15]

The Indoctrination Problem

Second, social studies in the former Soviet bloc, as taught in both middle and high schools, were understood less as detached empirical sciences and more as constituent parts of a messianic, fundamentalist and apologetic ideology. Though from the 1960s the Soviet Union no longer constituted a fully

---

13 Yuri Tarnopolsky, "Soviet Higher Education: A First-Hand Report", *Academic Questions* 1:2 (1998): 52–62.

14 Archie Brown, "Political Science in the USSR", *International Political Science Review* 7:4 (1986): 443–481.

15 Helen Shestopal, "Observations on the Transformation of the Political Science Community in Russia", *PS: Political Science & Politics* 32:4 (1995): 713–720.

developed totalitarian state, the burden of the past on higher education remains, especially in the social sciences, a heavy one.

Natural and technical sciences or mathematics in the Soviet Union were usually more or less isolated from their international communities too. In contrast to the social sciences, however, they developed, with varying success, their own national standards, schools, discourses and teaching styles. Moreover, they managed to establish Soviet Union- or bloc-wide communities with an identity and spirit that were often as advanced as or sometimes superior to their Western counterparts.[16]

This was only partly the case for the Soviet scholarly communities (if one can call them that) in disciplines such as economics and political science. The latter discipline, for instance, was, with the exception of foreign area studies and international relations, probably studied, conducted or taught with scholarly passion, curiosity and fascination by hardly anybody in the former Soviet Union. The university departments that constituted the Soviet equivalents of Western political science departments were often simply called "Departments of Marxism-Leninism". Social science departments in the Soviet higher education system did not fully constitute and were not even intended to represent centres of honest empirical research, open theoretical discourse, pluralistic methodological advancement, or scientific teaching. While some self-critical Western observers would, perhaps, argue that one can also speak of an 'indoctrination problem' in Western political science departments, what was happening in the former Soviet Union constituted a phenomenon of an entirely different magnitude.

These Soviet departments were *de facto* branches of the CPSU's ideological and propaganda apparatus, and there is, in many cases, still considerable institutional and personnel continuity between them and their re-named post-Soviet counterparts. Many of the former departments of Marxism-Leninism have, to be sure, been open to new ideas and cooperation with Western partners, and are actively introducing new textbooks and

---

16   Andrew Marks, "A 'Polytechnism' for the British Universities: Embracing a Revised 'Soviet' Model for Academia", *Higher Education in Europe* 27:3 (2002): 217–230.

research programmes. Still, the post-Soviet disciplines represented in these departments do not yet constitute integrated scholarly communities with an informed concern for the most valuable research, useful scholarly literature, and effective teaching techniques. In some post-Soviet Russian social science sub-fields, moreover, there is a new spirit of distinctiveness taking hold. This tendency has expressed itself in, for instance: the establishment of an aggressive 'Eurasian' version of the geopolitical approach to international relations;[17] the emergence of a new academic discipline called 'culturology' that attempts to systematise national stereotypes in a pseudo-scholarly fashion and to promote the 'Russian Idea' as a new meta-theory for Russia;[18] and the uncritical acceptance by a surprisingly large number of Russian social scientists of the abstruse, neo-racist theory of ethnogenesis developed by the late Soviet ethnographer Lev N. Gumilëv.[19]

---

17 Marlene Laruelle, "Pereosmyslenie imperii v postsovetskom prostranstve: novaya evraziiskaya ideologiia", *Vestnik Evrazii – Acta Eurasica* 1:8 (2000): 5–18; Marelene Laruelle, "The Two Faces of Contemporary Eurasianism: An Imperial Version of Russian Nationalism", *Nationalities Papers* 32:1 (2004): 115–136; John B. Dunlop, "Aleksandr Dugin's 'Neo-Eurasian' Textbook and Dmitrii Trenin's Ambivalent Response", *Harvard Ukrainian Studies* 25:1/2 (2001): 91–127; Andreas Umland, "Toward an Uncivil Society? Contextualizing the Recent Decline of Extremely Right-Wing Parties in Russia" (Cambridge, MA.: Harvard University Weatherhead Center for International Affairs – Working Paper no. 02–03) at: https://papers.ssrn.com/ sol3/papers.cfm?abstract_id=2890627: 36–39; Andreas Umland, "Kulturhegemoniale Strategien der russischen extremen Rechten: Die Verbindung von faschistischer Ideologie und metapolitischer Taktik im 'Neoeurasismus' des Aleksandr Dugin", *Österreichische Zeitschrift für Politikwissenschaft* 33:4 (2004): 437–454.
18 Julia Scherrer, *Kulturologie: Russland auf der Suche nach einer zivilisatorischen Identität*, (Göttingen: Wallstein, 2002).
19 Hildegard Kochanek, "Die Ethnienlehre Lev N. Gumilevs: Zu den Anfängen neu-rechter Ideologie-Entwicklung im spätkommunistischen Rußland", *Osteuropa* 48:11/12 (1998): 1184–1197; Marlene Laruelle, "Kogda prisvaivaetsya intellektual'naya sobstvennost, ili O protivopolozhnosti L.N. Gumileva i P.N. Savitskogo", *Vestnik Evrazii – Acta Eurasica* 4:15 (2001): 5–19; Bruno Naarden, "'I am a Genius', but no more than that': Lev Gumilev (1912-1992), Ethnogenesis, the Russian Past and World History", *Jahrbücher für Geschichte Osteuropas* 44:1 (1996): 54–82; Victor

In short, many of the older professors engaged in social science teaching and research in the former Soviet Union today seem, with some notable exceptions, to be too concerned with their own professional survival, status-preservation and re-definition – not to mention securing a decent livelihood for themselves and their families! – to be able genuinely to work as social science teachers with an overriding interest in, and strong ability to contribute to, the formation of a new generation of social scientists.

The Transition Problem

Third, the most important factor affecting how the post-Soviet social sciences can reform or establish themselves is their location in societies currently undergoing processes of profound transformation. Though this state of constant reform, transformation or, indeed, revolution is not a disadvantageous context for social science teaching and research in *every* respect, the numerous resulting problems far outweigh the few gains.[20] The extremely low salaries of university teachers and administrators, the laughable student stipends (mostly, moreover, merit and not need-based), and the pathetic budgets of university departments, academic libraries, and higher education administrative bodies constitute pressing challenges.

While the financial issue is certainly the most salient problem, it is not the only transition feature that negatively affects higher education in general and teaching of the social sciences in particular. For instance, students enter college coming from an equally crises-ridden high school system, and they leave university only to enter a tough, unstable labour market. The work places that do manage to provide a more or less adequate income by post-Soviet standards are for the most part those at foreign – mostly Western – commercial, governmental or non-governmental institutions. Thus, for many students in the former Soviet Union, the most realistic way to obtain

---

Shnirelman, and Sergei Panarin, "Lev Gumilev: His Pretensions as a Founder of Ethnology and his Eurasian Theories", *Inner Asia* 3:1 (2001): 1–18.

20 Scott, "Reflections on the Reform of Higher Education in Central and Eastern Europe", 111–114.

the financial rewards and social status of their Western peers is to emigrate permanently to some Western country. Apart from this large-scale 'brain-drain', there are further problematic circumstances, such as perceptions of moral decay, cultural alienation, ethnic tensions or fear of crime, that contribute to an overall climate of stress, pessimism, and insecurity. This has expressed itself in various ways in the everyday teaching process in post-Soviet higher education including—and, perhaps, especially—its social science departments.

3. Post-Soviet Higher Social Science Education

The following features of college teaching in the social sciences in the post-Soviet region focus largely on certain concrete negative effects of the three fundamental problems listed above. The somewhat dark picture emerging should, however, not be seen as the whole story about social science education in the former Soviet bloc. For instance, a key, positive repercussion of the post-Soviet transformation for the social sciences has been the steep rise in the popularity of university courses in such fields as business, law and economics, as well as, to a lesser degree, in journalism, public administration, political science, and sociology.

At the time of the Soviet Union, a common starting point for a career in industry, administration and even the CPSU apparatus had been a degree from one of the country's leading engineering schools, such as the specialised industry institutes in Moscow, or the large poly-technical institutes across the country. Today, in contrast, a higher degree in law, economics, or similar field is seen by many young people in the former Soviet Union as the best investment in their professional future. I met a number of students who were studying or planning to study for an additional degree, sometimes in a second social science field, as they believed that this would further improve their prospects in the labour market. Many students are well aware that a Western under- or post-graduate social science degree instead of, or in addition to, a diploma from a post-Soviet university will increase their chances of getting an adequate job—whether in their home country or abroad.

This is, at least in some respects, good news for social science college departments in general, and visiting lecturers from the West, in particular. Many of the brightest high-school graduates in the post-Soviet world enter higher courses in the social sciences, sometimes with the explicit intention of continuing their studies at a Western university. Incoming Western lecturers can thus usually count on finding a pool of highly motivated, diligent, and intelligent students in their host departments. A 1994–95 US Fulbright lecturer in political science at the average Russian provincial Yaroslavl State University reported that her second- and third-year students were "among the brightest" she had taught.[21]

Notwithstanding these positive effects, the negative repercussions of the three contextual peculiarities of post-Soviet social science higher education listed above are the more relevant ones. Below, I discuss these effects on the administrative, teaching, and studying processes.

Pathologies of Administration

The most consequential structural deficiency in the administration of many post-Soviet universities is rampant corruption—especially in the admissions process, but also in grading, thesis submission and defence, certification, and other issues.[22] Interestingly, this is not a new phenomenon. Like significant portions of post-Soviet organised crime, whose origins, perhaps unexpectedly, lie in the Brezhnev era, large-scale corruption in the higher education system emerged long before perestroika. A chemistry lecturer[23] who emigrated from the Soviet Union in the 1980s reported:

---

21   Stolz, "Teaching Democratic Principles in a Traditional Russian University: Fomenting a Quiet Revolution", 592–597.
22   Ray Johns, "Academic Corruption in Ukraine", *Ukraine Fulbright Alumni Association Newsletter* 6 (2001); Goldthau and Schütt, "Ursachen, Mechanismen und Auswirkungen von Korruption an russischen Hochschulen", in Umland, ed., *Geistes- und Sozialwissenschaftliche Hochschullehre in Osteuropa I*.
23   Tarnopolsky, "Soviet Higher Education: A First-Hand Report", 57.

In the 70s, as a result of a complete breakdown of Soviet idealism, both of the officially imposed and the genuinely spontaneous kind, higher education itself became an illegal business. Applicants were accepted to medical, commercial, and other prestigious institutes for giant bribes, with only a small number of such cases being reported in the Soviet press.

Soviet higher education administration was already affected by other corrupting features before the 1970s by virtue of being a part of Soviet society. Most prominently, there has long been and still is the unofficial Eastern Slavic institution of *blat*.[24] Not an entirely unknown phenomenon in Western societies, 'having a *blat*' is not an easily translatable concept, and could mean knowing somebody in a relevant position who owes you a favour, having a 'connection' to a relevant decision-maker, being in a position to trade goods or services you have access to, for example, for university admission of your children, or knowing well somebody who is in a powerful enough position to circumvent official regulations and practices on your behalf. Apart from these unofficial practices, high Party and state officials usually did not need *blat* to secure their relatives' irregular admission to, and safe passage through, their preferred higher-education courses.

What may have been still a relative novelty in the 1970s was the use of plain cash to gain university admission. And what is, probably, still a novelty in the newly independent states today is the magnitude of corruption involved in university admission, grading and certification.

Pathologies of Teaching

The primary, though probably not the only, reason for widespread corruption is the above-mentioned dire financial situation of post-Soviet higher education. This circumstance apparently also contributes to a second fundamental difference in how higher education in the humanities works in the post-Soviet region as compared to the West: the large number of hours students in Russia and other post-Soviet republics spend attending classes

---

24 Alena Ledeneva, *Russia's Economy of Favours: Blat, Networking and Informal Exchange* (Cambridge: Cambridge University Press, 1998).

each week. To somebody educated in the Western system, the time students and lecturers spend together in the lecture or seminar room every week appears ridiculous. Usually, students have at least three so-called *pary* ('pairs', i.e. double-hour, or eighty-to-ninety-minute lectures) per day, Monday through Friday. In other words, they spend approximately 15 'pairs', or 30 academic hours per week in class, sometimes more. This mode of teaching, it must be added, is not only characteristic of subjects such as foreign languages, mathematics, logic, or computer sciences — subjects that may indeed demand a large amount of teacher-student interaction. It is the same for teaching in normative philosophy, politics, history, social theory etc., i.e. subjects which, in Western universities, are heavily taught via various homework assignments.

On the surface, this situation seems, at least at the state universities of many post-Soviet countries, to be due to the obligatory standards set by their respective ministries of education. However, my impression is that the survival of this system is also related to the particular tradition that lecturers are paid, above all, according to the amount of time spent in class per week. Lecturers thus have an incentive to secure for themselves as many weekly teaching hours as possible. There even seems to be a kind of contest among academic staff members for the assignment of in-class teaching — something quite difficult to imagine among professors at many Western universities. The current degree of enlightenment in the Russian Ministry of Education is in turn illustrated by the fact that the heavily overloaded, *obligatory* weekly teaching plan for the state universities still contains not only physical education, but also idiosyncratic subjects like "security of information".

Not only does this incentive system run counter to the well-known didactic deficiencies of too much in-class teaching. The amount of in-class work that professors at all levels have to perform also leads to a rather heavy reliance on the traditional lecture method, i.e. on a teaching technique that is especially problematic from a didactic point of view. The semester-long lecture-series, moreover, is frequently combined with simple end-of-term oral examinations on the content of the lectures — a method that seems particularly prone to encouraging students to repeat their professors' arguments like parrots.[25] It is also not surprising that the above incentive system limits the lecturers' motivation to use writing assignments – whether at home or in class – in a serious way. Such written exams, essays or papers would have to be corrected outside class, i.e., it appears, often without extra remuneration. Another unfortunate result of the lecturers' heavy teaching load is that it leaves little time for research and publishing beyond those obligations that have to be fulfilled to receive a Candidate of Sciences (comparable to a British MLitt by research degree) or Doctor of Sciences (comparable to a Western PhD) degree.

Finally, the predominantly in-class teaching pattern, in combination with other factors, has various negative repercussions for the organisational aspects of higher education. Among them are a shortage of free lecture halls, and often overcrowded university facilities (libraries, reading rooms, cafeterias, toilets) during the day. Many students have, in addition to attending university for circa 30 academic hours per week, to work in order to cover their living costs. Thus their ability satisfactorily to complete whatever homework assignments they still get from local or foreign lecturers, such as take-home essays, term-papers, and other projects, is limited.

It must be added that there is, at least, one 'rational' explanation for the prominence of the traditional lecture method in the teaching of social sciences in the CIS: the simple unavailability or relatively high costs of suitable academic literature that could be assigned for reading at home. However, given the many new and fairly inexpensive textbooks that have appeared in recent years in all fields of the social sciences in Russia and Ukraine, and taking into account the still more or less regular opening hours

---

25 Ball, "Russian Students and History"; Stephen Rowland, "Teaching for Democracy in Higher Education", *Teaching in Higher Education* 6:2 (2001): 275–280; Salimi-Asl, "Strukturelle und kulturelle Rahmenbedingungen sozialwissenschaftlicher Hochschullehre in Kasachstan", Umland, ed., in *Geistes- und Sozialwissenschaftliche Hochschullehre in Osteuropa I.*

of university libraries, this argument is not as strong as it was in the early or mid-1990s. Still, in order to teach at the levels recommended by modern pedagogical research, the literature situation in Russia and Ukraine would have to improve significantly.

Pathologies of Studying

The most unfortunate repercussions of the isolation, indoctrination, and transition problems of post-Soviet higher social science education are those felt by students — whether as objects, or actors within the teaching process. Students are affected by the consequences of the above problems as learners, researchers, university members, and young citizens. As overworked, under-paid, and, sometimes, under-qualified university teachers may treat their obligations as a formality, their students behave accordingly. Put simply, the teaching process sketched out does sometimes lead to very little learning. As some lecturers seem to fake teaching, their students likewise fake learning. Arguably, going through post-Soviet social science higher education might well be the best way to learn how to confront post-Soviet public administration: do not take the many, rather formalistic prescriptions too seriously; instead, try to circumvent them with various forms of falsification, *blat*, bribes, or any other suitable means.

Many students in the post-Soviet world, at least in the social sciences, thus develop peculiar behavioural patterns that, to be sure, can be also observed at Western universities but are more widespread and accepted in post-Soviet student communities. They are, perhaps, even part of a specific post-Soviet student sub-culture. I dare to generalise that most students in post-Soviet higher social science education are, in comparison with students at Western universities, more deferential towards, and less critical of, authorities, such as teachers, 'great scholars' or the government. They arrive at opinions in a collectivistic way, rather than through individualistic discourse. They are, more so than Western students, inclined to focus on fulfilling the formal rather than the substantive aspects of assignments such as presentations or essays, and less inhibited in using cajoling or plain fraud to pass a course. In fact among some students there seems to be little appreciation of how unusual and unacceptable such behaviour is.

A few students, finally, internalise these kinds of practices to a degree that they also use them in dealing with Western lecturers or public organisations. They do so even though they have been explicitly warned that certain misconduct, such as plagiarism, will be penalised, or, even though they know that Westerners are much less in need of the 'presents' they might be offered in order to provide a certain grade, a 'pass' instead of a 'fail', or a letter of recommendation. Sometimes, the peculiarly post-Soviet 'common standards' in these matters are misinterpreted as being representative of general patterns in higher social science teaching world-wide. In other cases, students may plead for special treatment and lower standards in view of the specific, more complicated situation they admittedly confront in their countries as compared to students in Western countries.

To illustrate the above points, I would like to mention my two encounters with plagiarism in Russia and Ukraine: in one case, the student had copied by hand an essay from the internet, and, in the other, she had either found a suitable text on the World Wide Web, or had hired a Western graduate student to answer a question on a take-home assignment. These instances were not only unpleasant in themselves; neither was ever satisfactorily resolved. The two students refused to acknowledge their misdeeds, apologise, or resubmit essays of their own. Indeed, I was less surprised by the plagiarism itself than I was by the reaction (or absence thereof) of the students to my indignation.

4. Some Addenda for Future Visiting Lecturers

The above list of grave problems in higher social science education in the former Soviet Union might well be sufficient to discourage Western instructors from taking up an appointment in a post-Soviet university. It should be repeated, however, that in my experience these features are often more than compensated for by welcoming and friendly colleagues, helpful and understanding administrators,[26] and interactions with many highly motivated and able students.[27] The problems listed above also provide a rationale for such visiting lecturer programmes as the Civic Education Project (now reconstituted as the Academic Fellowship Programme), the Robert Bosch Foundation Lecturer Programme, the German Academic Exchange Service and the Fulbright Guest Professor scheme, and constitute the particular challenge that a Western visiting lecturer faces during a stint in the former Soviet Union. After all, why should the West be sending lecturers on a large scale to, for instance, Russia, if the above problems did not exist, or were not as grave?

Future potential visiting lecturers from Western countries certainly need to be warned that, when joining a post-Soviet social science faculty at an ordinary state university, they may enter a social micro-system the workings of which are not only different from comparable Western institutions, but also fundamentally problematic if measured by Western standards.[28] On the other hand, this is, of course, exactly the reason for their being there – to set an example of how to work differently, or, perhaps, even to try to change things for the better.[29]

---

26 Tatiana Suspitsina, "Mothers, Bosses, and Superwomen: The Construction of Identities of Russian Woman Administrators in Higher Education", *Higher Education in Europe* 25:4 (2000): 507–509.

27 Stolz, "Teaching Democratic Principles in a Traditional Russian University: Fomenting a Quiet Revolution".

28 Michael Deaver, "Democratising Russian Higher Education", *Demokratisatsiya* 9:3 (2001): 350–366; Goldthau and Schütt, "Ursachen, Mechanismen und Auswirkungen von Korruption an russischen Hochschulen: Ein Fallbeispiel aus Sibirien", in Umland, ed., *Geistes- und Sozialwissenschaftliche Hochschullehre in Osteuropa I*; Salimi-Asl, "Strukturelle und kulturelle Rahmenbedingungen sozialwissenschaftlicher Hochschullehre in Kasachstan", in ibid.; Stefanie Stegmann, "'Ich sitze auf gepackten Koffern': Frustrations(in-)toleranzen von Sprach- und Kulturmittlern", in ibid.

29 See Boris, "Teaching History in Belarus: Differences in Teaching and Learning Strategies"; Reuben Fowkes, ed., *Teaching Strategies in Higher Education: The Role of Innovation. Proceedings of the Second Regional Workshop* (Budapest: Civic Education Project, 1998), http://www.civiceducationproject.org/legacy/teachandlearn/doc/szeged98.pdf; Fowkes, ed., *Teaching Strategies in Higher Education: Effective Teaching,*

In some sense, the situation sketched out above is also what makes visiting lectureships in post-Soviet state universities such a unique experience. It is one of the few opportunities a Westerner has to become fully integrated into a post-Soviet public institution for a certain period of time. It is an—to some, perhaps, dubious—opportunity to get to know first-hand some pathologies in the thinking and behaviour of public officials that are more or less representative of post-Soviet state apparatuses in general.

Effective Learning. Proceedings of the Third Regional Workshop (2000); Gutbrod, "Wie vermittelt man Urteilskraft?", in *Geistes- und Sozialwissenschaftliche Hochschullehre in Osteuropa I*, Umland, ed.; Peters, "Wahlbeobachtung in Tatarstan: Möglichkeiten und Grenzen politischer Projektarbeit im heutigen Rußland, in ibid.; A. Salem, ed., *A Question of Method: Teaching in the Social Sciences at Post-Soviet Universities* (Budapest: Civic Education Project, 2002); Stolz, "Teaching Democratic Principles in a Traditional Russian University: Fomenting a Quiet Revolution".

The Development of Journalism Higher Education in Georgia: from Soviet to European

Marine Vekua

1. The Soviet System: Traditions and History

The Faculty of Journalism at Ivane Javakhishvili Tbilisi State University (TSU), which has been an independent faculty for over 30 years, has long been considered to be the principal school of journalism in Georgia.[1] Its development has been rapid and intense, often difficult but also very interesting. Today, the school has become a component part of the larger Faculty of Social and Political Sciences, and has the status of a separate department.

Media and journalism studies in Georgia, and indeed the country's entire educational system, has faced particularly difficult challenges since the collapse of the Soviet Union. University education did not meet European standards and requirements, technologies and facilities for education were rather old and poor, and study materials were rare and mostly fashioned according to localised standards. Curricula were full of highly generalised, over-theoretical content and media students could only complete their internship periods at a handful of newspapers, or at the state television and radio agencies. Academics faced constant economic insecurity: in order to survive they were obliged to work at various different universities at the same time, and for a very poor salary. All these developments bore on the quality of university education. For many and various reasons—e.g. the

---

1   Some of the text in this chapter has previously been published in my article, "Challenges of Media Education Standards in Georgia", *Journal of Education in the Black Sea Region* 2:2 (2017): 132–152, https://jebs.ibsu.edu.ge/jms/index.php/jebs/article/view/47/55; all such text has been modified considerably for its inclusion here.

Soviet collapse, the Civil War of 1991–1993, military conflicts in the West and northern parts of Georgia in Abkhazia and so-called South Ossetia in the early 1990s, refugee crises, etc.—school learning also significantly deteriorated, to the extent that those who came to the universities were insufficiently prepared for higher education. Very often this led academics to change the content of their classes and instead teach their students what they were supposed to have learnt at school, interrupting and even reversing the educational process.

In the Soviet Union, the social sciences, and especially journalism, were manifestly bound up with Soviet ideology, and were subject to great pressures of political control. In order to explain better what I mean I will tell you a story about my own personal experience. At that time I was a journalism student myself; teaching, studying and learning alike were all greatly dependent on a particular lecturer's personality: on their intellect, their ability to convey knowledge and understanding and, most importantly perhaps, on their courage. Freedom of expression and speech were the stuff of dreams and it was extremely difficult to say what you wanted to say openly, and to let others hear what they needed to hear. Yet for us there was something appealing in these restrictions: it was a strange, dangerous game. For example, towards the end of our undergraduate studies, a friend asked what he should bring back for us from the United States (he was a sportsman—a famous tennis player staying there for three months). Our response was to ask for *The Washington Post*. We had never seen it and our books gave no information about the Western press, other than to remind us how immoral and worthless it was. Having bought a copy of the newspaper, the tennis player realised that it would be confiscated at the airport terminal in Moscow, and that he might be arrested in turn. But he was a great lover of Soviet tricks and found a way out: he bought a huge dinner set for 24 persons and wrapped each piece of the set in a page of the newspaper. This is how the *Washington Post* arrived safely, and this is how we saw it for the first time. We then spent all night ironing out the sheets of paper. At the end of the term, everyone wrote brilliant and insightful annual theses on how 'immoral' the *Washington Post* was. Everyone was happy: the tennis player with his witty act, the students with their authentic US newspaper, and also university educational staff who were content with the students' critical attitude towards the Western press. The reality is that for students of the late 1970s, not least the first flush of Faculty of Journalism graduates from TSU, it was easy to appreciate the value and meaning of the freedom of speech.

Journalism studies in the early years following the Soviet collapse had certain advantages as well as disadvantages. In these years, students were much used to slow, careful study; the time needed for such an approach seems impossible now. On the other hand, rather than balancing theoretical knowledge and practical experience, the former was given priority over the latter, and as a result the field distanced itself from pressing practical concerns, including immediately commercial pressures. Beyond these considerations, as already mentioned, students acquired a knowledge which was closely linked with the style and emotional characteristics of lecturers themselves, with their care for their subjects, their educational attainment, their responsibility to use techniques appropriate to successfully conveying knowledge and understanding. In many cases lecturers, lacking support and resources, taught classes out of enthusiasm alone, especially in the hard times of the 1990s. Thus in this period teaching was more personal and more reliant on lecturers' personalities, to the extent that some collected a following and set up their own schools. In this way, the schools or their founders gained an air of cultural authority, something which in difficult times helped to maintain the field as a specialist, independent discipline.

2. Changes to the System from the 1990s to 2005

Far-reaching economic, social and technological changes from the 1990s onwards have greatly increased the importance of the media in contemporary culture, with important implications for journalism studies in terms of techniques, practices and knowledge. Georgian universities have responded to the new situation in different ways, not least by establishing programmes in the field at all levels from undergraduate to postgraduate.

What follows is a broad sketch of the system as it was from the late 1990s up until 2005.

Firstly, at the level of bachelor's degrees, undergraduates were schooled in social, and to a lesser extent humanitarian, studies but had poor professional journalistic skills: an ineffective way, arguably, to prepare reporters. Next, master's studies covered techniques and methods for research work, largely using theoretical models, but failed to teach their practical applications. Beyond this, the main purpose of studying at doctoral level, in a vague variant on Soviet postgraduate studies, was to prepare academics and researchers faced with teaching or working in the field. The process of awarding academic degrees also proved to be rather ambiguous: while in Soviet times degrees were awarded centrally by the Moscow-based Supreme Certifying Committee (*Vysshij Attestatsionnyj Komitet* or VAK), now no organisation—neither the universities nor the Ministry of Education— had such a function, leading to a gap in this area. However, in 2005, a number of educational establishments set up their own doctoral studies programmes and the power to award degrees went to the universities.

As noted above, in Georgia, TSU's Journalism Department is regularly identified as a principal school in the subject. From the late 1990s up until 2005, however, many private educational establishments emerged offering students alternative models of journalism education, initially at the level of bachelor's and master's degrees, and more recently at doctoral level. Some of the most notable of these include the journalism programmes at the Georgian Institute of Public Affairs, Georgian Technical University, Tbilisi Grigol Robakidze University and the University of Georgia.[2] The proliferation of programmes in this period partly explains why, in Georgia, it is now quite difficult to promote and develop journalism degrees without considering their relationship to market demands. The development of modern journalism means narrowing professional specialisations in terms of form (print, broadcast, new media), as well as in terms of content (the

2 See Marine Vekua, "Different Models of Higher Education in Journalism", https://silkroad.ibsu.edu.ge/previous/fourth.html (as of 31 July 2017).

reporting of culture, politics, health, etc.). But for small countries like Georgia, and thus for a small media market, having journalists specialised in narrow different fields is a luxury. Accordingly, media employees give preference to persons who at the same time have writing, reporting, editing, camera-working and other professional skills. Educational programmes have adapted to these circumstances, shifting towards the preparation of universal media professionals. Increasingly, target markets, whether they are global, local, regional or more particular ones, influence the meaning and purpose of journalism degrees, and the contents of specific curricula have begun to reflect this fact.

Among theorists and academics, there have been quite a number of responses to this issue, influencing the determination of materials and techniques at the level of journalism and media courses. For one group, communication is the dominant function of the mass media, and mass-media cultural forms — television for instance — are the main tool of this process. Another group sees the media as a manipulative system, meaning that journalism engenders the conditions under which public opinion is formed in the first place, and is thus close to propaganda. A third group gives priority to journalism's ability to mediate between the three main state powers and society — the so-called 'fourth government'. A fourth group identifies journalism first and foremost as an independent discipline, though one bound up with social and political processes.

These developments taken together have produced a situation in which many and various educative journalism programmes compete for attention. One solution has been to offer journalism education at all levels (bachelor's, master's, doctoral) with a curriculum geared towards professional training. Another sees journalism covered as part of a wider programme of study, generally taking in humanitarian and/or social subjects, and allowing for, say, degrees with a major in another field and a minor in journalism; this option is often found among those universities that have aligned or are aligning themselves with the Bologna Process. Running parallel with these tendencies, other institutions have pursued a high degree of specialisation, offering only master's degrees in journalism studies, and appealing particularly to people trained in other fields — those who want to change their careers or career plans. Beyond this, the so-called 'authors' schools' institutions, named after a person who has achieved recognition in journalism, or who is associated with a well-known media organisation, are a less common but still influential current; these schools generally do not issue to their graduates diplomas confirming any academic qualifications in journalism.

3.   Impact of the Bologna Process

Government Policy

Georgia currently aspires to join the European Union. As such, there is a pressing need for the country to develop and enhance EU standards and conventions with respect to human rights and the rule of law, and to fully embed these standards at an institutional level; the latter is a prerequisite for Georgia in terms of further developing and cementing its current relationship with the EU.

Georgia became a signatory to the EU Association Agreement on 27 June 2014, necessitating the country's integration into the EU free trade zone, an open economic trading bloc with up to 500 million citizens, all with rights to visa-free movement, employment, settlement and — crucially — study, anywhere within the free trade zone area. The latter will bring out issues of academic exchange and cross-border interaction in relation to the Georgian HE system. To this end, the Eastern Partnership Programme currently helps to ensure that educational rules and standards in Georgia meet European standards, while the EU Neighbourhood Policy sets ambitious objectives with respect to the country's commitment to pan-European educational values and standards, and to any necessary reforms within the field of education.

Between 1992 and 2005, the EU awarded Georgia an overall total of €505 million in grants. This financial assistance was channeled into many and various projects and programmes, among the most important of which were Technical Aid to the Commonwealth of Independent States (TACIS), the EC Humanitarian Office (ECHO), the European Initiative for Democracy and Human Rights (EIDHR), and the Macro-Financial Assistance (MFA) initiative. From 2007 to 2010, EU-funded programmes within Georgia mainly consisted of the National Indicative Programmes, most notably TEMPUS and ERASMUS, and, from 2016, the ERASMUS+ programme.[3] With respect to the package of reforms that Georgia implemented in order to meet EU-defined standards of civic life and governance, an important measure was the Development and Reforms Fund (DRF), established in 2004 on the initiative of ex-President Mikheil Saakashvili. The DRF aimed to support an active reform programme, and also had the ancillary purpose of attracting highly qualified professionals to public jobs in Georgia. From 2004 to 2006, the DRF played the principal role in supporting the reforms process within the Ministries of Justice, Defence, and Internal Affairs; in addition it actively supported the education of young Georgian professionals, enabling them to study at some of the most prominent universities globally—384 students received DRF financial support during this period, and the Fund continues to operate today.

An important challenge for Georgia now is to enhance the quality and standards of its higher education system as a whole, facilitating intercultural communications between Georgia and Europe. Georgian universities have developed an extensive network of institutional connections throughout the wider European educational system,[4] largely as the result of a fortuitous coincidence of interests between Georgian foreign policy on the one hand, and the goodwill of European partner institutions on the other. The ideal of

---

3   Lika Glonti and Marine Chitashvili, "The Challenge of Bologna: The Nuts and Bolts of Higher Education Reform in Georgia", in Voldemar Tomusk, ed., *Creating the European Area of Higher Education: Voices from the Periphery* (Dordrecht: Springer, 2007), 209–226.

4   See Giuli Alasania, "Education as a Priority—a Longstanding Tradition in Georgia", https://silkroad.ibsu.edu.ge/previous/fourth/4_02.pdf (as of 21 May 2016).

European integration has been central to Georgian educational policy for some time, and the Bologna Process has provided Georgia with an opportunity to advance this policy agenda, promoting as it does the positive exchange of educational values and policies between European countries. Unsurprisingly, therefore, Georgia joined the Bologna Process on 19 May 2005.[5]

A significant initiative was launched by the Georgian Ministry of Education and Science in 2013. Funds for undergraduate studies were increased – by GEL 96,700 million to approximately GEL ten million, with a number of such programmes being provided free of tuition fees – enabling students to study 4-year BA courses at state universities in a wide variety of disciplines. Among these are: agricultural studies, architecture, construction, engineering, biology, chemistry, physics, economics, mathematics, archaeology, educational studies, history, Georgian philology and philosophy. Further funds (GEL one million) were also made available for graduates of these programmes wanting to progress to doctoral-level study. In addition to these provisions, the overall number of state scholarships was doubled (costing an extra GEL 1.75 million), while in 2014 the range of disciplinary areas covered by the scheme was increased from 14 to 20.

Despite the consideration that a pluralist mass media may be regarded as integral to the ongoing process of democratisation currently underway as part of Georgia's integration with the EU, up to now the field of media studies has not been included within the state-funded degree programmes. Nonetheless, the fact that the government has prioritised higher education as such may serve to enhance the status of media studies, while journalism is, of course, a profession very much open to recruits from other disciplines, including those currently being funded by the state.

---

5   Lasha Khetaguri, "Sakartvelo da Boloniis procesi, 15 tsuti radio Tavisuplebastan ertad [Georgia and the Bologna Process: 15 Minutes with Radio Tavisupleba]", https://www.radiotavisupleba.ge/ (as of 21 May 2016).

Accreditation Matters

Education reform is a sensitive matter for any society. In the case of Georgia, the recent reforms have not met with unalloyed public enthusiasm, partly due to the government's relative reticence in informing the public of developments in this area, and partly because reform takes time and cannot be achieved immediately and at will. Nonetheless, a number of significant institutional and administrative changes have been implemented. First, legislation has been enacted aimed at codifying the guiding mission and administrative structures of Georgian universities, formally conferring on them financial and academic independence, and regulating the nature of institutional and commercial cooperation both between the universities, and between the university sector within Georgia and the wider European area. Notably, this legislation explicitly confirms the autonomy of universities within Georgia, something which had not previously been so clearly defined. Second, a newly formalised accreditation system is now in force for higher education,[6] and a National Education Accreditation Centre has been established to oversee it: this system has had an immediate effect, in that while previously some 220 HE institutions—of highly variable quality— were in operation within Georgia, this total has now been reduced to 72 (having decreased to 63 by 2010).[7] A third accreditation-related reform has been the division of the overall HE sector into a new tripartite structure; HE institutions are now accredited as full universities offering teaching at bachelor's, master's, and doctoral levels, or as teaching universities offering bachelor's and master's level programmes only, or as colleges restricted to

---

6   Lela Maisuradze, "Looking Beyond 2010—Perspectives for Georgia in the European Higher Education Area", https://silkroad.ibsu.edu.ge/previous/fourth/5_10.pdf (as of 21 May 2016).

7   Marine Vekua, "Journalism Education: in Search of the Best Approaches" (paper presented at the conference "Path to European Integration", Guram Tavartkiladze Teaching University, Tbilisi, 12 July, 2014).

offering professional-level or bachelor-degree programmes.[8] This measure has helped to ensure that the country's HE institutions and study programmes approximate to those offered in other European countries.[9]

Fourth, there has been the establishment of a state-funded student loan system, which has helped to ensure full access to HE for students of all socio-economic backgrounds. Fifth, a new Unified National Admissions Exams system has been established, remedying the previous situation which prevailed during the Soviet and immediate post-Soviet periods, where admission to HE institutions was effectively unregulated, and so notoriously prone to corruption. The sixth area of reform is related to the funding of scientific research: while scientific research in the Soviet era was conducted exclusively at state-funded and state-regulated research-only institutions, which operated under the oversight of the Academy of Science, now a Georgian National Science Foundation has been set up on a fully competitive basis, offering bespoke research grants to individual researchers based within the full range of HE institutions. It is hoped that this measure will help to enhance the hitherto relatively lacklustre record of scientific research within Georgia, as well as fostering new research collaborations with other European research centres. Lastly, there has been reform in the area of professional education, where previously tenuous institutional links between the HE and vocational sectors have been formalised and enshrined in legislation.

Partly as a consequence of this package of reforms, Georgia is participating fully in the Bologna Process, which of course sets agreed common standards for HE institutions across different countries; it has for some time also been formally involved in the activities of closely connected international organisations such as the Bologna Follow-Up Group Board and the London Communiqué Drafting Group.

---

8   See "Authorized Institutions", Ministry of Education and Science of Georgia website, http://www.mes.gov.ge/content.php?id=1855andlang=eng (as of 31 July 2016).
9   See http://www.ehea.info (as of 21 May 2016).

Curriculum Groupings

Curriculum design defines what students study, the content of any given educational programme, and the grouping of disciplines within particular institutions. In Georgia, the study of journalism had, by June 2010, settled into three distinct groups of curriculum organisation. The first of these is formed of Tbilisi State University's bachelor's and master's programmes, and the more or less similar versions of these programmes at a dozen or so other universities. This repetition is not as remarkable as it might appear, given the prestigious and pioneering status of TSU's Department of Journalism in the country, one which has developed new contents for its BA and MA curricula, implemented new teaching techniques, and offered a number of minors in different fields of social studies within the framework of the Faculty of Political and Social Sciences. In 2010, however, TSU announced that it would not offer a doctoral programme in journalism or mass communications. This was due to a variety of factors, among them the lack of suitable joint academic or exchange programmes with other institutions. Yet the chief cause of the collapse of doctoral provision at TSU within this field turned out to be political in nature. Many senior academics had been dismissed from the university for political reasons, and this left younger, less experienced colleagues unable to provide the depth of professional experience and expertise necessary to maintain a full doctoral-level programme. Nevertheless as many as 13 other Georgian universities have attempted to reproduce the TSU curriculum in journalism and mass communications, albeit with outmoded textbooks and teaching methods.

The second broad curriculum grouping within this disciplinary area has tended to take inspiration from approaches associated with US journalism schools. Examples include the respective media schools of the Georgian Institute of Public Affairs, the University of Georgia, and Caucasus University. These schools have used academic resources closely modelled on the US scene, employing American professors and using literature by American authors, replete with localised US examples and experiences. The grading system used by these institutions has also been similar to that of US universities; elective subjects are often far from the major or even the minor fields (i.e. music, dance, bridge, chess, etc.), while the majority of partner universities have mainly been from the United States. The third curriculum group is inspired by European educational standards related to the Bologna framework. Examples include Grigol Robakidze University and Guram Tavartkiladze Teaching University. This group has prioritised media production, with teaching based around the extensive use of university media facilities.

Such diverse curriculum groupings have had both positive and negative effects with regards to the teaching of journalism and media studies. Among the more positive effects has been the healthy degree of competition between the various journalism schools, which has arguably helped to maintain academic standards across the field, as well as encouraging individual journalism and media teachers to hone and develop their teaching skills in line with new standards of professionalism. Yet there have also been more negative effects, among them a perceived deficit in relation to prior knowledge and levels of educational attainment on the part of journalism and media students, one that university schools and their curricula have struggled to remedy. In addition, there has been a dearth of experienced media practitioners willing to devote their time to teaching, and in some schools a manifest lack of appropriate teaching resources. Other negative aspects relate to the absence of joint teaching programmes hitherto undertaken with universities in other countries and, more generally, the fact that some curricula have remained old-fashioned in their approach, their theoretical aspects being insufficiently integrated with their practical components.

Clearly any sustained programme of educational reform needs to be continuously analysed and scrutinised over time, all the more so as specific developmental milestones are reached. One such milestone occurred in 2010—five years after the initial adoption of the Bologna Process in Georgia—by which time it had become obvious that media education curricula in Georgia faced some serious difficulties. As we have seen, a full modernisation process has begun across the country's HE system—but education reform is an ongoing process, with continually shifting and evolving goals. Georgia must do more to develop its overall provision with respect to journalism education, and to bring the field into closer alignment with internationally agreed HE standards.

4. Recent Developments: 2005–2016

An important aspect of any process of national educational reform is the need to learn from the experience of other countries. In this regard, the experience of the Scandinavian nations is of particular relevance to the situation in Georgia. As of 2014, some 70 universities across the Scandinavian region offer bachelor's or master's study programmes in journalism. In Finland, for example, there is the Media and Global Communication programme at Helsinki University, or Tampere University's Journalism and Mass Communication programme. The teaching methods employed on such programmes have tended very much to prioritise the study of audio and visual texts, alongside the use of media technologies, and there has also been an emphasis on the study of foreign languages. Educators working within the field in Georgia can clearly learn much from study programmes such as these. They may also learn from the fact that many professional media companies in Scandinavia have established their own in-house training schools. One such firm is the Helsinki-based Sanoma Corporation (formerly SanomaWSOY), which has its own journalism school, while the Finnish public broadcaster Yle (or Yleisradio Oy) also has its own radio and television institutes.

As is well known, the state plays a key role in the Scandinavian education model, guided by a commitment to the three principles of lifelong learning, access and universality.[10] The result is distinguished by various prominent features: (1) most HE institutions are state-funded and cost-free to students; (2) three years of pre-university study are a feature (whereas in most

---

10 Alena Popova, "The Scandinavian Model: Why is It So Interesting?", www.alena popova.ru/deyatelnost/scandinavian-model.html (as of June 2016).

European countries it is two years); (3) the educational budget is nearly double that of other European countries; (4) universities do a great deal to form citizens with strong democratic standards and principles of freedom. (This process goes back to the 19th century when a 'public school' system was established in Denmark: for the first time in Europe two progressive innovations were involved in the educational process-dialogue as a teaching method and students' self-government as one of democracy's indicators.) It may be that Georgia can learn some important lessons from all or any of these features of education in Scandinavian countries.

An overview of the newly accredited study programmes within the field can provide a clearer picture of the dynamics of the current situation in Georgia. At present some 58 universities (out of a total of 72 accredited institutions) offer programmes in mass communications, compared with the 15 BA, 13 MA, two PhD and two professional programmes which were offered in 2005. Alongside the current HE-based programmes, Imedi TV, Maestro TV and Radio Tavisupleba (the word means 'Liberty' or 'Freedom') have all now opened specialist media schools. The new curricula bear certain salient features concerning the quality of training now on offer. These include a notable number of partnerships between universities and media organisations, the active involvement of radio and TV companies, magazines, newspapers and professional organisations, like the journalists' union, in the development process of many of the programmes on offer, and the promotion of exchange schemes and joint programmes with many other countries. Additionally, many journalism study programmes now actively foster the training of more specialised or technical workers, such as media managers, advertising executives, public relations specialists and media technologies managers. Further, as these study programmes have evolved, campus-based studio and publishing facilities have greatly improved in technical sophistication: many universities now offer bespoke radio and TV stations, and on-campus magazine publishing facilities. Alongside these more positive developments, there are also difficulties: among them, the question of how far many school leavers are equipped for university study;

the issue that up to now only one university—TSU—has offered journalism study at doctoral level; the inadequacy of information imparted by universities about the details of study programmes offered to prospective students; and the lack of teaching in the areas of photojournalism and documentary practice.

Innovative Methodologies

As already noted, the application of standards associated with the Bologna Process has impacted on virtually all aspects of Georgian higher education, including the area of pedagogy, resulting for example in teaching techniques that seek to elicit student-centred learning. Traditionally, university teaching tended to concentrate on conveying theoretical knowledge at the expense of competence in its practical applications. Now, however, journalism and media programmes employ more diverse teaching techniques designed to encourage active participation on the part of students, ones that go beyond more passive and less engaged styles of tuition. In practice this has meant more interactive working methods, such as problem-based learning (PBL), the use of visual material, mock press conferences, classes taught by invited speakers, in-class dialogues and debating, brainstorming, case studies, spider diagrams, topic narrowing and choosing, mind-mapping, and the practice of role-playing. Such methods have supplemented rather than replaced traditional methods, like induction, deduction, analysis, synthesis, and so forth. The overall aim has very much been to achieve a productive balance between the practical and theoretical aspects of given courses of study. On the more practical side, many Georgian universities now encourage the production of student magazines, on-campus TV programmes, and radio and multimedia productions. There has also been a renewed emphasis on the use of external internships as a means of equipping students with some degree of practical industry experience.

Such student-orientated teaching necessitates the use of a relatively complex system of assessment, one which can adequately gauge a given student's progress with regards to both the acquisition of theoretical knowledge and to the level of practical attainment, as well as the efficacy of a given lecturer's teaching. In practice the main source of guidance in these areas has been the Georgian National Framework of Qualifications, according to which a student's performance can be assessed through a variety of traditional and non-traditional modes. These include written essays and individual or group presentations, alongside more innovative and practice-based methods such as the preparation of newspaper articles, the recording of interviews, the preparation of bulletins and programmes for broadcast, and the editing and production of newspapers and magazines, etc. Throughout, the aim is that assessment should be reliable, valid, unbiased, clear and systematic.

Study Conditions

Students in Georgia are becoming increasingly mobile and self-directed in terms of their choice of study programme or university in the country. They also show more interest in studying abroad, often taking up places on international exchange programmes. In response, universities in Georgia, not least those institutions adopting the guidelines set by the Bologna Process and Lisbon Recognition Conventions,[11] have found themselves competing with one another for students, and have learnt to market and sell their study programmes as particularly illuminating and attractive. This does not necessarily imply a triumph of image over substance when it comes to Georgian universities offering BA and MA journalism courses. Rather, students on such courses may expect to experience a variety of technological and methodological innovations. For example, two BA programmes – at Grigol Robakidze University and Guram Tavartkiladze Teaching University (GTTU) – offer creative writing workshops and, as mentioned earlier, a great many places now have their own on-campus radio and TV stations available for student use. Others (such as the Georgian Institute of Public Affairs and the David Aghmashenebeli University of Georgia) offer opportunities for

---

11 For more information on the Bologna Process and the Lisbon Recognition Convention, see http://www.ehea.info/ (as of 31 July 2017).

live TV broadcasting, while many host student-made print media of various kinds; taking up such opportunities often leads to professional internships for media and journalism students. The support structures for these programmes take in the full range of archival and digital resources, including libraries, multimedia teaching facilities and wireless Internet access. These are supplemented by career-oriented activities, such as student conferences and competitions (e.g. the Centaur international student TV festival, national student competitions in advertising, etc.), and professional corporations (like GTTU's Reporter Club) that hold student press conferences and host master classes and public lectures. In these ways, university teaching, professional training and various supplementary practices help students to pursue journalistic careers.

Digital Technology for Pedagogical Purposes

Plainly digital technology can be an important tool in the learning process, and should be embedded as an essential component of all study programmes. As an education resource, IT helps to foster new learning and teaching cultures, for instance by facilitating communication between students and staff, access to course resources in a digital environment, group activity among students, digital literacy, and the simplification of academics' administrative work — all much more cheaply, immediately, and accessibly than in the offline world. Consequently, software tools such as Blackboard, DAQ, ELVIS II, LabVIEW LAMS, Moodle and Scorm are widely used as teaching aids in Georgian universities.

Working Conditions and Academic Integrity

Georgian academics often collaborate with other academics nationally and internationally, placing emphasis on the exchange of views and experiences, the pooling of expertise and the setting up of joint research and teaching projects. Increasing numbers of manuals, textbooks, teaching aids and reference guides in journalism studies have been authored by Georgian academics in recent years, working alone or in teams, among them the book

Jurnalistika [Journalism], published in 2013 and co-authored by over a dozen academics from nine universities in Georgia and France.[12] Georgian academics, locally and internationally, are of course variously involved in writing grant applications, presenting papers at academic conferences, and publishing articles in academic journals. Such collaboration across institutions and across national borders offers ways to ensure the utility of peer review, creating circumstances in which intellectual rigour, professional practice and ultimately academic integrity can flourish.

Universities, Students, Employees and Their Intersections

Journalism and media study programmes must try to meet the demands of two quite distinct target markets, fulfilling students' training and professional needs, while also reflecting and accommodating the expectations of the professional media organisations and networks for which students will one day work. At the same time, such programmes must satisfy academic and intellectual standards, which are integral to university education as such. One response to ensuring that all these requirements can be met has been to involve employers in the design of journalism and media studies curricula; many Georgian universities have established close working relationships with media and news organisations, sending them questionnaires to solicit their feedback, organising roundtables and thematic meetings in which they actively participate, and embedding them in the activities of careers centres and employability services, etc. To illustrate this point, what follows are the details of a 2014 questionnaire compiled by GTTU, aimed at eliciting feedback responses from the professional media, which would then have a role in updating and improving its journalism and media study programmes. Nearly a hundred respondents — taking in managers, producers, editors and journalists — from 14 leading media organisations responded to the following questions:

---

12 Marine Darsavelidze, Gilles Rouet, Marine Vekua et al., *Jurnalistika* [Journalism] (Tbilisi: Meridiani, 2013).

1. Should graduates be able to analyse texts and draw appropriate conclusions?

2. Should graduates be able to analyse verbal and visual information and draw appropriate conclusions?

3. Should graduates know the grammar and syntactic norms of their native language [Georgian]?

4. Should graduates know any foreign language?

5. Should graduates be able to speak fluently live on TV or radio?

6. Should graduates be able to communicate easily with respondents, colleagues, employers, etc.?

7. Should graduates be aware of media-regulating laws?

8. Should graduates safeguard the principles of professional ethics?

9. Should graduates safeguard employers' ethical codes?

10. Should graduates be able to control themselves in critical situations?

11. Should graduates be able to: (1) focus on the most pressing problem; (2) find ways to obtain information; (3) develop synthetic accounts of their topic; (4) choose the target audience well; (5) define correctly the aims of practical work; (6) make action plans, identify priorities and define their sequence; (7) find and work on necessary sources of information; (8) find appropriate illustrations; (9) correctly identify respondents; (10) prepare and conduct interviews; (11) montage and prepare (in the case of electronic media) their material for airing; (12) work to deadline?

12. Please express your views – what other skills or competences are vital for graduates?

13. What in your view are the weaknesses of graduates?

14. When employing graduates, what position do you usually offer them: (1) journalist/reporter; (2) assistant editor (not editor-in-chief); (3) junior or trainee manager; (4) press speaker; (5) public relations specialist.

Employers' answers to such questions can play an important part in the form and content of educational programmes, enabling academics to more effectively foster students' development of skills in, for instance, communicative efficacy, ethical practice, investigative tactics and interviewing techniques. The participation of potential media employers in curriculum design can yield very useful and telling results, and should be actively encouraged.

Student Feedback

Being able to assess the effectiveness of study programmes is important to the educational process — affecting for instance the choice of topics to be studied as well as the manner, type and location of teaching. A network of feedback is useful here (meaning that lecturers and students might reciprocally influence each other); such feedback systems can also provide a test for how far the aims and criteria of a study programme have been met in practice. In Georgia, as elsewhere, one of the most common methods for determining strengths and weaknesses at the levels of courses, programmes and modules is the student questionnaire. To take another example from GTTU, here is a questionnaire offering BA Journalism students the chance to (anonymously) assess the effectiveness of their course:

1. Are the aims of your module clear?
2. Is the lecturer well-prepared and does he/she deliver interesting classes?
3. Does the lecturer use examples/illustrations in discussing their subject?
4. Does the lecturer answer questions from the audience clearly and thoroughly?
5. How would you assess the material offered?
6. Is the lecturer sufficiently fair in assessing students?
7. Does the lecturer follow the syllabus plan?
8. Do the course materials fit with the contents of classes?
9. Does the lecturer show how theoretical views might be used in practice?

10. Is the lecturer available for consultation outside classes?

11. Are additional teaching resources (projectors, Internet, etc.) used?

12. Does the lecturer communicate clearly?

13. Are you happy with the university's library resources?

14. Are you happy with your studying conditions?

15. How could the lecturer improve your independent study?

Such questions can always be adapted to changing demands: the point, however, is that the responses may be very important to the quality of educational programme and learning process alike, and should be taken into account.

There are also other feedback mechanisms. Acquiring knowledge about their objects of study is not in itself enough when it comes to students' personal development, and for this reason students at Georgian universities are often invited to assess their development at important focus points in their courses. GTTU students, for example, make use of a Personal Development Plan (PDP) as a tool, taking responsibility for their studies and associated aims and in the process developing useful self-appraisal skills. Beyond this, all programmes are required to submit a self-assessment report annually to the National Centre for Education Quality Enhancement, and by extension to the Georgian Ministry of Education and Science. The rationale is to help ensure common standards across the HE system as a whole, as well as to encourage 'best practice'.

Faculty Management

When at the end of 2004 the Georgian Law on Higher Education was adopted "as a driving force towards integrating Georgia with the Bologna Process",[13] various aspects of the Georgian higher education system—and this was especially the case with teaching—were necessarily reformed in line both with legal obligations and with institutional fiat on the part of HE institutions

---

13   For further detail about the Law on Higher Education, see e.g. http://www.bologna-bergen2005.no/EN/national_impl/New/041230_Georgia.pdf (as of 31 July 2017).

themselves. Taken together, these considerations have fuelled a degree of prescriptiveness with regard to the structure and form of every such institution, down to their administrative units, budgets, etc. One result which took place in 2005 saw a number of universities merging previously established faculties into one. For example, 22 faculties at TSU were merged into six new ones. The aim was not simply to create larger faculties; rather the process was intended to simplify and improve faculty management and administration, creating circumstances for the improvement and maintenance of teaching, research and learning, the protection of academic freedom and student rights, the fostering of lifelong learning and students' employment prospects, and the more efficacious development and use of material resources.

The advantage of this enlargement of the faculties is the way it hands students extraordinary opportunities for choosing curricula, major/minor specialisations, option modules, particular academics, etc. But some institutions recombined faculties without sufficient consideration or debate. For example, business, law and social science can be united into one faculty, but this could result in academic ambiguity, and thus further administrative complexities. Smaller universities sometimes justify such decisions on the grounds of greater simplification of administration and management; ideally, however, such a merging of faculties should be based on logical relations between otherwise different fields.

5.   Afterword

In the Soviet period in Georgia, journalism courses had their positive and negative features. Among the more positive ones were that: (1) access to these courses — and education generally — was free of charge; (2) such courses offered deep and wide elementary (though highly generalised) knowledge; and (3) at Tbilisi State University, the only place in Georgia offering courses in the subject at the time, student numbers were small, about 40 per academic year on average (compared to 200 or so currently), allowing for teaching in small groups and the more personal attention that comes with it. Among the more negative aspects were that: (1) the educational process was excessively entangled with ideology; (2) there was an imbalance between theory and practice, and little prospect of participating in exchange programmes, in student and staff mobility, and/or in collaborative projects internationally; and (3) digital and more broadly technical resources were poor, while the contents of curricula fell far short of meeting the needs of journalistic practice.

In Georgia today, the main purpose of the media schools and their accompanying programmes is to give professional training in journalistic practice. This is a natural result of journalism higher education in Georgia constantly adapting its content, quality and presentation to changing circumstances, above all to social change, the preoccupations of governments and the demands of media companies.

Dedifferentiation and Ecological Dominance: The Case of Russian Higher Education

Joseph Backhouse-Barber

1. Introduction

Higher education has historically existed as an institution that occupies an idiosyncratic position in Western society.[1] On one hand it functions as a fundamentally constituent part in the reproduction of the institutional and normative structures of society.[2] On the other hand, according to the liberal model on which it was conceived, higher education is ostensibly billed under egalitarian terms, with the aim of promoting social mobility and fostering critical thought.[3] Soviet higher education in Russia (SHER), on the other hand, unlike the Western university, had no precursor in civil society — it was derived from, and indeed retained, a direct systemic connection to Communist ideology as prescribed by the Soviet government.[4] Soviet academics were expected to uphold an official political position. Any personal political attitude was ideologically subordinated to what were enforced as "communal needs".[5] Thus where the Western higher education system was, first and foremost, ideologically rooted in the liberal,

---

1 I would like to thank A. Salem for making comments on a draft of this chapter, from which I have benefitted. Salem's classes on critical and philosophical theories were also beneficial intellectually, while their supplementary material was interesting and useful for the purposes of this study.

2 See Pierre Bourdieu, *Distinction: A Social Critique of the Judgement of Taste*, trans. Richard Nice (London: Routledge & Kegan Paul, 1986); and Stephen J. Ball, *Class Strategies and the Education Market: The Middle Classes and Social Advantage* (London: Routledge Falmer, 2003).

3 See Robert F. Butts, *A Cultural History of Western Education: Its Social and Intellectual Foundations* (New York: McGraw-Hill, 1955).

4 See Alex Kuraev, "Soviet Higher Education: An Alternative Construct to the Western University Paradigm", *Higher Education* 71:2 (2015): 181–193.

5 Ibid.

enlightenment notion of the individual, the Soviet form was conversely based on a concept of the collective.[6] Initially it is possible to offer a basic comparison. On one hand, if beneath the ostensible value function through which liberal higher education is instituted there exists a subterranean disciplinary function,[7] then a comparison can be drawn between this *unspoken structural* function and the *spoken structural* function of Soviet higher education. In both cases there is an orientation to the reproduction of the whole social body. On the other hand, the 'object' taken to be reproduced informs the prescribed outcome, and the possible descriptions of both systems, differently.

This chapter will compare and contrast the Soviet form of higher education with the post-1991 forms that have emerged as a result of the fall of the Soviet Union, and the consequent neoliberal reforms that have been, and are being, implemented. It will attempt to do so by utilising Luhmannian systems theory against a background of Habermasian critical theory. The impetus to use the work of these two thinkers in this context is twofold. Firstly, there is obviously the belief that their work can be of particular use in understanding the subject matter at hand. Secondly however, the reverse is also true. It is the hope of the author that the subject matter can, in return, be useful in constructing and understanding a relationship between the 'descriptive' concerns of systems theory on the one hand, and the concerns that motivate Habermasian critical theory on the other. Substantively these intentions will be born out in a framework that attempts to describe and contrast neoliberalism as it was generated, and now exists, in the West, with the ideology of the Soviet Union as it existed in Russia. Neoliberalism and

---

6   See Butts, *Cultural History of Western Education;* and George Avis, ed., *Making of a Soviet Citizen: Character Formation and Civic Training in Soviet Education* (London: Routledge, 1987).

7   See Sarah Amsler, Joyce E. Canaan, Stephen Cowden, Sara Motta, and Gurnam Singh, "Why Critical Pedagogy and Popular Education Matter Today", http://www.lu lu.com/items/volume_67/8291000/8291569/1/print/Critical_Pedagogy_Popular_ Education.pdf (as of 5 April 2016).

the Soviet Union will then be presented as the joint social histories that produce the higher education system in Russia today.

2. Neoliberalism and Education in the West: A Brief History

To begin, neoliberalism can be traced back to the ordoliberals of 1930s Germany.[8] Their pursuit of competitive law as a means of protecting freedom,[9] along with Schumpeter's[10] criticism of the notion of the 'common good',[11] began to bring into question the basic assertions underlying the normative function of state-democracy, of which the welfare state is a prime example.[12] Drawing on Schumpeter, Kenneth Arrow and later James Buchannan questioned whether any kind of single value, or 'general will', on which a welfare state must be based was at all compatible with the conditions necessary for freedom; at the same time, the Chicago school were presiding over a resurgence of free market economics.[13] The combination that emerged was partly a divergence from traditional liberal economics à la Hayek,[14] where the self-regulation of the economy was fetishistically elevated, but was also highly critical of welfare state socialism as a means of acting in the interests of a collective will. On Hayek's classical liberal model the economy was presented as a self-stabilising network capable of mass integration

---

8   See Michel Foucault, *The Birth of Biopolitics: Lectures at the Collège de France 1978–79*, trans. Graham Burchell (New York: Palgrave Macmillan, 2008).

9   See Massimiliano Vatiero, "The Ordoliberal Notion of Market Power: An Institutionalist Reassessment", *European Competition Journal* 6:3 (December 2010): 689–707.

10 Joseph A. Schumpeter, *Capitalism, Socialism, and Democracy* (London: Allen & Unwin, 1950).

11 Schumpeter's criticism was founded on the basis that the 'common good' was untenable due to the idiosyncrasies manifest in a population.

12 See Foucault, *The Birth of Biopolitics*; also Wendy Brown, *Undoing the Demos: Neoliberalism's Stealth Revolution* (New York: Zone, 2015).

13 See Mark Olssen, "Neoliberal Competition in Higher Education Today: Research, Accountability and Impact", *British Journal of Sociology of Education* 37:1 (December 2015): 129–148.

14 See Friedrich A. Hayek, *The Road to Serfdom* (London: Routledge Classics, 2006).

without—and this is crucial—state intervention. Thus the assimilation to
market dynamics was not required to be actively carried out since it was a
'natural' process of integration. However, the neoliberal variation had no
such faith in passive socio-economic process. Effectively neoliberalism
retains the strong economic primacy of classic liberalism, but instead of
negating state intervention, the state was enlisted in aid of furthering market
efficiency. The effect of these positive interventions in education have
become well known, and much contested. Through processes of
commodification and regulation higher educational paradigms are sculpted
to the convenience of market logics. Unsurprisingly, universities begin to
resemble businesses with a thoroughly developed, managerial architecture,
and act accordingly by employing incentivised structures geared to
suppressing costs, and maximising 'productivity'.[15] In the context of the
Western university, the genealogy of this form of higher education can be
traced back to and, as problematic as it is, placed within a historical context.
It is a product of indigenous ideology. The institutional and normative
structures that constitute and enable its existence are likewise products of a
historical process in which they can locate themselves directly.[16]

3.   Soviet Russian Higher Education:
   A Habermasian Distinction

In the case of the changes taking place in Russian higher education since
1991, this cannot be said, at least not without divergence. Notably, there are
some quite remarkable continuities between the Soviet form of higher

---

15   See Michael Burawoy, "Redefining the Public University: Developing an Analytical
   Framework", http://publicsphere.ssrc.org/burawoy-redefining-the-public-universi
   ty (as of 7 April 2016). See also Charles Thorpe, "Capitalism, Audit, and the Demise
   of the Humanistic Academy", *Workplace: A Journal for Academic Labour* 15 (September
   2008), http://ices.library.ubc.ca/index.php/workplace/article/viewFile/182219/1
   82230 (as of 7 April 2016); and Louise H. Jackson, *Mythologies of Neoliberalism: an
   Analysis of Widening Participation to Higher Education* (PhD thesis, University of Exeter,
   2015).
16   I am drawing here on Foucault, *The Birth of Biopolitics.*

education, and the proliferating neoliberal form in the West. It is possible to see the similarities as being more than just coincidental. Instead, a common origin can be proposed:[17] the use of proxy metrics and the formalisation of teaching practice can be explained as symptoms of the "erosion of the structures that insulated scholarship from the demands of state policy and economic imperatives".[18] This analysis is consistent with a long line of critical theory that problematises the systematic operations of the capitalist state and economy regarding their impact on social life.[19] In the closing chapter of Jürgen Habermas's *The Theory of Communicative Action*, an interesting distinction is made in this regard.[20] The developmental path of organised capitalism, as Habermas describes it, can broadly be seen to branch off in two general directions. The main, and by far the most prolific form at this current juncture, is the political order of welfare-state democracy. Born out of the functional necessity of generating legitimacy in the context of an increasingly rationalised lifeworld on the one hand, and the substantive contents necessary to ameliorate class conflict, on the other, welfare-state democracy ostensibly functions to stabilise the relationship between the economy and lifeworld. However, in the face of the economic crises that are a feature of capitalism[21] the mode of production in certain instances can be maintained

---

17 See Craig Brandist, "A Very Stalinist Management Model", *Times Higher Education*, 29 May 2014, https://www.timeshighereducation.com/comment/opinion/a-very-stalinist-management-model/2013616.article (as of 2 August 2016); and Craig Brandist, "The Risks of Soviet-Style Managerialism in UK Universities", *Times Higher Education*, 5 May 2016, https://www.timeshighereducation.com/comment/the-risks-of-soviet-style-managerialism-in-united-kingdom-universities (as of 13 May 2016).

18 Ibid.

19 See Jürgen Habermas, *The Theory of Communicative Action, Volume 2: Lifeworld and System, A Critique of Functionalist Reason*, trans. Thomas McCarthy (Cambridge: Polity, 1987); and Herbert Marcuse, *One-Dimensional Man: Studies in the Ideology of Advanced Industrial Society* (London: Routledge, 2006).

20 Habermas, *The Theory of Communicative Action*, 384–386.

21 See Hyman P. Minsky, "The Financial Instability Hypothesis", in "The Capital Development of the Economy and the Structure of Financial Institutions" (paper

in the face of social disintegration only through authoritarian or fascistic political orders. Taking as its point of departure bureaucratic socialism, as in the case of Soviet Russia, and also various moments in the history of capitalist modernisation, state party dictatorship has emerged. What is common to both of these trajectories is the precondition of the initial differentiation of the sub-systems of economy and state.[22] The necessity of this differentiation lies in the practical limits of the communications required to integrate growing, increasingly urbanised populations. On a Habermasian perspective, by allowing the normative constraints around certain 'mediatised' communications — namely money and power — to become relaxed, the limitations that consensus places on the speed and magnitude of coordination are partially bypassed. The macro dynamics of money and power 'uncouple' from lifeworld contexts as functional systems facilitating the mass co-ordination necessary to reproduce modern society. For Habermas the primary difference between the two trajectories made possible by the initial differentiation of a capitalist state and economy is the evolutionary primacy afforded to either subsystem. While in the former case this relates to the direction generated by the intrinsic dynamic of growth internal to the economy, in the latter case the relation is reversed. The state sub-system achieves a position of autonomy in relation the economy, evidenced in Soviet Russia by the operation of a command economy.[23] Superficially it seems analysing SHER and its neoliberal incarnation in this way is a fruitful approach. The use of proxy metrics, excessive formalisation, and a general shaping of education in functional terms regarding economic

---

prepared for the session "Financial Fragility and the U.S. Economy" at the annual meeting of the American Economic Association, January 2–5 1992, New Orleans, Louisiana), *The Jerome Levy Economics Institute Working Paper*, 72, (1992), http://www.levyinstitute.org/pubs/wp72.pdf (as of 17 September 2017).

22   This is an important theme in Habermas's book, *The Theory of Communicative Action*, which I draw upon here.

23   See Mark Harrison, "Coercion, Compliance, and the Collapse of the Soviet Command Economy", *The Economic History Review* 55:3 (2002): 397–433.

requirements are phenomena common to both.[24] They become intelligible as processes engendered through the dominance of either the state or the economic systems in the integration and reproduction of society. In both cases, on a Habermasian view, the state and economy each necessarily require the other: the state must always rely on the self-steering performances of the economy, just as the economy relies on the organisational performance of the state. Thus the functionality of both systems is always necessary, and the respective effects on education are comparable.

4. Soviet Russian Higher Education: A Systems-Theoretical Perspective

This 'branching off' from the dominant trajectory is somewhat evident in Soviet ideology, in that it was a radical departure from what existed previously. Consequently, as aforementioned, SHER had no precursor in civil society, unlike the Western university model.[25] The role prescribed to Soviet education, derived from the ideology of Soviet Marxism, therefore had little recourse to established cultural institutions from which to reproduce itself. Thus, the metamorphosis of the system of higher education in Soviet Russia was almost exclusively driven by functional economic concerns, and ideological authority.[26] This is well illustrated in the context of education by the use of the 'class principle' to displace ruling class monopolisation of university places, and replace it with a more collective 'functionality' based around *providing* for a planned economy.[27]

---

24 See Brandist, "A Very Stalinist Management Model"; and Brandist, "The Risks of Soviet-Style Managerialism in UK Universities".

25 See Kuraev, "Soviet Higher Education".

26 See Leslie W. Ross, "Some Aspects of Soviet Education", *Journal of Teacher Education* 11:4 (1960): 539–552; and Yaroslav I. Kuzminov, Dimitry S. Semenov, and Isak D. Froumin, "The Structure of the University Network: From the Soviet to Russian 'Master Plan'", *Russian Education and Society* 57:4 (2015): 254–321; and Kuraev, "Soviet Higher Education".

27 See Kuzminov, Semenov and Froumin, "The Structure of the University Network".

Ideologically, this was part of a process that can be regarded as akin to de-hypostatisation. The organisation of concrete interventions, themselves a product of hypostatisation, was used to propagate the abstract, ideological principles of Soviet Marxism foundational to the Communist Party. Collective life was a target of change *through* objective structures of administration.[28] Obviously, this does not discount the directly symbolic aspect of Soviet ideology in SHER. Rather, ideological positions in higher education were 'administered' by the value selections of the Communist Party, as part of the societal reversal and distortion of the cyclic relationship between the public, politics and administration common to democratic systems.[29] This is evident in Kuzminov, Semenov, and Froumin's observation that SHER did not feed back into the state or the economy at all.[30] Rather, SHER was restricted to providing answers, and not asking questions by operating, in effect, as an organisation subject to the Communist Party whose functionality was defined by problems labelled within the political system. This necessarily involved selections convenient to Soviet politics. Sociology was infamously repressed, alongside other potentially critical subjects.[31] The Luhmannian systems-theoretical concept of dedifferentiation is useful here.[32] Through a 'programme' of socialism, the internal logics of the political system, penetrated and thus determined the organisation of higher education. A 'programme' in this sense is, simply put, a method used by what Luhmann conceptualises as autopoietic, operationally closed,

---

28 See Stephen J. Collier, *Post-Soviet Social: Neoliberalism, Social Modernity, Biopolitics* (Princeton: Princeton University Press, 2011).

29 See Niklas Luhmann, *Die Politik der Gesellschaft* (Frankfurt: Suhrkamp, 2002): 278–280; and Evelyn Moser, "The Logic of the Soviet Organisational Society: Political Control, the Soviet Village, and World Society", https://www.fiw.uni-bonn.de/publika tionen/FIWWorkingPaper/fiw-working-paper-no.-4 (as of 23 June 2016).

30 Kuzminov, Semenov and Froumin, "The Structure of the University Network".

31 See Kuraev, "Soviet Higher Education".

32 For an introduction to the particular meaning of 'system' in this context, see Niklas Luhmann, *Social Systems*, trans. John Bednarz, Jr. (Stanford: Stanford University Press, 1996): 12–16.

systems in order to construct and adapt to their environments. As a programme, socialism can potentially affect two levels of a system's functioning: the semantic or the operational.[33] At the semantic level, the programme functions as a means of amplifying the scope for learning and adaptability within a system, by expanding the capacity for environmental references. The evolutionary existence of a programme, in this sense, is variant, while the operational distinctions through which a system relates to itself — a system 'code' — are relatively invariant. This 'invariance' will be returned to shortly. Dedifferentiation occurs when the *operations* of a system (the assignment of code values) become determined by a programme. The autonomy of a functional system is disregarded through the elimination of its operational specificity. Soviet society can be seen as an example of this on a large scale: through the programme of socialism, the operations of various functional systems became 'organisations' subordinate to the political system.[34] To understand this, it is necessary to return to the idea of 'invariability' in relation to the operations of society. The use of code values in operations as invariant is possible as long as 'crossing over' (e.g. from better to worse, beautiful to ugly) between value selections remains possible; that is code values are not determined by other selections.[35] As long as it is possible to code an operation on either side of a value distinction, the code, and by extension the system, can persist, since the ability to 'cross over' that confirms a code and permits its invariance is what, at a basal level, produces a system's specificity, and what is thus the basis for its self-reference. In short, it is what fundamentally distinguishes a system from its environment. Thus,

---

33 For an explanation of these terms in this context see Niklas Luhmann, "Complexity, Structural Contingencies and Value Conflicts", in Paul Heelas, ed., *Detraditionalisation: Critical Reflections on Authority and Identity at a Time of Uncertainty* (Cambridge, MA.: Blackwell Publishers, 1995); also Niklas Luhmann, "Why Does Society Describe Itself as Postmodern?", *Cultural Critique* 30 (Spring 1995): 171.

34 See Niklas Luhmann, "Answering the Question: What is Modernity? An Interview with Niklas Luhmann", in William Rasch, *Niklas Luhmann's Modernity: The Paradoxes of Differentiation* (Stanford: Stanford University Press, 2000), 204–205.

35 See Luhmann, *Social Systems*, 444–445.

once a system determines the assignment of a code value on the basis of other-reference and precludes its specificity, it can no longer operate under the conditions of autonomy that this specificity allowed. In the case of the stratified societies of the pre-modern period, when all value selections were moralised according to the distinction 'good/bad' by virtue of being organised as properties of a certain strata, particular functional codes could not exist as invariant since the possibility of 'crossing over' specific to them, that facilitated invariance, was eliminated:[36] the moral code of good/bad determined all other value selections. Soviet society was organisational rather than stratified,[37] but nevertheless a similar logic applies. The programme of socialism with its own necessary value selections became the reference point for the determination of values relating to a system's coding. Thus the specific code that was at the core of the autonomy of functional systems — that is the code as the particular form that interrupts circulatory self-reference and facilitates autopoiesis — was denied its necessary invariance. In presenting this analysis one thing should be made abundantly clear: the process of dedifferentiation through the programme of socialism was not 'orchestrated' in the humanist sense. The changes that took place occurred through the internal dynamics of each system. It is a foundational aspect of a Luhmannian theory of autopoietic systems that only the system itself can determine its own organisation, and that the environment can, at most, perturb the process.[38] In this case the environmental pressure that psychic systems placed on society were 'resolved' through operations within society that lead to dedifferentiation in the way described above — in other words, systems, including the education system, dedifferentiated themselves. The education system's code is better/worse[39] (or similar), and thus its autopoiesis relies on the ability to apply this code invariantly to both 'successful' and 'unsuccessful' operations. As already noted, the specificity

---

36 Ibid., 397–398.

37 See Luhmann, "Answering the Question: What is Modernity?", 204.

38 See for instance Luhmann, *Introduction to Systems Theory*, 88, 89.

39 See Luhmann, *Social Systems*, 244.

of this form of organisation is essentially what allows the education system autonomy. Programmes in the education system define the content of what is subject to the bivalence of the coding. Through programmes the education system constructs and connects itself to social demand. The education system's functionality lies in this ability to 'connect' society with an aspect of its environment, namely the bodies and minds of people. This does not mean that education is in any way determined by its environment as a product, or that it is subservient to systems found there. It simply means that the internal dynamics of education are organised in a certain way, by virtue of the internal relationship between self-reference and other-reference. The education system's code supports the construction of, and is thus concerned with, 'careers' through a socially selective function, such that an individual can perform better or worse, not only in relation to others, but in relation to themselves temporally. By prescribing what is coded as better or worse on the basis of the *politically* oriented demands selected through the programme of socialism, the education system immediately lost its organisational specificity, and hence its autonomy, ultimately leading to dedifferentiation. This is illustrated extremely clearly by the stark reorientation of SHER from a European liberal university model—education for education's sake—to one pragmatically oriented to realising a political goal through mass, vocational training.[40] The semantics of education remained intact, but the operational logics that provide for internal organisation became assimilated to the political system. Communications that semantically persist as education are coded at the operational level by the political system. In simple terms, education's function of 'cultivation' was assimilated as a mechanism of collective organisation, or in a word, politics. Again, this can be evidenced quite clearly by the fact that Communist Party officials stationed at each university were considered as decision-makers equal to the Rector.[41] As has been said, SHER did not 'feed back' into the economy or state at all because

---

40   See Kuraev, "Soviet Higher Education".
41   Ibid.

the actual *institutions* of education—what Moser would call the "material level"[42] of a system—were still organised through the programme of socialism, and so were dealt with in terms of semantically specific organisations *subject* to the Communist Party. Hence, the most common diagnosis of Soviet education has been that it was simply a tool to further the hold of Soviet ideology over society.[43] None of this is to suggest that 'learning' was somehow replaced with politics in terms of the individual— or in systems-theoretical terms, the psychic system—but that the communications that enforce the relevant selections were no longer produced by an education system that is self-organising. Higher education in the Soviet Union was no longer operating under the weight of education's own internally organised history, but became a semantically specific form of politically relevant legitimation and membership. Thus it is no longer sufficient to regard Soviet higher education only in terms of coercive principles.[44] Higher education in the Soviet Union was not repressed or impinged upon *by* the political, but came to be *produced as political* at a basal level.

5.   Reconceptualising Neoliberalism: Ecological Dominance

Notably, the process of dedifferentiation that took place in Soviet Russia was a different process than that which is taking place in relation to Western higher education under neoliberalism, though there are, as already mentioned, strong similarities between the two. The distinction that Habermas offers can also be re-evaluated here. From a Luhmannian systems-theoretical perspective, functionally differentiated society cannot be characterised by the simple domination of one sub-system over others, by virtue of the operationally closed, autopoietic nature of the systems that

---

42   See Moser, "The Logic of the Soviet Organisational Society".

43   See Anthony Jones, ed., *Education and Society in the New Russia* (New York: M.E. Sharpe, 1994).

44   In the broader sense, this is what Foucault rightly dismisses as the 'repressive hypothesis' of power. See Michel Foucault, *The History of Sexuality, Volume 1: The Will to Knowledge,* trans. Robert Hurley (London: Penguin, 1998).

constitute it. The explanation of Soviet society using a concept of dedifferentiation partially resolves this conflict through an explanation of the operational assimilation of sub-systems other than the political system — here education — to political organisation, made possible through the programme of Soviet socialism. Soviet dedifferentiation was a product of relatively extreme environmental pressure regarding human activity, and as such remained a relative outlier compared to the world society of which it was a part. Again, this does not describe the conditions for, or the realities within, neoliberalism. Neoliberalism aligns with the trend towards structural differentiation identified numerous times as an aspect of modernity.[45] Regarding the Habermasian distinction, neoliberalism sits firmly within the parameters of what he delineates as the form of modernity — developed capitalism — characterised by the primacy of the economic sub-system.[46] Despite the seeming conflict that this understanding engenders with a systems-theoretical account of autopoietic systems, the association of neoliberalism with economic 'primacy', and thus Habermas's distinction, may still prove fruitful in the context of utilising systems theory in understanding the changes to higher education in Russia.

To do so, it is first necessary to reconceptualise neoliberalism in a way that allows for the possibility of economic dominance, but that is reconcilable with a systems-theoretical understanding of society in terms of the dedifferentiation of the Soviet education system. As noted earlier, neoliberalism in the West is characterised by a turn towards economic 'rationality' in areas of society other than the economy. It is distinguished from its predecessor *liberalism* by its change in stance towards state intervention. Rather than negate state intervention altogether, the state is enlisted to positively enforce economic competition. This does not necessarily prescribe an economically determinist concept of society. Following Luhmann, modern capitalist society can be understood as

---

45 See Dietrich Rueschemeyer, "Structural Differentiation, Efficiency, and Power", *American Journal of Sociology* 83:1 (1977): 1–25.

46 See Habermas, *The Theory of Communicative Action*.

functionally differentiated. This means that due to the specificity that allows autonomy, the economy, like other functional systems of society, is reliant on the complex performances of other functional systems (e.g. law) that it has no control over. However, in a developed capitalist society the relationship between different functional systems is complex and contingent. Given the different operative dynamics of each system, there can be disparity in the ability of systems to structure the environment of other systems.[47] From this asymmetry it becomes possible for an ecological relation of dominance to arise, where no systems actually dominate.[48] This paradoxical situation is possible because, although functional systems remain autonomous and thus completely indeterminate to one another, the relative pressure they exert on the autopoiesis of systems other than themselves is not necessarily equal. In biological terms ecological dominance refers simply to a certain tax on making up more biomass than others, and the reasoning is relatively similar here. The distinctive logic of an international capitalist economy gives it many reasons to assume for itself a position of relative dominance in respect to the other functional systems of society.

Jessop offers several explanations as to why this could be the case, though there is not enough space to discuss them all here; in fact Jessop takes an analysis based on ecological dominance to a point that possibly becomes incommensurate with a Luhmannian approach as a whole.[49] However, without fully endorsing Jessop's position, one factor appears particularly salient: the economic system's ability to increase the complexity of its operations primarily on the basis of self-reference, or, more specifically, to

---

47   See Bob Jessop, "The Relevance of Luhmann's Systems Theory and of Laclau and Mouffe's Discourse Analysis to the Elaboration of Marx's State Theory', https://bobjessop.org/2014/02/09/the-relevance-of-luhmanns-systems-theory-and-of-laclau-and-mouffes-discourse-analysis-to-the-elaboration-of-marxs-state-theory/ (as of 19 July 2016).

48   See Niklas Luhmann, *Political Theory in the Welfare State*, trans. John Bednarz (New York: Walter de Gruyter, 1990).

49   See Jessop, "The Relevance of Luhmann's Systems Theory and of Laclau and Mouffe's Discourse Analysis to the Elaboration of Marx's State Theory".

base its operations on the irritations produced by competition between capitals. This can be further divided into two factors. Firstly, actualisations produced as other-reference within the capitalist economy can be made immediately available as a relation between elements marked as self-reference, thus enlarging the scope for reproduction of the system as a whole. Secondly, the negative value of the asymmetrical code payment/non-payment used in the economy,[50] which serves a reflective function, can be further observed on the basis of this distinction between capitals. A coding of non-payment can be immediately related to another operation, possibly coded as payment, by distinguishing between competing capitals, thus allowing a negative code value to act on the one hand in a reflective function, and on the other as an operation relatable to further operations. By virtue of this ambivalence regarding the assignment of code values the economy is granted an extremely high level of internal flexibility. These factors contribute to a situation where the economy can be understood to be a greater source of adaptive pressure on the surrounding systems, than any of them are individually. The logic of dominance in this case is quite simple. The generalised pressure that the economy exerts on the systems in its environment is increased when its effects become part of the pressure that they in turn place onto their environment. This does not mean that the same process does not happen for all systems in society, but that there is, for the reasons given, a discrepancy regarding *the degree to which* it takes place. The change in attitude toward state intervention that characterises neoliberalism is thus simply the point in the development of this economic ecological dominance regarding the evolution of the political system.

Unlike the economy, the education system cannot channel other-reference into a relationship between elements of self-reference, nor can it continue operations on the basis of a diversion from a negative code value. Hence the education system develops programmes that produce the 'contents' of careers so that they 'fit' primarily into a context structured

---

50   See Luhmann, *Social Systems*, 461–462.

through economic functionality, such that a positive coding of 'better' (or equivalent) in the education system is likely to relate to communications that are positively coded as payment in the economic system. This is why, for instance, whether a career is judged as successful or not is generally closely correlated with the magnitude of an individual's salary, except in rare circumstances.[51] The neoliberal focus on maximising 'productivity' in higher education, and the consequent competition between institutions are thus understandable as programmatic performances by the education system related to the ongoing conditioning of this correlation. The fact that this relationship is becoming increasingly explicit is something that will be considered later on. In the context of this analysis, neoliberalism appears as a description that society can ascribe to itself as a product of developing economic ecological dominance. This allows the Habermasian distinction based on the primacy of economy or state to be formally preserved. The comparison now available is between the Soviet dedifferentiation of educational communications into politics, and the ecological dominance of the economy that characterises neoliberal educational forms, of the sort being implemented in Russia after 1991.

6.   Continuing Dedifferentiation, Ecological Dominance, and Alienation

The collapse of the Soviet Union brought to an end the hermetic closure of Soviet society to the Western world. Western access to the Soviet structures of higher education was coupled with an unprecedented acceleration in the pace of their change.[52] However, despite the Soviet organisational form no longer existing *per se*, it must be remembered that the opening up of society

---

51   In these instances, the disjunction between a 'successful' career and a large salary is often swiftly remedied by the adaption of the economic system. The rapid rise in the salaries of professional sportspeople, such as footballers, would thus be an example of the flexibility of the economic system.

52   See Artemy Magun, "Higher Education in Post-Soviet Russia and the Global Crisis of the University", http://www.isa-sociology.org/universities-in-crisis/?p=508 (as of 4 July 2016).

to neoliberalism, and its subsequent reorganisation, was constituted out of social structures that already existed, and therefore did not entail their complete destruction. The Soviet form of education as an organisation under political control thus must be recognised contextually in terms of understanding the neoliberalisation of higher education as it actually exists in post-Soviet Russia. As Stark accurately points out, post-Soviet organisations and institutions were rebuilt "not *on the ruins* but *with the ruins* of Communism".[53]

On one hand, the obvious creation of privatised educational institutions[54] is backed by clear indications of the kind of communication that functional differentiation suggests. The orienting of education towards 'careers' is one such indication. For example, Morgan and Kliucharev list continuing adult education along with professional and vocational training as core tenets of modernisation policy in Russian education;[55] and Yuri Reznik emphasises the "humanisation" of education as a central shift in ideology according to the idea of "development".[56] In both cases the individual is dealt with using a concept that is distinct from — but not necessarily independent of — other systems. A 'career' is only possible as a coherent concept as long as it retains its identity *vis-à-vis* other communication systems. A career cannot be understood in purely economic terms (though it often implies them), nor entirely in terms of power (in a political sense). An individual can pursue a 'career' *in law*, or *in politics*, but to the degree that it is a career it can only be understood against itself: that is, against the 'careers' of other individuals or directly against itself temporally. In other words, a career makes 'sense' as a

---

53   David Stark, "Recombinant Property in East European Capitalism", *American Journal of Sociology* 101:4 (January 1996): 995.

54   See Natalia Kyui, "Expansion of Higher Education, Employment and Wages: Evidence from the Russian Transition", *Labour Economics* 39 (April 2016): 68–87.

55   John Morgan and Grigori A. Kliucharev, "Higher Education and the Post-Soviet Transition in Russia", *European Journal of Education* 47:1 (March 2012): 3–8.

56   Yuri Reznik, "The Reform of Higher Education in Post-Soviet Russia: 1987–1997", http://files.eric.ed.gov/fulltext/ED441388.pdf (as of 26 July 2016).

concept because it invokes itself. This formulation of the career concept, of which humanised development is a semantic variant, is thus an example of educational self-reference.

On the other hand, however, the dedifferentiated structure of the Soviet Union persists in higher education in various ways, legally and illegally. Corruption[57] is perhaps the most obvious although complex example, and occurs in post-Soviet Russian higher education in many different forms. Nepotism, cronyism and favouritism are examples of Soviet politico-social structures persisting illegitimately or "illegally".[58] However, many similar processes occur legally through the political system due to the persistently significant role of the 'state'.[59] In these cases, various aspects of society remain as organisations under political control.[60] In the case of the instances of corruption mentioned above, communicative structures confirmed through the political structure of the Soviet Union in turn continue to structure communications relating to education, via the networks that formed under political dedifferentiation persisting through a mechanism of trust.[61] Hence, communications lose their education-specific logic. Other forms of corruption in Russian higher education are not as easily accounted

---

57   See e.g. Ararat L. Osipian, "Replacing University Entry Examinations with Standardised Tests in Russia: Will It Reduce Corruption?", http://static1.1.sqspcdn. com/static/f/275549/9729934/1291751711550/Osipian2_UCEA2007.pdf?token=Rx Q6lCJgNTYhlnMyqWMJG9mLLy4%3D (as of 1 August 2016); Ararat Osipian, "Vouchers, Tests, Loans, Privatisation: Will They Help Tackle Corruption in Russian Higher Education?", *Prospects* 39:1 (March 2009): 47–67; and Ararat Osipian, "Education Corruption, Reform, and Growth: Case of Post-Soviet Russia", *Journal of Eurasian Studies* 3:1 (January 2012): 20–29.

58   Ibid.

59   The state, in this sense, is a self-description of the political system. See Balazs Brunczel, *Disillusioning Modernity: Niklas Luhmann's Social and Political Theory* (Frankfurt am Main: Peter Lang, 2010).

60   See Philip Casula, Jeronim Perovic and Ivo Mijnssen, *Identities and Politics During the Putin Presidency: The Foundations of Russia's Stability* (Stuttgart: Ibidem, 2009).

61   See Niklas Luhmann, "Familiarity, Confidence, Trust: Problems and Alternatives", in Diego Gambetta, ed., *Trust: Making and Breaking Cooperative Relations* (New York: Blackwell Publishers, 1988).

for in this way. Bribery and embezzlement, for instance, do not fit so easily into an understanding based solely on the dynamics of Soviet politics persisting. They do however, fit with a broader definition of dedifferentiation as Luhmann describes it. In these cases, what is clear is not the direct continuation of Soviet political structures, but those communications that constituted them being rendered through the economic system. The logic of dedifferentiation still applies. Communications pertaining to educational organisation are assimilated as economic: that is according to payments. In these instances, in Luhmann's terms, the educational code of better/worse becomes determined according to an economic coding of payment/non-payment. For example, a tutor could take money in order to pass a student, thus denying the education system the autonomy that it requires to exist, at least regarding that student's career. In this sense post-Soviet Russian higher education feels the effects of its history in two ways. Firstly, as a continuation of dedifferentiation according to Soviet organisational forms, legally and illegally, through cronyism and the organisational role of the state; and secondly as a diversion of communications onto other differentiated systems (in this case the economy). This second effect paradoxically combines dedifferentiation with differentiation and presents itself as a kind of communicative instability,[62] the wider effects of which were palpable in the 1990s Russian crisis. This second effect also highlights the reality of a post-Soviet Russian society that cannot be analytically reduced to a simple either/or confrontation between Soviet and neoliberal forms of organisation. Where simpler forms of corruption can be presented as a 'relic' destined to pass as Russia 'modernises', this kind of educational corruption is more intimately bound up with processes of neoliberal reform. As Magun explains, "the collapse of

---

62 In the context of a structurally differentiated society, "stability now has to be grounded primarily in flexibility, changeability, decidability". See Luhmann, *Theory of Society, Volume 1*, trans. Rhodes Barrett (Stanford: Stanford University Press, 2012), 301.

Communist ideology created a climate of anomie where corruption [...] was not generally perceived as reprehensible".[63]

However, in the context of neoliberalism characterised by the ecological dominance of the economy, there are reasons to assume for it a positive role in producing conditions of educational instability, of which corruption is symptomatic, beyond the negative effect of dismantling Communist ideology. In doing so, there is also occasion to further clarify, in the face of Luhmannian systems theory, the Habermasian distinction between state and economic primacy[64] that has quietly framed the analysis so far. Through the emphasis on individual responsibility, political and economic liberalism undermines the confidence required for participation in systems, by attempting to replace it with what Luhmann calls the condition of trust.[65] Alienation is the consequence of attempting to base participation in a system on the distinction between trust and distrust, when participation in that system actually requires confidence. In short, the trust/distrust distinction often calls upon the operation of confidence as a presupposition of participation. In certain cases,[66] liberalism thus actively produces alienation as a consequence of its operation by prescribing 'choice' to a condition of necessary confidence. Neoliberalism extends this further, simply as a consequence of its enforcement of an economically conditioned rationality that, by its very nature, must base itself on a concept of competition that presupposes the rational 'choice' of individuals, but also must act to guarantee (to produce) the same condition.[67] This process can be analysed in terms of the ambivalences that constitute what Habermas calls "the colonisation of the lifeworld". On the one hand, to the degree that lifeworld

63 Magun, "Higher Education in Post-Soviet Russia and the Global Crisis of the University".
64 See Habermas, *The Theory of Communicative Action*.
65 Luhmann, *Familiarity, Confidence, Trust*.
66 That is, if the condition of trust is *recognised* in psychic systems as a condition of necessary participation.
67 See Foucault, *The Birth of Biopolitics*.

processes become integrated systematically—in a Habermasian sense[68]—through the sub-systems of the economy and state, individualised actors are increasingly likely to orient themselves strategically; that is, instrumentally in terms of a 'choice' between consequences. On the other hand, the degree to which this can take place must find its limits in the conditions necessary for the continued symbolic reproduction of the lifeworld, since lifeworld integrity is entirely necessary to maintain the intersubjective 'anchoring' of the state and economy in the lifeworld through legal institutionalisation. 'Colonisation' happens when lifeworld reproduction becomes impinged upon, as intersubjectively constituted areas of life are reified as systematically structured fields of choice for individualised actors, ultimately endangering the basic conditions of systematic functioning.

7. Neoliberalism: Alienation and Instability

Neoliberalism sharpens the tension of this ambivalence by disengaging the state in practices that attempt to respond to and preserve the symbolic reproduction of the lifeworld, and instead promotes action that often enforces the process of colonisation. Decisions made strategically, based on systematised relations, are constituted on the condition of what Luhmann delineates as "trust".[69] The requirement of intersubjective lifeworld contexts in which systematised relations ultimately anchor themselves is analogous to the presupposition of 'confidence' required for participation in these cases. The anchoring that Habermas describes can be looked at in systems-theoretical terms as a process internal to the respective social system. In Luhmannian terms, social systems 'anchor' themselves in other (psychic and social) systems as a construction internal to themselves. The relationship between systems, in this sense, exists variously: as various operations within various systems. The point at which this can be problematised is the

---

68   It should be noted that Habermas uses 'system' in a different way to Luhmann, as analytically distinguished from what he calls the Lifeworld. See Habermas, *The Theory of Communicative Action,* for a full explanation.

69   Luhmann, *Familiarity, Confidence, Trust.*

efficiency of the operation that constructs this relationship as continuing the autopoiesis of the given system in the face of environmental perturbation. The possibility for alienation occurs when the recursive constructs relating to these relationships internal to a *social* system are resolved as environmental perturbation by *psychic* systems. In the context of neoliberalism, the condition of trust, as a choice, produced by certain communications cannot fulfil the participatory requirement of confidence. If this is recognised, distinguishing a condition of alienation (or something similar) thus becomes necessary for the psychic system to observe the trust/distrust selection enforced by the social system in terms of a lack of confidence from the perspective of necessary participation. In other words, only by recognising its own disenfranchisement can a psychic system continue to operate in the context of the enforced selection between trust and distrust becoming primary. Thus, in instances where alienation arises to observe the trust/distrust distinction as primary, the condition of confidence becomes even more improbable. This is reconcilable with a Habermasian concept of reification through an understanding of psychic systems constructing concretised selections. The use of alienation as an operation to observe choices relating to necessary participation means that psychic systems must construct 'rigid' selections that narrow the scope of actions available to them, and then recognise them as being enforced. In the simplest terms, reification is the recognition of social systems.[70] For Habermas, reification presents itself as a problem related to the symbolic reproduction of the lifeworld by reducing communicative rationality — which is dialogic — to instrumental rationality — which is monologic. For Luhmann, the condition of a lack of confidence unleashes the possibility of "deteriorating effects which diminish the range of activities available to the system".[71] In

---

70   This recognition can also be looked at in terms of what Habermas classes as the structural differentiation of the lifeworld: into personality, culture, and society. In Luhmannian terms psychic systems become *simultaneously* aware of their individuality, *and* the social context that allows for it — which must thus necessarily be participated in.

71   Luhmann, *Familiarity, Confidence, Trust*, 97.

other words, in the same way that reification limits the scope of communicative action necessary for the reproduction of the lifeworld in Habermas, alienation in Luhmann limits the scope of operations available for social systems to reproduce themselves. The evidence of this limiting effect, in Luhmannian terms, can be found throughout Western society in the self-descriptions of each functional system. As the range of operations available to each system is limited through the processes described above, then there is necessarily a shrinking of the scope for self-description available to each system. In the context of the ecological dominance of the economy, this conditioning is likely to construct descriptions related to this. Hence neoliberalism presents itself to itself. The proliferation of 'economic paradigms' into more and more areas of society — from politics[72] to law[73] — that is a prevailing concern among theorists and critical commentators from Marx onwards can thus be regarded as the product of the burgeoning relationship between economic ecological dominance on the one hand, and the construction of alienation within psychic systems on the other.

Education, and higher education in particular, are no exceptions to this.[74] The neoliberal phenomena, broadly understandable as the 'marketisation' of higher education, is thus a performance of the education system in the face of environmental perturbation structured by this economic ecological dominance, on the one hand, and by the limitation of self-descriptions available to it through the loss of conditions of confidence and the production

---

72 See Alfredo Saad-Filho and Deborah Johnston, eds., *Neoliberalism: A Critical Reader* (London: Pluto, 2004).

73 See David S. Grewal and Jedediah Purdy, "Introduction: Law and Neoliberalism", *Law and Contemporary Problems* 4:77 (2014): 1–23; and Jafaar Aksikas and Sean J. Andrews, "Neoliberalism, Law and Culture: A Cultural Studies Intervention after 'the Juridical Turn'", *Cultural Studies* 28:5–6 (2014): 742–780.

74 See e.g. Mark Olssen and Sean J. Peters, "Neoliberalism, Higher Education and the Knowledge Economy: From the Free Market to Knowledge Capitalism", *Journal of Education Policy* 20:3 (2005): 313–345; and Mike Molesworth, Richard Scullion and Elizabeth Nixon, eds., *The Marketisation of Higher Education and the Student as Consumer* (New York: Taylor and Francis, 2010).

of alienation in psychic systems, on the other. Increasingly the programmes that the education system constructs to deal with its environment, by focusing on aligning the binary code of the education system with the function of the economic system, actually reflect this semantically.[75] In other words, where 'productivity' and competition between institutions can be understood as evidence of the conditioning of educational dynamics by economic ecological dominance, the explicit reference to these dynamics and to the economy can be understood as the way the loss of conditions of confidence affect educational self-description. For instance, the touting of links with business by universities as a merit, and the publication of graduate earnings across subjects, are examples of this economic conditioning surfacing semantically within the education system. Unsurprisingly, this can be observed in post-Soviet Russian higher education. For example, commercial and administrative tasks are routinely given precedence over research and teaching,[76] because being able to meet the demands of a 'modern' economy has paradoxically remained the utmost of concerns in Russian institutions of higher education. Whereas under Soviet conditions of dedifferentiation this was a role determined by politics in the context of inclusivity regarding the economy, current Russian institutions are increasingly forced to 'sell' themselves in a 'competitive' global 'market'.[77]

---

75   The difference being in the way that success is described. The limiting of self-descriptions available to the education system is evident in the declining 'taboo' status assigned to discussion of financial matters — a general trend that Deleuze and Guattari might call 'the decoding of flows'. See Gilles Deleuze and Felix Guattari, *Anti-Oedipus: Capitalism and Schizophrenia*, trans. Robert Hurley, Seem Mark, and Helen R. Lane (Minneapolis: University of Minnesota Press, 1983).

76   See Magun, "Higher Education in Post-Soviet Russia and the Global Crisis of the University".

77   See Oleg Alekseev, "Climbing the Global University Rankings", http://www.univ ersityworldnews.com/article.php?story=20140702115809236 (as of 18 August 2016); Andreay Yakunin, "Government Investment is Increasing, but Russian Universities Need Business Too", https://www.timeshighereducation.com/world-university-rankings/2014/brics-and-emerging-economies/analysis/russian-universities-need-business-too (as of 18 August 2016).

Indeed, at the turn of the millennium, higher education in Russia was described solely in these terms in a government report, as an "effective capital investment";[78] whilst the GIFO project sought to restructure education in aid of its regulation by consumer demand.[79] The publication HERB[80] is reflective of this, as the education system attempts to describe itself effectively in an increasingly narrow context, and thus manages to make abundantly clear the inclusion of Russian higher education in a global education system where 'competition' becomes a woefully inadequate conceptual tool. At the same time, not all communications related through educational institutions are produced through the education system itself, but are instead produced, by various methods, through other systems – the problem being that neoliberal reforms, with their characteristically alienating effects, in the context of the transitionary state that Russian education finds itself in, offer little purchase on what identifies as the anomic state of Russian educators.[81] To return to the Luhmannian distinction above, the collapse of the Soviet Union destroyed confidence; neoliberal reforms attempted to replace that with trust, based on a 'choice'.[82] Given the structural remnants of Soviet society that exist to such an extent in Russian higher education, dedifferentiation, of which corruption is an example,[83] is allowed to remain possible insofar as it is produced as a choice within society, in the context of the alienation of necessary participation that neoliberalism conditions. The shrinking of the scope of activities available to the educational system

---

78 Tatiana Gounko and William Smale, "Modernisation of Russian Higher Education: Exploring Paths of influence", *Compare: A Journal of Comparative and International Education* 37:4 (August 2007): 533–548.

79 Ibid.

80 See the journal *Higher Education in Russia and Beyond*, https://herb.hse.ru/en/archive.html (as of 18 August 2016).

81 See Magun, "Higher Education in Post-Soviet Russia and the Global Crisis of the University".

82 Luhmann, *Familiarity, Confidence, Trust*.

83 See Osipian, "Replacing University Entry Examinations with Standardised Tests in Russia"; Osipian, "Vouchers, Tests, Loans, Privatisation"; and Osipian, "Education Corruption, Reform, and Growth".

through the processes described above, means that its ability to react with a more compelling account of its environment is hindered. Thus the education system remains, in the context of Russian institutions of higher education, unstable.

8. Conclusion

This chapter has undertaken an admittedly broad-brush analysis of the realities that produce, and condition, Russian higher education as it existed under the Soviet regime, and as it exists now. In doing so it has sacrificed the level of specificity that is necessary to construct the current realities of Russian higher education in anything approaching their full complexity. However, it has done so for a reason. If the broad theoretical project of Luhmann is to be brought to bear — fruitfully and in consideration of Habermasian concerns — on such a specific subject, then the job is a large one. The paths from the general to the specific must be trodden one by one, and there are many diversions. This chapter, then, is a first tentative step. What, hopefully, it has been able to provide, in light of its intentions, is a description that includes difference, alongside similarity. On one hand the Soviet form of higher education, and that produced under neoliberalism, are fundamentally different realisations borne out by different organisational forms. On the other hand, the problems they faced, and face, remain remarkably similar. The Soviet form of higher education proved unstable because Soviet dedifferentiated society was itself unstable in the context of a world society of which it was a part. The neoliberal form of higher education in Russia is unstable because it combines these structures with a problem of instability that neoliberalism itself presents in world society, whereby the lack of conditions of confidence limits the flexibility of functional systems, including education. For these reasons it is possible to find continuities in the descriptive concerns of systems theory, and the pragmatic concerns of critical theory. Alienation can be problematised as reification. Perhaps, in light of this, systems theory can provide alienation as a worthy site of uncertain protest, as an anarchistic leap into the unknown — or perhaps not. Either way the meeting of systems theory with the concerns of critical theory in this context provides many avenues to investigate—from the dynamics of the instrumentality that characterised Soviet education, and still characterise neoliberal reforms, to problems of continuing dedifferentiation in education as a 'coping mechanism' of society.

Pedagogies, Technologies and Social Formations

Robert Ferguson

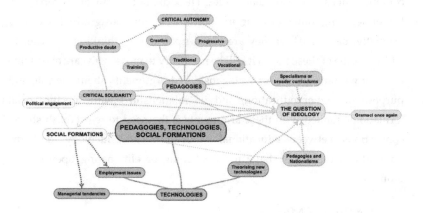

1. Introduction

The purpose of this chapter is to identify and debate some of the key contradictions, tensions, opportunities and serious weaknesses in developments in higher education across the ex-Communist countries and much of the rest of Europe, with special reference to the humanities and social sciences. The approach taken is to highlight issues which are taken from a range of contexts and educational approaches. I do not offer direct critiques of ex-Communist countries. I ask readers to accept the relevance and urgency of some comparative considerations. It is my assertion that an oblique approach to education challenges will often generate more productive thinking and strategic outcomes. My wish is to stimulate debate, argument, and the evolution of relevant and appropriate pedagogies. The core of my argument will depend upon two things: a recognition of the key role which the new technologies are playing or are likely to play in higher education in all the above countries and regions; and at the same time the tensions and influences of social and national barriers which impede critical thinking. The motivation behind my discussion of new technologies is not based upon an inherent wish to praise or to condemn, though the latter is sometimes hard to resist. The chapter will try to suggest some forms of appropriate pedagogy which will facilitate both critical thinking and social commitment as core curricular values. These are not exactly at the top of the list of learning outcomes for undergraduate and postgraduate courses generally, particularly if they are based upon critical thinking. In order to address some of these issues it will be necessary to move with care over some well-known but not always well-considered arguments about the role and purpose of higher education, and its relationships with specific social formations. Linked with these arguments is the need to re-establish strong connections between educational innovations and ideology, and the implications these may have for weakening or eliminating open critical thought.

2.   The Rule of Money

I will begin in the United States with reference to the important research of Professor Ellen Schrecker. One of her more recent works is entitled *The Lost Soul of Higher Education*.[1] Schrecker has spent much of her academic life researching the repression visited upon the academic and wider community in the United States by the House Committee on Un-American Activities. She is also an astute observer of the intellectual and structural constraints that have been built up, layer by layer, in higher education in the United States of America.

> Beginning in the late 1960s and 1970s, while most professors attended to their classes and careers, the institutions that housed them were evolving into ever more bureaucratised organisations with an increasingly market-oriented set of priorities that reinforced the university's long-standing hierarchical structures while weakening its traditional intellectual and educational commitments. In the process, moreover, professors were losing much of their power to determine the educational

---

1   Ellen Schrecker, *The Lost Soul of Higher Education: Corporatisation, the Assault on Academic Freedom, and the End of the American University* (New York: New Press, 2010).

policies of their institutions and to protect their own academic freedom and that of their colleagues.[2]

Schrecker's work has, over the years, patiently and with a fine sense of what constitutes educational freedom, identified the multitude of ways in which higher education can be manipulated and constrained for ideological purposes. But here, of course, we are talking about the United States of America, which has usually been interpreted as a bastion of freedom by those educationalists and politicians of a less than liberal persuasion. There is now a substantial amount of research which considers the ways in which the free market and commodity production have first insinuated themselves, and then brazenly staked massive claims in the structures of higher education.[3] There may well be those academic staff from the ex-Communist countries who will comment with some justice that we in Western Europe and North America do not know how lucky we are. The constraints, repression, persecution and imprisonment of those who dared to speak out against specific so-called Communist regimes were of another order to what might seem mere free market inconveniences, when compared to the gulag. But these arguments are not only counterproductive and perilously close to truisms: they also miss the point that times are changing very fast and there are those who are now interpreting the future of higher education as the future of the new technologies. Little else matters. Innovation is the new freedom. Entrepreneurialism is the new substitute for critical analysis. Management will conquer all. And profit will insinuate itself as the driving force of all education, whether through provision of (private or sponsored) courses or hollow promises of future economic success to tomorrow's graduates. Money and the promise of money is the name of the game. And what a game it is.

---

2 Ibid., 154.
3 See especially Naomi Klein, *No Logo* (London: Harper Perennial, 2005); and Henri Giroux, "Democracy's Nemesis: The Rise of the Corporate University", *Cultural Studies – Critical Methodologies* 9:5 (August 2009): 669–695, http://journals.sagepub.com/doi/abs/10.1177/1532708609341169 (as of 1 September 2015).

In order to clarify some of the issues which, I argue, need to be on the minds of social theorists as they seek for appropriate pedagogies and relevant social understanding I will move to another region where education is very high on the agenda. On 18 May 2015 the UK's *Guardian* newspaper contained a 28-page pull-out report entitled "Education in Brazil". The piece was authored by 'The Report Company', which took sole responsibility for its content.[4] On their website The Report Company explain what they do:[5]

> We cover significant developments and milestones in countries around the world, interviewing the people behind the news—from heads of state and government ministers to CEOs of major corporations and local personalities. Printed and distributed with leading media around the world on a regular basis, our features reach a knowledgeable, smart and affluent readership that is keen to find out the other side of the story.
>
> Through a series of exclusive interviews, we ask influential personalities worldwide to share their vision on how their nation relates to the world and how they position their businesses to succeed against a challenging economic backdrop. As well as raising awareness about the investment opportunities available in their economy, we give them the opportunity to dispel misconceptions about their nation's brand whilst exploring how best to manage perceptions at an international level. We discuss the role the private and public sectors can play in strengthening political and business relations with leading global investors and where intersections of interests can be found.

The purpose of the report on education in Brazil is to cultivate interest, attract investment and generally 'talk up' the aspirations of influential educationalists and entrepreneurs. Brazil, as we know, is a vast country and it is attempting, as the report suggests, to address major educational and economic issues head on and with optimism. This is not, however, why I am referring to the report and the undoubted sincerity and energy which many of the contributors demonstrate in their contributions. My interest is in the language they use, the discourses they construct, and the rhetorical flair with which they evade or avoid some key issues. I do not presume to criticise educational development in Brazil. I do, however, wish to take Brazil's

---

4   See https://www.theguardian.com/the-report-company/brazil-education (as of 1 September 2017).

5   See http://www.the-report.com/about-us/ (as of 1 September 2017).

overall strategy for development, at least as outlined in the Report, as a metaphor for the situation facing many of us in higher education. "Education in Brazil" is not an educational publication. It is a multi-layered and sophisticated advertisement. For the social theorist and the (re)searcher for relevant pedagogies, a little introspection would not go amiss here, before we turn again to the harsh realities of our educational worlds.

I will now take a series of phrases and terms which are used by various contributors to the report. It is the cumulative energy of these linguistic turns which interests me. It could be argued that they become the building blocks of the new common sense, and then of what I have referred to elsewhere as the "discursive reserve".[6] These are phrases such as: to modernise and compete; to innovate; innovative solutions; vocational training; schools should help students find a place in the market; before everything, we train our students to think like entrepreneurs. And then there are the brief asides which touch upon recognisable educational concerns which are not so dependent upon rhetorical flourishes. Perhaps the most telling is in an unsigned piece under the title "A New Plan for Education in Brazil". It is worth quoting at length:

> Every year, three million children enter the Brazilian education system, but only 500,000 of them will go on to leave high school with a sufficient level of Portuguese to enter the jobs market and only 137,000 with adequate maths. *Add to these basic subjects the 21st century skills of critical thinking, teamwork, digital knowhow and problem solving and it is clear that the government urgently needs to address its public education shortcomings if Brazil is to develop. Education for all is a noble cause, but it remains hollow rhetoric if these growing classrooms are not empowering their occupants with knowledge.*[7]

So this somewhat lengthy report has seen fit to mention very briefly such approaches as critical thinking and even empowerment. But, as with so many of the claims made here, the terms used are simply taken for granted. They are code words for a utopian vision of profit-generating capitalism where occupants will live and work happily in a prosperous economy. But what is

---

6   Robert Ferguson, *Representing 'Race': Ideology, Identity and the Media* (London: Edward Arnold, 1998).

7   No author attributed; emphasis added.

critical thinking? And problem-solving? And empowerment? And digital knowhow? To ask such questions may seem impolite and might even spoil the party. But we have to take that risk. In order to do so it is necessary to mention a name whose absence from this report cracks and shatters the educational silence: that of Paulo Freire.

The fact that Freire is not mentioned, and that he was and is the most valuable universal educational export so far produced in Brazil, is something more than an oversight, and is in a real sense alarming and tantamount to a scandal. Freire was concerned with education for liberation. He did not depend upon exhortations to break into the job market or to hone one's entrepreneurial skills. He abhorred what he called the 'banking model' of education, where empty heads had to be filled with approved 'knowledge'. He wrote with clarity and a refreshing lack of jargon:

> Education either functions as an instrument which is used to facilitate integration of the younger generation into the logic of the present system and bring about conformity or it becomes the practice of freedom, the means by which men and women deal critically and creatively with reality and discover how to participate in the transformation of their world.[8]

If we look back over the terminology used in the report, it is also important to learn at least one more lesson from Freire: the need to problematise the terms with which we are addressed and indeed those we use ourselves. A most cogent definition of the term suggests that it is a defamiliarisation of common sense. This brings me full circle in relation to the terminologies so often used unproblematically to sell us the educational future in discourses about education.

This introductory discussion has mentioned just one of many possible routes into the conceptualisation and theorisation of educational processes. Freire is eminently quotable and, of course, he does not solve all our pedagogical problems, whether at the primary, secondary or higher education levels. But, and it is a big but, he makes us reconsider just what we

---

8   Paulo Freire, *Pedagogy of the Oppressed*, trans. Myra Bergman Ramos (New York: Continuum, 2000), 34.

think we are doing. With this is mind, and hopefully carrying with us the baggage of a little introspection, we can turn to questions of higher education and the new technologies 'where you are', as the newscaster says.

3. Technologies and Social Formations

There was a time when educational planners and politicians made a habit of invoking such terms as 'empowerment' and 'problem-solving' as core to the educational process. More recently the phrase 'critical thinking' has found its way into the administrators' lexicon. These terms were and are more commonly used in relation to pre-university education. I suggest that they are now little more than a nod in the direction of serious educators who have been concerned with 'liberatory' thinking and the promise of a world freed from oppression and exploitation. They are empty phrases in their present usage—a low key substitute for sound and fury. Serious attempts to address and even to do something about oppression and exploitation are today mainly associated, in popular educational discourse, with one or another lunatic fringe. Sane educators and planners stay on the path of righteousness. And that path is, of course, the path of technology, or more esoterically, the new technologies. It is to the latter that I will now give some attention.

One of the main advantages, in a troubled world, of concentrating on the promise of technology, is that it means that one can leave a direct engagement with politics out of everything, and concentrate on planning. Computer technologies, digital communication, mobile learning, multimodal literacies, are going to do the trick. But the trick, it would seem, is to ignore reality in favour of a new world of promise to be provided by technological savvy, computer literacy and preparation for a jobs market which is unlikely ever to materialise. And 'reality' anyway is little more than one amongst many perceptual and psychological constructs for those who inhabit the worlds of representations which have become devoid of referents outside of themselves.

This negativity should not be taken as a denial of the significance of new technologies. Nor is it a Luddite argument. Plainly the new technologies have considerable potential as tools for liberation. But that would have to be in social formations which are very different from the ones which most of us inhabit right now. One of the key factors which is undermining educational potential and development is the stress placed on the new technologies as a means of increasing production, especially of consumer goods. For the educator, however, the new technologies are providing educational and research tools which far exceed the wildest dreams of progressive pedagogues in the twentieth century. We now have the means to access and analyse (empirically) countless data and search libraries with a speed that was previously literally unthinkable, except to writers of science fiction. This should be rephrased, perhaps, to say that those with access to the new technologies — specifically the Internet — possess such means. I will say more about this in relation to the development of appropriate pedagogies; but first it is pertinent to ask what we might learn from the history and development of technologies.

For Howard Segal:

> the real lesson to be learned from the serious study of technology's past is that technological progress and social progress do not necessarily go hand in hand but often conflict. The same lesson, of course, can be derived from the serious study of such contemporary technological advances as pesticides, organ transplants, nuclear weapons, and space shuttles. A course or program in technological literacy that suggested this might nevertheless risk loss of foundation, corporate, governmental, or even college and university support. So might a course or program that led newly enlightened citizens to control (their) technology by, say, opposing the nuclear power plants or nuclear weapons they now truly understood.[9]

Segal has been a quiet but consistent voice asking searching questions about technologies. He is not alone, of course. Segal's conclusion is that the new technologies are a mixed blessing. Brian Winston, on the other hand, takes a somewhat more radical approach in his important work *Media Technology and*

---

9   Howard P. Segal, "The Cultural Contradictions of High Tech: Or the Many Ironies of Contemporary Technological Optimism", in Yaron Ezrahi, Everett Mendelsohn and Howard Segal, eds., *Technology, Pessimism and Postmodernism* (Dordrecht: Kluwer Academic Publishers, 1994), 208.

Society.[10] It is worth quoting the conclusion to this work because it carries within it some small seeds of hope for all our educational futures:

> I hold our situation to be, basically, that business, media, alienation, nuclear families, right-wing governments, technologically induced health hazards, traffic jams, deep-fried food, dating, poverty — all these and much else, continue as usual. No revolution — just 'the constant revolutionising of production, uninterrupted disturbance of all social conditions, ever-lasting uncertainty and agitation', as the Communist Manifesto put it.

> Thus the pile of debris at the feet of Klee's *Angelus Novus* grows ever closer to the heavens. Only a good *historical* understanding of how it got there can help us clear it away.[11]

Between the overly tolerant Segal, and the caustic political analysis of Winston, there is much that can be learned and done. Since they wrote their pieces the world of digital technology has raced ahead by leaps and bounds. Education (and social theory) has to find its place between ever more sophisticated computer games, hundreds of shades of training software, and the tendency in much of the 'developed' world to construct a whole society of white rabbits who, without everything that digital media technology

---

10 Brian Winston, *Media, Technology and Society: A History from the Telegraph to the Internet* (London: Routledge, 2000).

11 Ibid., 342. Winston is referring here to Walter Benjamin's famous 'Ninth Thesis on the Philosophy of History', which runs as follows: "A Klee painting named 'Angelus Novus' shows an angel looking as though he is about to move away from something he is fixedly contemplating. His eyes are staring, his mouth is open, his wings are spread. This is how one pictures the angel of history. His face is turned toward the past. Where we perceive a chain of events, he sees one single catastrophe that keeps piling ruin upon ruin and hurls it in front of his feet. The angel would like to stay, awaken the dead, and make whole what has been smashed. But a storm is blowing from Paradise; it has got caught in his wings with such violence that the angel can no longer close them. The storm irresistibly propels him into the future to which his back is turned, while the pile of debris before him grows skyward. This storm is what we call progress". Walter Benjamin, "Theses on the Philosophy of History", trans. Harry Zohn, *Illuminations: Essays and Reflections*, in Hannah Arendt, ed. (New York: Schoken, 1969): 257–258.

provides, will be late for very important appointments.[12] The new technologies and digitisation can either 'do' or offer so many services, so many games, so much surveillance, and so much of educational relevance. For the social theorist who happens to be a university or college lecturer this poses two major issues: how much to theorise and then teach about, and how much of the technology to utilise when engaging in this very process. Which brings us to questions of pedagogy.

4.   Pedagogy and Power Relations

Pedagogy is an elusive term, but whether we like it or not, it informs a great deal of what we do in education. It can be defined as the principles, practice or profession of teaching. If we happen to be concerned with the social sciences, then we can afford to extend the definition of pedagogy to every kind of teaching that takes place in our social existence. I began this chapter with the promise that I would explore some key contradictions in higher education. The first which needs exploration is whether it is epistemologically acceptable to mention the term teaching without linking it with the word learning. My contention is that it is not and nor should it be. What we have to face in higher education is that teaching can take place in a multitude of different ways, and we can learn from many more sources beyond those who are designated as our teachers. Once again, however, this is something of an educational truism. Some sceptics might wish to suggest that there are individuals involved in something called teaching, where very little learning takes place at all. This is amusing perhaps, but mistaken. What we learn from bad teaching is that not all teaching has to be delivered from a lectern. Perhaps the most worrying thing about bad teaching is that we may even learn how to become a bad teacher ourselves!

---

12 The reference here is to the white rabbit in Lewis Carroll's *Alice in Wonderland.* The White Rabbit is very famous in popular culture for his line "I'm late! I'm late! For a very important date!" in the 1951 Disney film. He appears at the very beginning of the book, running close by Alice on the riverbank and muttering, "Oh dear, oh dear! I shall be too late!".

For some writers and thinkers concerned with higher education there has been an interest in a form of alternative pedagogy which denies the need for teachers. The most daring, or stupid, or misguided version, depending on one's reading of it, has to be the one set out by Rancière in *The Ignorant Schoolmaster*.[13] Coming from an intellectual milieu where Althusser — his one-time tutor with whom he contributed to *Reading Capital*[14] — was concentrating on dissecting the operations of ideology, while Foucault was dismembering the operations of power, Rancière came to adopt the role of an educational Icarus as he flew dangerously close to the illusory sun of educational equality (not to be confused with equality of opportunity or educational provision), using the concept of 'equal intelligence' as a parasol. This golden glowing orb promises to fulfil our wildest liberal educational aspirations. If we are all already equal in intelligence, then all that is needed is to put the learner in front (metaphorically or literally) of what might be interesting and let them get on with it. It is not even necessary that the teacher should know anything about the subject. This is the mirror image of the teacher as an authoritative person (not to be confused with the authoritarian), of which Harold Entwistle wrote in relation to the works of Gramsci.[15] Rancière argues that one should not be bound by experts, and that the poor and disenfranchised should feel that it is within their capacities to teach themselves whatever they want to know. The precise details of how this might take place are beyond the scope of this chapter, but at the least they provide a thread which can be linked with the concepts for liberation put forward by Freire. Rancière should have begun by following Freire and *problematising* the term intelligence. Key to the argument of Rancière is that the learner should not be subordinated to the intelligence of another: that

---

13 Jacques Rancière, *The Ignorant Schoolmaster: Five Lessons in Intellectual Emancipation* (Stanford: Stanford University Press, 1991).

14 Louis Althusser and Étienne Balibar, *Reading Capital*, trans. Ben Brewster (London: New Left, 1970).

15 See Harold Entwistle, *Antonio Gramsci: Conservative Schooling for Radical Politics* (London: Routledge & Kegan Paul, 1979).

"there is stultification whenever one intelligence is subordinated to another [...] whoever teaches without emancipating stultifies".[16] It does seem possible that Rancière is missing a significant point here. It is perfectly possible to be a rebel, to question and to learn from someone who can be questioned and doubted (or agreed with), without being stultified. What would be wrong would be for an educator to make false promises or to attempt to efface their own power, presence, education and experience. One might almost say 'Better the Jesuit or Marxist you know than the Liberal that you do not'. It would surely be more acceptable, though still problematic, to suggest that a teacher or lecturer will have been most successful when their presence is required only as an equal. To pretend that that could be a starting point, even with acceptance of the UN declaration of Human Rights, is to live in denial. Power relations do not disappear because we stop talking about them. Nor does the power which has to be associated with ideology. And a superior intellect (I am avoiding the use of the term intelligence here) can be a genuine inspiration.

There have been oppositional exceptions which are remarkable, and it is still a salutary experience to read *Letter to a Teacher* by The School of Barbiana.[17] Barbiana is a community of about twenty farmhouses in the hills of the Mugello region in Tuscany. It happened quite a few years ago, but it still offers many educational challenges and insights. I will cite only the opening of the book for the simple reason that it demonstrates the crucial importance of context and social formation in the development of appropriate pedagogies of liberation. A pedagogy can be both successful and emancipating in one context, and stultifying in another. Unless we consider this we end up chasing just another methodological rainbow. The opening words of *Letter to a Teacher* are:

Dear Miss

16 Rancière, *The Ignorant Schoolmaster*, 18.
17 School of Barbiana, *Letter to a Teacher*, trans. Nora Rossi and Tom Cole (Harmondsworth: Penguin, 1970).

> You won't remember me or my name. You have failed so many of us. On the other hand I have often had thoughts about you, and the other teachers, and about that institution which you call 'school' and about the boys that you fail. You fail us right out into the fields and factories and then you forget us.[18]

The group of writers of this book were boys from Tuscan peasant families. They voice their opinions without fear or favour, even if we may find some of these opinions questionable now. They back up their views with a considerable amount of statistical data, which in itself would be a notable achievement for any secondary student. The tone of the opening is hardly complimentary to the teaching profession of the time. It is also a response to years, possibly generations, of subjugation. These boys are an example of an educational paradox. They have been motivated by their subjugation! This is no way to structure state education, but it is a first class example of how the motivated student cannot or will not be held back from learning. The pedagogy they adopted is also one which could hardly be replicated; but it illustrates the opposite of anomie as it is fired by a sense of injustices to be put right, and a kind of solidarity which is absent from the pedagogy of entrepreneurialism:

> Life up there was hard too. Discipline and squabbles until you didn't feel like coming back. But there a boy who had no background, who was slow or lazy, was made to feel like the favourite. He would be treated the way you teachers treat the best student in the class. It seemed as if the school was made for him. Until he could be made to understand, the others would not continue.[19]

To our potentially jaded educational sensibilities all this may seem either utopian or romantic. What I am arguing, however, is that these boys (and they were very conscious that no girls from the community attended their classes) were not problematising academic matters and pedagogy as a top priority. They were problematising their social and economic situation. This in turn generated a pedagogic response which was based upon context and conditions. There is certainly a lesson here for all educators at all levels of the

---

18 Ibid., 6.
19 Ibid., 8.

contemporary education systems of Europe. It is the social and economic which are likely to be the most important formative influences for education in the future. The problem we then face is who decides what is meant by 'social' and 'economic'. I will return to this matter at the end of the chapter. For the moment it is important to note that what the motivation of the students of the School at Barbiana meant was that they would not be stopped from learning. The pedagogy they developed was appropriate to their needs and circumstances then and there.

5. New Technologies of Communication

I have been drawn, over the years, towards a pluralist view of the development of pedagogy. Perhaps it would be better to suggest that all learning and teaching should incorporate a range of pedagogies, and that these will include aspects of what has been called both progressive and traditional approaches. I will now move to a consideration of the new technologies and digitisation.

The first point to note is that by the time we designate technologies as 'new' they are usually quite well established, and for the younger students they are not 'new' at all. We have now passed through the time when we could just gawp at the power of digitisation and information storage capacities, or the speed of computers and the capacity of our RAM. For the educationalist, whether at school or university level, the questions which have to be addressed are concerned with how this 'new' age of multiple technologies impacts upon our understandings, experiences and the ways in which we work with our students. I will be concentrating now upon teaching, learning and research in the social sciences and humanities at university level.

There are clearly certain positive aspects of course design and delivery that have been facilitated by the new technologies. There has been much innovation in approach and methodologies and aspects of course design, whether taught face to face, at a distance, or through what have become known as mixed mode approaches. As previously noted, the new technologies have also meant that many learners potentially have access to information on a scale previously undreamed of. This is indisputable. What is perhaps disputable is that the new technologies will carry within them the seeds of liberation and a more just and equitable society. They might: but it is no more inevitable that they will, than that the coming of the ballpoint pen would bring about education for freedom. To think that way, especially for an educator, is dangerous. So far the new technologies and social media have been at their most effective in mobilising groups for social action. They have also been instrumental in naturalising the bland, the superficial, and a strong tendency towards the non-contemplative. The White Rabbit syndrome is becoming an inherent part of computer usage for many students and citizens. We are all late for a very important date (as in the sense of appointments). But it is usually the wrong date. If we consider some of the contradictions which need to be faced in the ex-Communist countries, they will bring us closer to the metaphorical 'date' or dates which should be central to education and research interests, especially, though not exclusively, in the humanities and social sciences.

These contradictions are about certain underlying principles of education, history, cultures, economics and politics. The new technologies can be instrumental in identifying and exploring these contradictions. They can also act as a technological smokescreen (e.g. we are all entrepreneurs now) behind which the real educational challenges are hidden or stultified.

There are global issues which throw up a wide range of contradictions in the face of the often false or misguided promises and premises of education. These issues include the growing gap between the rich and the poor, the caste system, the class system, the future of employment, the ecology of the planet, atomic weapons, racism, religious intolerance, peace, tolerance, justice, and the list goes on and on. Yet the remarkable thing is that the issues identified here — and there are many more, of course — are often blissfully absent from the agendas of educational planners and managers. They are also absent from the agendas of far too many teachers and researchers. Remember the fleeting reference to the 21st century skills of critical thinking which are alluded to in an aside in the report from Brazil discussed at the beginning of the chapter. In fact the crucial issues for a meaningful education in a democracy are becoming footnotes and asides — whilst managerialism and technological rhetoric are plastering over the contradictions.

If we consider the learning and teaching of history for a moment, then what happens highlights the enormous gulf which has to be crossed before any genuine liberating education can be considered. If we live in a country where different histories are taught as *History*, then we have a serious problem. If we live in a country with different curricula to match different versions of History, then we have a serious problem. If we live in a country where our first language is the second national language and where History is a euphemism for tunnel vision, then we have a serious problem. We have to move to an understanding that to approach the study of History, we must recognise that it exists only as combinations of *histories* which evolve over time. These histories are, of course, intimately linked to politics and nationalisms and other social and economic interests. For those who might say that this thinking smacks of some kind of relativism, I would reiterate what E.H. Carr said about mountains: "It does not follow that, because a mountain appears to take on different shapes from different angles of vision, it has objectively either no shape at all or an infinity of shapes".[20]

We know, also, that there is much competition and rivalry between different versions of history, and different histories. Eric Hobsbawm offered a sober and lasting comment on this:

Historians, however microcosmic, must be for universalism, not out of loyalty to an ideal to which many of us remain attached but because it is the necessary condition for understanding the history of humanity, including that of any special section of humanity. For all human collectivities necessarily are and have been part of a larger and more complex world. A history which is designed *only* for Jews (or African Americans, of Greeks, or women, or proletarians, or homosexuals) cannot be good history, though it may be comforting to those who practise it.[21]

20   Edward Hallett Carr, *What is History?* (Harmondsworth: Pelican, 1978), 26–27.
21   Eric Hobsbawm, *On History* (London: Weidenfeld & Nicolson, 1977), 277.

There are two key terms here, which are pertinent to my argument. The first is the reference to living in a "larger and more complex" world. The second is that of universalism. It would seem that as the internet and the new technologies facilitate communication and a potential sense of global community, there is a tendency for the teaching of history to become insular and localised. One has only to consider the Balkans to find copious examples. Only certain ecological issues seem to generate some kind of universalist appeal. But we also know that it is not only the learning and teaching of history which is at stake. The design and production of relevant and contextual curricula, which incorporate but are not dependent upon the new media, have to become core activities for both educators and researchers. How this can come about is beyond the scope of this chapter.

6. Productive Doubt and Critical Solidarity

It is not the easiest of tasks to try to knit together a range of economic, social and ideological issues with the educational hype surrounding the use of digital media and the new technologies. But this is the task which has to be undertaken if education and educational research is not to cruise into the still and shallow waters of technological certitude where it will become becalmed. When it comes to pedagogy, there is some hope in the generation of what I call productive doubt, and in a move beyond the liberal notion of critical autonomy. It will mean first that we must constantly problematise the concept of being critical. This has to go beyond some crass and untheorised notion of constantly carping about the world. Critical thinking certainly has to demonstrate some element of independent thought, but it is not a great deal of use to anyone if that is all it does. And this is where the concept of critical solidarity comes in. Critical solidarity recognises that for action to occur in the world there have to be alliances, agreements, and shared strategies on a wide range of issues. But it also insists that these forms of cooperative action are based upon considerations which are seldom if ever reducible to the preordained. I must not think a particular way because I am British, or a man, or white. Critical solidarity has to strive for universality.

All of these activities can take place with or without digital technologies. The latter are contextual but not fundamental. On the other hand, it is perfectly possible for the digital technologies to be invoked, developed and exploited in ways which either ignore or actively work against political involvement. This must not be misunderstood. I have already argued that one of the main strengths of the digital and social media is that they can be central to social and political activity. This must not be confused with their structured and planned *educational* usage. It will never be good enough to say that the digital media will revolutionise education. It might be more accurate to suggest that they can revolutionise the forms of ideological and discursive domination which in the past have been the business of more traditional media. Change without change. In order to stop this happening some alternative strategies will need to be developed. One kind of strategy would be that brought about through the practice of critical solidarity and pedagogies which are deemed appropriate for such practice. It is not the digital media which have to be radicalised, however, it is the educational and social thinking which inform their usage.

Whether it will be possible to work through the contradictions raised here and bring about a happy marriage of the new technologies and radical democratic thinking is yet to be ascertained. Whether the high aspirations linked with new technologies and articulated in the Brazilian example are workable or even desirable needs further debate. We also have to consider future employment patterns in the light of such fundamental texts as *Farewell to the Working Class* and *The Jobless Future*.[22] And in the context of the ex-Communist countries we have to consider whether one educational and ideological cage has been torn down only to be replaced by another which is full of promises. And not much more.

At the same time, in the social sciences and humanities, we have to accept that empirical data continue to form an intellectual bedrock for those who

---

22 André Gorz, *Farewell to the Working Class: An Essay on Post-Industrial Socialism* (London: Pluto, 1987); and Stanley Aronowitz and William DiFazio, *The Jobless Future: Sci-Tech and the Dogma of Work* (Minneapolis: University of Minnesota Press, 1994).

would study political economy, and who will not be put off by the fact that the very phrase has lost the power of attraction it once held. This has been well put in the conclusion of Thomas Picketty's *Capital*:

> From the outset, political economy sought to study scientifically, or at any rate rationally, systematically and methodically, the ideal role of the state in the economic and social organisation of a country. The question it asked was: What public policies and institutions bring us closer to an ideal society? This unabashed aspiration to study good and evil, about which every citizen is an expert, may make some readers smile. To be sure, it is an aspiration that often goes unfulfilled. But it is also a necessary, indeed, indispensable goal, because it is all too easy for social scientists to remove themselves from public debate and political confrontation and content themselves with the role of commentators on or demolishers of the views and data of others.[23]

For those like Freire and other educationalists concerned with concepts of liberation and resistance, there has been a stress on discovering how to participate in the transformation of our world. This chapter is designed to stimulate discussion and analysis and possibly some action. I have tried to do this through some arguments, and by drawing upon the positions of educational thinkers as well as historians and social theorists. I hope I may have generated the wish for public debate and possibly for action. I hope also that questions of pedagogy will always find their place as equals alongside any debates about the new technologies. My concluding reference is to a recent work by István Mészáros. I include it because it poses a challenge to all educators, and demands everyone's response. Perhaps this book and this chapter might open a few doors to such debate?

Mészáros is referring here to the pressures upon those who would acquire an education to conform:

> Nevertheless, by internalising the ubiquitous outside pressures, they must adopt the overall perspectives of commodity society as the unquestionable limit of their own aspirations. Only the *most conscious collective action* can extricate them from this paralysing predicament.

---

23   Thomas Picketty, *Capital in the Twenty-First Century*, trans. Arthur Goldhammer (Belknap Press: London, 2014), 574.

Viewed from this perspective, it is clear that formal education is not the *primary* ideological cementing force of the capital system; nor is it capable of providing, *on its own*, a radical emancipatory alternative to it. A main function of formal education in our societies is to produce as much conformity or 'consensus' as it is capable of within and through its own institutionalised and legally sanctioned limits. To expect from commodity society the active enactment — or even the mere toleration — of a mandate given to its formal educational institutions which would invite them to fully embrace the great historic task of our time: that is, the task of *breaking capital's logic in the interest of human survival*, would be a monumental miracle. This is why remedies, also in the educational field, 'cannot be *formal*: they must be *essential*'. In other words they must embrace the totality of educational practices of established society.[24]

24 István Mészáros, *The Challenge and Burden of Historical Time* (New York: Monthly Review, 2008), 228-229.

Marketisation as Social Control: Critical Reflections on Post-Soviet Higher Education

Tom Driver

1. Introduction

Education is a fundamental prerequisite for all freedoms, allowing for the expansion of one's conscious perception and enabling individual agency.[1] In an essay contrasting common and good-sense, the philosopher Henri Bergson remarked that what a society gives by way of education, it expects back in wisdom.[2] At the heart of education, as a subjective *process* rather than a *static* object, there should be communication and dialogue, nourished by the 'critical matrix' of 'love, humility, hope, faith and trust'.[3] Such traits enable the development of one's thinking capacities and the possibility of achieving what Freire termed *conscientisação*, critical consciousness, as opposed to a massified thinking characterised by a disengaged, manageable conformity.[4] Critical thinking demands that one connects the abstract to the concrete with relation to the social, political and historical context of one's contemporary world. This chapter will conceptually explore the conditions and space for critical thinking, following the profound transformation of post-Soviet higher education from a socialist-state model to a neoliberal, market-based one. Developing over many decades and expanding to win

---

1   I would like to thank A. Salem and Joe Backhouse-Barber who read earlier drafts of this chapter and offered detailed criticisms and suggestions that have helped to improve it. I should add that the research was partly inspired by A. Salem's lectures and seminars about critical sociology and its philosophical basis, along with many of the texts accompanying them.

2   Henri Bergson, "Good-Sense and Classical Studies", in Keith Ansell Pearson and John Ó Maoilearca, eds., *Henri Bergson: Key Writings* (London: Bloomsbury Revelations, 2014), 421.

3   See Paulo Freire, *Education for Critical Consciousness*, trans. Myra B. Ramos (London: Bloomsbury, 2013), 42.

4   Ibid., 17 (translator's note).

over minds and hearts across the world, the impact and importance of the Soviet Union should not be understated. Following a brief exploration of the historical and theoretical context, the chapter seeks to conjoin social theory with the concrete, practical realities of the market model of higher education, relating ideas drawn from Frankfurt School thinking and from post-structuralism to secondary material from universities across Europe, but especially from post-Soviet Russia. Although the arguments may be relatively abstract, their purpose is to raise suspicion and promote critical reflection on common-sense assumptions about the market model of higher education and the wider discourse of marketisation.[5] I will argue that the implicit mechanisms of this discourse enable social and political control, and place significant constraints on critical thinking. The embrace of market freedom in Russia's post-Soviet universities could then be seen as a difference in degree, rather than a difference in kind.

2. The Historical and Theoretical Context

In order to understand the appeal and power of the Soviet project we must grasp its political and ideological *modus operandi* in relation to human subjects (selves). It was arguably built on the foundations laid by the French Revolution, with the assertion that reason and revolution would lead the struggle of the working classes towards a rational and free social order.[6] Given the pressing need for rapid industrialisation and the materialists' desire for objective mechanical laws, a scientific technocracy drove itself into the revolution's subsequent, technocractic structure, leading to formal, impersonal policies and laws made by specialist, technical experts. Rehmann

---

5   'Discourse' here refers to the socio-cultural construction and dissemination of values and ideas which are implicit in texts and representations. This entails consideration of the disciplinary matrices within a given society, as shaped by dominant political ideas and relations of power and subjectivity (or formations of self). See Norman Fairclough, *Discourse and Social Changes* (Cambridge: Polity, 1992).

6   See Peter Kenez, *A History of the Soviet Union from the Beginning to the End* (Cambridge: Cambridge University Press, 2006).

has argued that this led to the institutionalisation of a rigid "Marxist-Leninist philosophy", and should be seen as a neutralisation of ideology,[7] reducing the power of ideas to an operative function within the established state of affairs. Abstract thinking and subjective consciousness were not recognised and understood as immanent to all thinking beings, to be enriched and expanded from the actual to the potential. Instead thought—especially critical thought—was subordinate to and coerced by systemic requirements, seen merely as an instrument 'from without' for the top-down implementation on individuals of a 'socialist ideology', as opposed to 'bourgeois ideology'.[8] Soviet technocratic, social engineering provided and enabled the conditions for a totalitarian system and, with the rise of Stalinism, rigidities quickly set in, while room for critical thought was severely restricted.[9]

It is important to note, as Alexei Yurchak insightfully has, that the culture and day-to-day meaning of the late Soviet lifeworld was far more complex than many simplified accounts suggest. Reductive dichotomies of official/unofficial norms and values, and of the absolute disposition of the state versus the people, fail to recognise the actual importance of many socialist ideas and the meanings they gave to people's lives, even if they were routinely transgressed.[10] Yurchak also notes a profound educational shift in the early Soviet period, which continued until its collapse, marked by Stalin's broad campaign "to eradicate the remnants of idealist avant-garde thinking" and replace it with the "realism of objective scientific laws".[11] This shift is crucial for the argument of this chapter. Higher-educational policies needed

---

7   Jan Rehmann, *Theories of Ideology: The Powers of Alienation and Subjection* (Chicago: Haymarket, 2013), 67–68.

8   See John Thompson, *Ideology and Modern Culture* (Cambridge: Polity, 1989), 45.

9   Rehmann, *Theories of Ideology*, 67.

10   Alexei Yurchak, *Everything Was Forever, Until It Was No More: The Last Soviet Generation* (Princeton: Princeton University Press, 2005).

11   Ibid., 45.

to provide the "affirmative action"[12] for the technical demands first of industrialization, and later of the war-economy. This meant that open, abstract and critical thought was possible, so long as it did not clash with the Party's ideological line (such as the requirement for rapid industrialisation); and most crucially, so long as it could be assimilated within the wider demands of the economy.

The political problems associated with this were that authority and total power were consolidated within the Party. Arendt made the compelling case that a distinct feature of totalitarian regimes is the necessary need to close off competing, potentially subversive thoughts and realities. No sacrifice is too great, the ends justify the means, driven by the conviction that one has "found the key to history" or the "solution to the riddles of the universe".[13] Following the domination of Stalinism and Nazism, enormous intellectual effort has been put into ensuring that the total subordination of individuals to master plans does not reoccur. To protect against the potential degradation of critical thought, the space for free thought is essential, as expressed in "Popper's nightmare"[14] of a closed society in which:

> The holistic planner overlooks the fact that it is easy to centralise power but impossible to centralise all knowledge which is distributed over many individual minds, and whose centralisation would be necessary for the wise wielding of centralised power. But this fact has far-reaching consequences. Unable to ascertain what is in the minds of many individuals, he must try to control and stereotype interests and beliefs by education and propaganda. But this attempt to exercise power over minds must destroy the last possibility of finding out what people really think, for it is clearly incompatible with the free expression of thought, especially of critical

12 See Sheila Fitzpatrick, *Education Policy and Social Mobility in the Soviet Union 1921–1934* (Cambridge: Cambridge University Press, 1979), http://catdir.loc.gov/catdir/samples/cam031/78058788.pdf (as of 11 July 2016).

13 See Hannah Arendt, *The Origins of Totalitarianism* (New York: World Publishing, 1962), 457.

14 See Richard Gombrich, "British Higher Education Policy in the last Twenty Years: The Murder of a Profession", http://www.atm.damtp.cam.ac.uk/mcintyre/papers/LHCE/uk-higher-education.html (as of 2 August 2016).

thought. Ultimately it must destroy knowledge; and the greater the gain in power, the greater will be the loss of knowledge.[15]

The "holistic planner" (concerned with a whole system), here refers to the Hegelian notion that through the power of freedom and reason, society is to be understood and comprehended in its absolute totality. Dialectical logic is predicated on the idea that there is a two-way relation between objective knowledge and the subjective knower,[16] "the development of the objective world is throughout interwoven in the development of consciousness".[17]

Modern Western philosophy has been greatly affected by the Cartesian separation of mind and body, theory and practice, in which knowledge of the mind and knowledge of sense perception are seen as at odds. Cartesian dualism and the subsequent rise of modern science and industrial capitalism have led to a significant proliferation of knowledge based on sense perceptions, and to the replacement of abstract qualities for mechanical quantities which can be fixed and measured.[18] Modernity is closely linked to the changed understanding of the material world, and to empirical practices derived from the natural and social sciences, in particular mathematics and formal logic (common sense). This *res extensa* (knowledge based on sense perception) has profound consequences for higher education, and can be linked to the prioritising of funding for STEM subjects (science, technology, economics and medicine) over the creative arts and philosophy. It can also lead to an unending formalisation and multiplication across many disciplines of empirical and, in particular, positivistic research, which though they may be critical in themselves can delimit the space for more abstract critical thinking. Opposed to formal logic (common sense), dialectical logic insists on the need for dialogue between both theory and practice, the need

15   Karl Popper, *The Poverty of Historicism* (London: Routledge, 2013), 82–83.
16   See G.W.F. Hegel, *The Phenomenology of Mind*, trans. J.B. Baillie (London: Macmillan, 1910), 39–40.
17   See Herbert Marcuse, *Reason and Revolution* (Boston, MA.: Beacon, 1960), 105–106.
18   See René Descartes, *World and Other Writings*, trans. Stephen Gaukroger (Cambridge: Cambridge University Press, 1998).

to act like beings of thought and to think like beings of action. What exists is only fixed, stable and mechanical in its *appearance*; its *essence* is ultimately qualitative and transformative. Mediation allows the flow, development and realisation of a substance or a concept's greater form.[19] The Hegelian-Marxist dialectic becomes problematic in the notion of totality (total system). The significance of this for critical thought lies in the dogmatic assumption that the whole is the truth, that one has all the answers, inevitably leading to the treatment of individuals as cogs in a machine, and a closing off of space for critical, free thought. Critical thinking "falls back into the same one-dimensionality",[20] becoming subordinate to power and enclosed in its own totalising universe of discourse. Hence, Adorno warned, "the whole is the false",[21] recognising that dialectical thinking is not a *total* system but a method of thought and critique that does not abandon philosophical reflection.

For all its limitations, the existence of the Soviet socialist project as an alternate system to capitalism effectively maintained a global balance of power, keeping either system from overstepping its mark. This would all change in 1991: the moment of Fukuyama's proclaimed End of History,[22] and of a remaking of world order. The collapse of the Soviet Union and its satellite states provided the enabling conditions for the extension of free-market capitalism, itself becoming holistic. The collapse also marked Russia's absorption into the supranational, juridical framework of global market capitalism, or as Hardt and Negri call it, "Empire".[23] Entry into this order is conditional on submission to the pillars of neoliberal free-market

---

19   See Marcuse, *Reason and Revolution*, 124.

20   See Christian Garland, "Adorno: Negation as Theory and Method", https://pages.g seis.ucla.edu/faculty/kellner/Illumina%20Folder/garland%5Badorno.htm (as of 30 August 2016).

21   Ibid.

22   Francis Fukuyama, *The End of History and the Last Man* (London: Penguin, 1992).

23   Michael Hardt and Tony Negri, *Empire* (Cambridge, MA.: Harvard University Press, 2000).

theory: *laissez-faire* liberalisation, privatisation, financial deregulation, and an opening up to foreign direct investment.[24] Before descending into the practical realities of neoliberalism in higher education, it is important to consider the theoretical differences brought about by Russia's radical transformation. In this context what is at stake are the political concepts of freedom and democracy, with their subsequent discursive practices. The 'window of opportunity' created by this historical moment was taken up zealously by intellectuals, policymakers, think-tanks and financial technocrats who understood this opportunity as "the apotheosis of a century-long intellectual battle between advocates of planning and advocates of markets".[25] In philosophical terms, this was the termination of the argument for a *telocratic* order, in which there is an end goal or state to be attained, towards which the rest of the social whole is to be steered.[26] This is in contrast to a *nomocratic* order, based on the market and the institutional framework provided by the rule of law, and the absence of the pursuit of any specific social ends.[27] At the heart of this argument (and of the ideological Cold War) were the antagonisms between what the thinker Isaiah Berlin termed the "two concepts of liberty":[28] positive, and negative liberty (freedom).

Classical liberalism functions as a nomocratic order, based on the market and on the non-totalisible nature of the economic world. With no general will or shared *telos* (end goal) for society, liberalism functions with a negative conception of liberty (freedom *from*), emphasising the need for the self-limitation of governmental power.[29] Negative freedom demands the *political*

---

24 See Iain McLean and Alistair McMillan, *Dictionary of Politics* (Oxford: Oxford University Press, 2003).

25 See Stephen J. Collier, *Post-Soviet Social: Neoliberalism, Social Modernity, Biopolitics* (Princeton: Princeton University Press, 2011), 131.

26 See Raymond Plant, *The Neo-Liberal State* (Oxford: Oxford University Press, 2009), 6.

27 Ibid.

28 Isaiah Berlin, "Two Concepts of Liberty", in *Four Essays on Liberty* (Oxford: Oxford University Press, 1969).

29 Plant, *The Neo-Liberal State*, 6.

freedom of the individual from coercive, collectivised notions of the greater good; as Berlin notes, this means that it is not incompatible with *economic* enslavement.[30] Given the bureaucratic, coercive structure of sovereign nation states, the self-limitation of governmental intervention is understood as indispensable to respect for the operation of the free market, and to facilitating its 'natural order' and 'harmony'.[31] Negative freedom is not about ideas or emancipatory action, but simply about the independence of individuals *from government*. In contrast, positive liberty (freedom *to*) is an enabling freedom, striving towards self-mastery and control over one's own destiny.[32] Central to the struggles of both the French and Russian Revolutions, it is a juridical and revolutionary approach to freedom, asserting the inalienable rights of subjects (selves). It radically calls into question the power and legitimacy of a government, and poses the question of a social contract honouring the rulers and the ruled. This shared contract or general will can of course become extremely problematic. In order to pursue and achieve a certain end, for example a collective Communist society, state intervention and coercion becomes necessary, and individual freedom becomes negated (denied). Due to the informal, fluid, unpredictability of social and economic life, *telocratic* master plans encounter struggles and disputes. Technocratic adjustment to the plan, particularly when faced with prolonged social unrest, can easily regress into tyrannical force. No sacrifice is too great, and inevitably knowledge, education and critical thinking must be subordinated and must not come into conflict with a society's ultimate *telos*.

3.   The New Market Order and Higher Education

This brings us to the contemporary importance of neoliberalism, which is something quite different. While still predicated on market discourse, Hayek

---

30   Ibid., 3.

31   See Harry Landreth and David C. Colander, *History of Economic Thought* (Boston, MA.: Houghton Mifflin, 2012).

32   See Berlin, "Two Concepts of Liberty", 8.

saw the *nomocratic* (absence of a specific end goal) foundation as essential to a free society;[33] this is not simply Adam Smith and classical liberalism revived.[34] Originating with the German ordoliberal movement early in the 20th century, neoliberalism's intellectual journey towards global hegemony began with the formation of the Mont Pelerin Society in 1947.[35] Responding to the monstrous political realities of fascism and Stalinism, as well as the welfare-state consensus in the West, it was the power and legitimacy of the state that was of primary concern to their thinking. What was required was a new economic rationality, stemming from market-based institutions, which could provide consent and legitimacy to the procedures and institutions that make up the state. It is a *decentralised* conception of political order *centred* on the economy and law; it produces a 'permanent political consensus' among the individual agents who consent to this 'economic game of freedom'.[36] It resembles an inverted social contract, enforced by the rule of law, which acts as a highway code for the market order. From their inception, neoliberal ideas have had a constructive/destructive relationship with freedom. Some degree of collective organisation is necessary to regulate a society based around this economic-juridical system (market economy and rule of law); the state must constantly intervene to produce freedom, simultaneously consuming freedom.[37] In needing to manage the delicate balance between self-limitation and social control, neoliberalism is a governmental style. It is less about *what* governments may touch or intervene in within society but about *how*.[38]

---

33 See Plant, *The Neo-Liberal State*, 6.
34 See Michel Foucault, *The Birth of Biopolitics: Lectures at the Collège de France 1978–79*, trans. Graham Burchell (New York: Palgrave Macmillan, 2008), 116.
35 See David Harvey, *A Brief History of Neoliberalism* (Oxford: Oxford University Press, 2007).
36 See Foucault, *The Birth of Biopolitics*, 84.
37 See Karl Polanyi, *The Great Transformation: The Political and Economic Origins of Our Time* (Boston, MA.: Beacon, 2001).
38 See Foucault, *The Birth of Biopolitics*, 133.

Foucault suggested that we understand this as a "sociological liberalism",[39] in its saturation and dispersal of political power across society. This means that we need not remain at the abstract level of social theory in our study of post-Soviet higher education, but must explore and engage with the everyday practical realities of the market model of higher education. The neoliberal state is at once built on a market economy (market, negative freedom) and active, vigilant state intervention in the form of unending market policies. Such political intervention, unlike in the Soviet Union, does not take the form of crude, individual subordination to a party line or ideology; it operates through a porous, vast expansion of economic rationality into the social environment. Political power operates through these discursive practices that accompany marketisation. This literally means that public and private institutions, social relations and the social world itself are to be embedded in the political economy of the commodity market. To give some examples: the idea of citizenship is to be modelled on the ideal consumer; politicians are transfigured as personalities and managers of public life; and higher education becomes training for the market through operation of the entrepreneurial university.

The two interlinked bases of this control are competition, and the individual as enterprise-unit, which, using human capital, must rationally calculate and maximise its competiveness, efficiency and marketability. Here individuals are conditioned not as objects of exchange and mass consumption, but as entrepreneurial subjects of specialised consumption.[40] In his essay on the *Two Conceptions of Liberty*, Berlin stated that positive freedom aims to grant one's wish to become an active subject rather than a static object.[41] Classical liberalism's mantra of *laissez-faire* negative freedom is here turned on itself. Juridical, coercive, positive freedom *to* is actively stimulated by the state so as to produce the optimal conditions, environment and subjects for the market. This paradoxically still requires (at least the

39   Ibid., 146.
40   Ibid., 146–147.
41   See Berlin, "Two Concepts of Liberty", 8.

appearance of) governmental self-limitation, the need for negative freedom *from* the state, in the form of for example financial deregulation and the privatisation of public institutions. Henceforth, the argument of this chapter will be that if the Soviet-state system is to be characterised by overt, political terror, then the neoliberal-market system may be criticised as being based on covert, bio-political control. An early, symptomatic example of this is that market reformers operating on Russia's transition to a market system rarely actually used the term 'neoliberal'[42] throughout the transition. By 'covert', we mean a far more subtle power, not quite a traditional theory of the state or of ideology, but an art of government and governing through the formation of subjectivities.

To reflect on the conditions and space for critique within higher education in post-Soviet Russia requires a consideration of the trajectories set in motion elsewhere by the marketisation of universities as entrepreneurial institutions. This process, tied to complex global forces, originated and was most prominent in Europe and the US. The logical discourse of marketisation and the paradigm of market governance has subsequently accelerated to become (in varying forms) the dominant institutional framework both nationally and internationally.[43] The market reform of public services, and in particular of higher education, began in the UK under Thatcher's government in the 1980s.[44] It operates by transforming the traditional, prestigious connotations of universities and higher education into modernised, commercial imperatives, reformed strictly along the free-market model.[45] This has led to the establishment of many more institutions

---

42 See Collier, *Post-Soviet Social*, 131.
43 See Harvey, *A Brief History of Neoliberalism*.
44 See Gombrich, "British Higher Education Policy in the last Twenty Years: The Murder of a Profession".
45 See Charles Thorpe, "Capitalism, Audit and the Demise of the Humanistic Academy", *Workplace: A Journal for Academic Labour* 15 (September 2008): 103–125, http://ices.library.ubc.ca/index.php/workplace/article/viewFile/182219/182230 (as of 30 August 2016).

of higher education, and to a significant increase in student numbers, despite large cuts to state funding. This was achieved through the marriage of the university system with private enterprise and with governmental audit agencies, allowing for a vast expansion of education, understood as a market service. There has been a great deal of literature written on this topic, given its magnitude and significance for wider society.[46] We will now consider some critical accounts of the 'freedom' that these marketised changes have achieved in British higher education: changes which for many signal not educational liberation but constraint. Standards are argued to be deteriorating, with many universities facing economic insecurity, attributed to serious under-funding in proportion to participation.[47] The expansion of higher education also brings with it the detrimental introduction of exponentially increasing tuition fees, which may simply negate or nullify the increased educational equality brought about by widening access in the first place.

Furthermore, such achievements are relative to other counterweights that the market brings to the table, like the total subordination of intellectual life to a cold, instrumental rationality, dictated by the measure of money.[48] Marketisation, or commodification, involves the reduction of a phenomenon or process to the numerical value of price and exchange. The hegemony of measurement, of fixed, static metrics, requires formalisation in the methods and language of social research, which must meet strict, instrumental 'aims and objectives'. Analogous to the expansion of business and marketing into social research, this can lead to a reorientation of higher education, calling the creative, abstract imagination to order. Comte, the father of positivism, himself took pride in his philosophy, demanding the "subordination of imagination to observation",[49] to that which is rather than that which could

---

46   See Ralph Fevre, *The Demoralisation of Western Culture: Social Theory and the Dilemmas of Modern Living* (London: Continuum, 2000).

47   See Thorpe, "Capitalism, Audit and the Demise of the Humanistic Academy", 103–125.

48   See Alex Callinicos, *Universities in a Neoliberal World* (London: Bookmarks, 2006).

49   See Marcuse, *Reason and Revolution*, 347.

be. Measurement, and its notorious love affair with modern capitalism, is intrinsically tied to the logistics and operations of marketisation. Deduced from the formal discipline of economics and the mathematical formulae that inform it, market metrics function purely quantitatively. There can be little space for those essential characteristics of Freirean *conscientisação* (critical consciousness) in a closed universe where only money talks. When applied to higher education, this can lead to a stripping away of the moral and qualitative content of social and educational relations.[50] Academics are competitively pitted against one another for funding, students are embodied consumers, and education is seen purely as an instrumental service available on the market. With staff demoralised and students disengaged, the ultimate casualties are our critical faculties, which require communication and dialogue, alongside the time, space and thinking tools for critique. This view has been set out by, for instance, Stefan Collini who argues for the need to completely rethink both the purpose and value of the university institution.[51] The funding and value of education should not simply come from a university's ability to make more money, but should be appreciated for its more qualitative provisions.[52]

Behind the appeal and discourse of the market is a dogmatic belief in its superiority in reducing bureaucracy, and increasing efficiency, here meaning economic cost-cutting, as in a business which must better balance its books regardless of the social and moral consequences. Applying this model to educational establishments which require trust and the space for reflective thought results in the rise of what Charles Thorpe describes as an audit culture.[53] Formal audits replace trust and thinking space with a technology of surveillance and an emphasis on control. Critique and free-thinking must be made subordinate to meeting targets and ensuring efficiency within

---

50   See Ralph Fevre, *The Demoralisation of Western Culture*.
51   Stefan Collini, *What are Universities For?* (London: Penguin, 2012).
52   Ibid.
53   Thorpe, *Capitalism, Audit and the Demise of the Humanistic Academy*.

universities, in a manner analogous to the Taylorist work discipline of the industrial factory system.[54] Following marketisation processes, formal audit agencies such as the Research Assessment Exercise, its successor the Research Excellence Framework, and the Quality Assurance Agency, have been introduced to implement the corporate-managerial shake-up of higher education. They require academic research to be formalised, reduced and simplified (i.e. pinned down) before being submitted for 'quality assessment', in a process akin to routine governmental practices.[55] Accompanying the implementation is the operation of pseudo-markets and the vast expansion of a rather costly internal bureaucracy tied directly to state institutions. As with the economic rankings of corporations, competitive league tables are central to how an institution is viewed/funded, and subsequently to what it can achieve. Further, achievements are themselves predominantly recognised in relation to the authority of the market. Referring to neoliberal transformations of higher education, Gombrich concludes that the "substitution of something called 'quality control' for the true quality of professionalism is make-believe of Orwellian dimensions".[56] Neoliberalism's appropriating powers result in an aporetic (or in Marcuse's terms one-dimensional) world in which meaning is lost, and where:

> at the nodal points of the universe of public discourse, self-validating, analytical propositions appear which function like magic-ritual formulas. Hammered and re-hammered into the recipient's mind, they produce the effect of enclosing it within the circle of the conditions prescribed by the formula.[57]

That formula is the orthodox free market, now deeply ingrained within higher education. Behind the Orwellian newspeak of words such as 'excellence', 'world-leading' and 'quality', there lies a rigid quantitative score that provides a pseudo-rationale for the legitimacy of 'authoritarian

---

54 Ibid., 108.
55 Ibid., 105.
56 Gombrich, "British Higher Education Policy in the last Twenty Years: The Murder of a Profession".
57 See Thorpe, *Capitalism, Audit and the Demise of the Humanistic Academy*, 109.

management techniques' that ensure compliance to this order. In practice, these phrases simply refer to the competitive measurement of academic work as it scores in the market paradigm. Resistance has arisen in the UK in the form of the Campaign for the Public University[58] and the Lincoln Social Science Centre.[59] Both are strongly opposed to the rigid formalism and market-induced constraints on educational freedom.

Such opposition must be at the very heart of a critique of the entrepreneurial university and more widely of global marketisation. As the conditions for freedom and democracy become increasingly threatened, we must recognise the internal contradictions unfolding. The discursive practices of the new market order were institutionally implemented on the grounds that in a complex global society only markets could protect education, freedom and democracy. The emphasis lies not in terror but regulatory control, albeit a far subtler form of control than under the Soviet system. Despite significant educational constraints, the Soviet system did produce some magnificent pieces of cultural and literary theory,[60] such as Vygotsky's founding theory of cultural-historical psychology. The restrictions on education stemmed partly from the Party imposing its own line, but more restrictive was the erosion of the demarcation that "insulated scholarship from the demands of state policy and economic imperatives".[61] When examining documents from early Soviet education under Stalin, Craig Brandist came to a troubling realisation. The controlling, bureaucratic nature of the documents actually matched those of the contemporary free-market model, to the extent that he labelled them "a very Stalinist management

---

58 For the Campaign for the Public University, see, http://publicuniversity.org.uk/ (as of 25 November 2016).
59 See the Social Science Centre, Lincoln, http://socialsciencecentre.org.uk/ (as of 25 November 2016).
60 See Craig Brandist, "A Very Stalinist Management Model", *Times Higher Education*, 29 May 2014, https://www.timeshighereducation.com/comment/opinion/a-very-stalinist-management-model/2013616.article (as of 2 August 2016).
61 Ibid.

model".[62] Whilst there may not be crude political censorship or direct state repression, the many parallels must provoke uneasy questions in relation to the fate and demise of critical thinking within universities. Divisive competition between both institutions and intellectuals, the subordination of abstract thought to static metrics, the hinging of research to the wider corporate economy, and the importation of industry-style performance management are all incompatible with "academic freedom and intellectual integrity".[63] The subtlety of this control lies in its fluid nature: there is no rigidly imposed ideological line. The market rests on deeply ingrained discursive practices: it is post-ideological, not *for* anything outside of maximising efficiency, profits and utilities. Located in the hyper-reality of an all-consuming social world, higher education (and society as a whole) must assimilate to the spatial domination of advertising and marketing, the result being that the space and conditions for any kind of critique, thought and action that might deviate from the discourse of the market, wither away. Charles Thorpe rightly argues that in the creed of entrepreneurialism, higher education is being transformed from an autonomous component of civil society into merely a policy instrument for the marketised-state.[64] The model resembles control through decentralisation: this a far more subtle expansion of state power and control than previously.

4. A Critical Reflection on the Post-Soviet Transition

These transformations of higher education have not occurred in a vacuum; they are symptomatic of the conditions now demanded across the world for entry into the totalising system of global capital. During the Cold War, capitalism had to appear to some extent as the torchbearer of freedom, democracy and decentralisation, as the vehicle for free thinking and critique. Following the stagnation and breakdown of the Soviet planning system, and an education system tied directly to the state, free-market fundamentalism

---

62 Ibid.
63 Ibid.
64 See Thorpe, "Capitalism, Audit and the Demise of the Humanistic Academy", 104.

was seen as *the* solution. Post-Soviet Russia felt the full force of the marketisation process, with particular emphasis on higher education. Whilst these processes are not everywhere identical, one task of this study, in relation to the space for critique, is to interpret the structural aspects of the changes — the unintended consequences.

At least in theory, Russian higher education has become decentralised, diversified and autonomous from state power, with increased student participation and institutional coordination with international universities.[65] The Bologna Process introduced in the early 1990s was specifically geared towards the marketisation of higher education. We will now consider some of the discursive practices entailed, such as the introduction of the New Public Management model[66] derived from Western Europe, whose effectiveness we just discussed. In a paper by Repneva, it is argued that emphasis again lies on the usual suspects: an "increase of quality, effectiveness, efficiency and performance".[67] The hope is to bring Russian higher education into line with European and American practices, via reforms that can "generate human capital, enhance economic productivity and provide the skills needed to thrive in a market economy".[68] Advocates of the reforms invoke the desire to establish an education system that demonstrates "quality", is "equitable", "highly competitive", and has the "most significant impact on growth".[69] There is also the dubious

---

65 See Ben Eklof, Larry Holmes and Vera Kaplan, *Educational Reform in Post-Soviet Russia: Legacies and Prospects* (London: Frank Cass, 2005).
66 See Maria Repneva, "Higher Education Reform in Post-Soviet Russia: Rapid Emergence of Private Higher Education", http://essay.utwente.nl/62761/1/Thesis_Repneva.pdf (as of 3 August 2016).
67 Ibid., 8.
68 The term 'human capital' refers to the previously mentioned extension of an all-pervasive economic rationality deep into the social world, based on the market utopia of the human enterprise. See Eklof, Holmes and Kaplan, *Educational Reform in Post-Soviet Russia Educational Reform in Post-Soviet Russia*, 2.
69 See Stephen P. Heyneman, "A Comment on the Changes in Higher Education in the Post-Soviet Union", *European Education* 42:1 (Spring 2010): 76–87, http://www.

endorsement of using state incentives to improve educational quality,[70] which seems to imply that if reform is in the name of the market, governmental power ceases to be in operation. In 2014 the journal *Higher Education in Russia and Beyond*[71], which is focused on the Russian Academic Excellence Initiative, also known as the "Global Competitiveness of Leading Russian Universities Program", was launched by the National Research University Higher School of Economics. This aims at "making Russian universities world-class research universities".[72] Conforming to global trends in signification, this propositional language attempts to denote a higher-educational free-market utopia.

In historical terms we must acknowledge the still relatively recent period in which markets and global capital have been in operation in the former Eastern bloc. As Pachuashvili notes, this also means that wide-ranging analysis of higher education across the region is not straightforward, with universities and countries in a state of flux.[73] However, with an insight into the discourse of the market and the theoretical framework of neoliberalism, it is possible to identify certain recurring changes across post-Soviet higher education. Across the region and university institutions, there has been the conditional, systemic need to become more competitive, through an increase in the presence of the private sector and the laws of the market.[74] The Head

vanderbilt.edu/peabody/heyneman/PUBLICATIONS/SH%20Changes%20in%20Ed.%20PostSoviet%20Union.pdf (as of 21 August 2016), 84.

70 Ibid.
71 See Oleg Alekseev et al., "Making Way to Global University Rankings: Russian Master Plan", *Higher Education in Russia and Beyond* 1 (Spring 2014), https://www.hse.ru/data/2014/05/16/1321296879/HERB_01_Spring.pdf (as of 18 August 2016).
72 Ibid., 2.
73 Marie Pachuashvili, *The Politics of Higher Education: Governmental Policy Choices and Private Higher Education in Post-Communist Countries. A Comparative Study of Hungary, Georgia, Latvia and Lithuania* (Budapest: Central European University, Department of Political Science, 2009), 41, http://stage1.ceu.edu/sites/pds.ceu.hu/files/attachment/basicpage/478/mariepachuashviliphdfinal.pdf (as of 15 August 2016).
74 Ibid.

of the Laboratory for Universities Development at the Higher School of Economics, discusses post-Soviet educational transition and Project 5–100, aimed at placing Russian universities near the top of global rankings,[75] ones based not on conformance with a strict, ideological party line but on market efficiency and publications in the most popular journals. These changes are described as a progressive "move towards global market presence";[76] however we should recognise their resemblance to other governmental, audit policies in operation in universities across Europe. These are bureaucratic agencies, which demand formalisation and the reduction and ranking of intellectual work in the name of competition and enterprise, adhering to pervasive market measurements which can be controlled, predicted and manipulated with great ease. Post-Soviet market reforms have also been aimed at shifting higher education from an administrative-command system to a law-governed system,[77] to eliminate structural rigidities. Yet what should be clear from a critical interpretation of the bureaucratic nature of the market education model is that such distinctions are not so clear-cut.

Given its *telocratic* (end goal) foundations, the Soviet Union was constrained by a heavy bureaucracy and by the centralised power required to achieve the end *telos*. Eklof notes that students were merely "cogs in a machine" tied to a "command system".[78] Following the repression and terror of totalitarian states, in which the market was subordinate to the social plan, neoliberal ideas were founded on the negation of collectivised, positive notions of freedom, in favour of individual autonomy from the state. However, as argued earlier, neoliberalism is not simply negative freedom from the state. With a global, juridical-institutional framework in place, it can

---

75 See Dmitry Semyonov, "Russian Excellence Initiative in the Post-Soviet Context", *Higher Education in Russia and Beyond* 1 (Spring 2014): 15, https://www.hse.ru/dat a/2014/05/16/1321296879/HERB_01_Spring.pdf (as of 18 August 2016).
76 Ibid.
77 See Eklof, Holmes and Kaplan, *Educational Reform in Post-Soviet Russia*, 8.
78 Ibid., 5.

grant many revolutionary, juridical (positive) freedoms, provided they are expressible through the market; it can grant collectivised-individual consumption. The Bologna Process has been at the heart of post-Soviet marketisation since 1991. The central ideas behind the educational plan are now simply tied to market demands,[79] matched with a "surge in market orientated studies",[80] and affirm the idea of a more subtle form of state control operating through a synthesis of education and the economy. A complete reversal of the formula occurs with, as Foucault puts it, the "state under the supervision of the market rather than a market supervised by the state".[81] As we explored earlier, this distinction between the two conceptions of freedom may in itself be too simplistic. In reality, positive and negative freedom should not be seen as incompatible, separate and mutually exclusive systems.[82] The two concepts are (at least partially) entwined, synthesised in the global market and international rule of law. Many socio-cultural practices and representations derived from the market discourse allow for autonomy and individuation, the only condition being that one conforms to and obeys the market utopia of individualism, the enterprise-unit and specialised consumption. Through the subtle operation of a regulatory, disciplinary power, alternate ideologies, worldviews and, most detrimentally, critique can all be comfortably absorbed or simply refuted as authoritarian. It is now the business sector who call on individuals to rebel, be different and express themselves! Any public figure who speaks of a collective good that goes beyond the market (as with traditional leftist politics), is denounced as dangerous and backward.[83]

In theory, freedom from the promised *telos* of a Communist utopia, i.e. the transition to a neoliberal model of higher education, would open up

---

79   Ibid., 14.
80   Ibid., 12.
81   See Foucault, *The Birth of Biopolitics*, 116.
82   Ibid., 42.
83   See Ulrich Beck, *Risk Society: Towards a New Modernity*, trans. Mark Ritter (London: Sage, 1992).

educational horizons to a wealth of new, critical ideas. Since 1991 central authorities in Russia have allowed regions and municipalities choice over what and how they teach. In the social sciences, the "straight-jacket of Marxism-Leninism"[84] has been replaced by the introduction of, for example, sociology, global education, civic education and religion.[85] It could be argued that such changes are important in the era of globalisation, and that rising demand is matched by the rise in university participation across Russia. However, there has also been a vast growth in industries productive for the market, such as law, economics, business administration, marketing and computer technology.[86] This can be seen as a kind of hidden curriculum, perfectly analogous to individual enterprise, seeking to maximise human capital, and rationally anticipating and calculating what the market wants. This shift not only affects these subjects themselves but also extends into other areas of education, combining harmoniously with the quantitative research methods of the social sciences. Whilst this shift may simply seem like one of the necessary requirements demanded by globalisation, we should try to remember that processes of globalisation do not have to be wholly synonymous with neoliberal marketisation: this is apparent in the very fact that academic and intellectual work — hardly commercial activities in themselves — reorient themselves towards the demands of global capitalism.[87] The suggestion is that the free market does in fact have a *telos*, and an entrepreneurial social plan for its achievement. An example can be found in the title of a journal previously cited, which reads; "Making Way to Global University Rankings: Russian Master *Plan*"[88] (my italics). Androushchak and Yudkevich also argue that, despite the disappearance of the Soviet education system, with a slight switch of words and criteria, some

---

84   See Eklof, Holmes and Kaplan, *Educational Reform in Post-Soviet Russia*, 6.

85   Ibid.

86   Ibid., 12.

87   See Andrew Ryder, "Reform and UK Education in the Enterprise Era", *Higher Education Quarterly* 50:1 (January 1996): 54–70.

88   Alekseev et al., "Making Way to Global University Rankings: Russian Master Plan".

Gosplan (State Planning Committee) central planning agencies are still used. Again, although this occurs without a rigid ideological line, there is the governing of universities by an internal hierarchical bureaucracy, tied to the state, with "the academic community playing a minor role in decision making".[89]

Since 1991, there has been a strong incentive to "de-ideologise" the educational curriculum.[90] In the spirit of critical thinking, this must raise suspicion and enquiry into what replaces the rigid Marxist ideology of the Soviet system. Magun denounces the sense of *anomie* present in post-Soviet higher education, which is leading to an increase in corruption and a cynical disengagement. Priority is given to administrative tasks ahead of teaching and research, while commercial effectiveness determines hiring policies.[91] As we have seen, given the post-ideological nature of the market, ideological disorientation may not be an obstacle to reforming higher education, given that market freedom does not need to physically subordinate individuals to its political ideas, but instead rests on the bio-political, active production of the optimal conditions and environment required for its functioning. An institutionalised nihilism, following the volatile flows of capital and data, reflects and reinforces an environment of perpetual uncertainty and insecurity. The globalisation of financial markets and the huge expansion of ICT and transportation have led societies into what Bourdieu called the "absolute reign of flexibility".[92] This includes higher education, where recruitment is short term or temporary and where there is an *individualisation* of a *structural* wage relation, so that conditions are precarious and solidarity

89   Gregory Androushchak and Maria Yudkevich, "How Post-Soviet Russian Academia Struggles with the Past", *International Higher Education* 69 (Fall 2012): 4, https://www.hse.ru/pubs/share/direct/document/65976889 (as of 4 August 2016).
90   See Eklof, Holmes and Kaplan, *Educational Reform in Post-Soviet Russia*, 9.
91   Artemy Magun, "Higher Education in Post-Soviet Russia and the Global Crisis of the University", International Sociological Association, 4 June 2010, http://www.isa-sociology.org/universities-in-crisis/?p=508 (as of 30 August 2016).
92   Pierre Bourdieu, *Acts of Resistance: Against the New Myths of Our Time*, trans. Richard Nice (Cambridge: Polity, 1998), 97.

is reduced in the name of competitiveness.[93] There need not be a sovereign, centralised power ready to terrorise those who do not comply, and/or enforcing some crude ideological false consciousness. Students, workers, universities, all must compete on the market; life itself becomes a competitive consumptive act, constantly stimulating and satiating one's innermost desires, and making resistance difficult. Despite the general weakening of trade-union activity and participation, interestingly, union membership and resistance within the public sector and higher education remains high.[94]

Magun condemns the current paradigm as a "global crisis of the university", in which the market metrics of formalisation and standardisation have caused great harm to higher education in post-Soviet Russia and beyond. Formal, technocratic measures necessary for marketisation are unable to tackle corruption within institutions, and are wholly inadequate to the task of mobilising universities and society to the task of critical thinking.[95] These concluding assertions about the space for critical thought are applicable to post-Soviet Russian education; they are certainly not confined to it, however, but reflect global shifts in power and control. With Russia, however, especially given the nature of its political history and its radical market transformation, there may also be signs of something much darker. Pomerantsev, who has written on the country's transition to a market economy, describes a warped development that has not produced a "democratic capitalism", but rather a "postmodern dictatorship"[96], a soft totalitarianism, characterised by marketisation and the

---

93 Ibid.
94 See Chris F. Wright, "The Future of Workplace Relations" (Acas Future of Workplace Relations Discussion Paper Series, September 2011), http://www.acas.org.uk/media /pdf/g/m/What_role_for_trade_unions_in_future_workplace_relations.pdf (as of 28/11/2016), 3.
95 Magun, "Higher Education in Post-Soviet Russia and the Global Crisis of the University".
96 Peter Pomerantsev, "Russia: A Postmodern Dictatorship?" (paper written for the Global Transitions Lecture Series of the London-based Legatum Institute in association with Institute of Modern Russia, October 2013), http://www.

infusion of postmodern ideas, such as the end of meta-narratives, and simulations, into the very heart of politics. With the rise and predominance of both mass culture and mass media, the real becomes that which can be simulated,[97] in a process that offers new forms of social control, and societies in permanent flux under an informational overload. In this situation "nothing is true and anything is possible";[98] the very narrative of the real is undermined, we are saturated with information, and there is an implosion of meaning. Critique, opposition, and ultimately resistance can easily be appropriated in a less rigid and more fluid political universe, allowing large parts of society to safely let off steam, while a stronger and more sustained resistance remains part of a marginal, insulated discourse.

Reflecting on the market reforms and on contemporary higher education in Russia, Magun argues that they have "created an odd society where neoliberalism was a *form* that allowed (post)Soviet institutions to continue to exist—on condition that they reorient themselves towards making business".[99] This view raises doubts about commonsense assumptions that a higher education system based on the market model is *a priori* more free and democratic than other models. It also raises questions about how far global marketisation is leading to regressions towards divisive nationalisms or promoting authoritarian leaders elsewhere—whether with Putin in Russia, Trump in the US, or the resurgence of far-right groups across Europe. All these, paradoxically, are actually fully compatible with free-market democracy, while being perceived by some as strong defenders against the volatility of global markets and the dominance of international financial technocrats. Of course in political terms there have been great changes in the transition from Soviet paradigms to contemporary market ones. Soviet

li.com/docs/default-source/publications/pomeransev1_russia_imr_web_final.pdf? sfvrsn=4 (as of 23 August 2017).

97 See Jean Baudrillard, *Simulacra and Simulation*, trans. Sheila Glaser (Ann Arbor: University of Michigan, 1994).

98 Pomerantsev, "Russia: A Postmodern Dictatorship", 11.

99 Magun, "Higher Education in Post-Soviet Russia and the Global Crisis of the University".

technocrats were working with a strict, repressive, ideological framework, whereas market technocrats exert tyranny through economic forecasts and growth charts. Politically the two paradigms are very different, but there are converging plateaus shared by both systems, including the enabling of political order, social control and the reduction of individual agency and autonomy over one's own destiny.

5. Conclusion

Returning to Berlin's essay on liberty, he states unequivocally that "conceptions of freedom directly derive from views of what constitutes a self",[100] a human subject. In other words, the social, and life itself, continue to be sites of political and economic struggle. The triumph of the market and market freedom simultaneously meant the triumph of a certain political understanding of what it means to be human. In his lectures on neoliberalism, Foucault considered it as the realisation of bio-politics, in which the primary, overarching political concern is the biological destiny of the human species.[101] In applying the economic grid to all aspects of human and social life, culture itself becomes intoxicated with political power. What matters is the individual, the consumer, one's lifestyle; this is 'common sense'. There is no need for idealism, critical thinking or education as an end-in-itself; Gramscian 'good sense' is an unprofitable expense. With the economisation of the social world, all that remains for the market's indefinite realisation is the formation of an ideal subjectivity, an economic sense of one's self and the world around us. That self is *homo economicus* (economic being), comprised of economic efficiency, marketability and human capital.[102] *Homo economicus* is an introspecting, self-interested, mechanical conception of self, predicated on rational calculation; marketisation can satisfy its innermost desires. Liberalism (both classical and contemporary) is

---

100 Berlin, "Two Concepts of Liberty", 10.
101 Foucault, *The Birth of Biopolitics*.
102 Ibid.

dependent on Adam Smith's "invisible hand of the market",[103] the crucial term being "invisible", referring to the dispersed, unknowable and ultimately *non-totalisable* nature of the economic world. With the impossibility of an all-seeing and all-knowing economic rationality, socialism and telocracies (societies with a collectivised, end goal) are rendered impossible; any overt attempt to plan and administer the social world, including education, is precluded. The structural imperatives of marketisation, global in scope, ensure compliance. Hence the prior constraints on Russian higher education can be removed, provided that it is integrated within the wider framework of the free-market. *Homo economicus*, the individual as enterprise-unit, at the centre of the market model of higher education, lives and represents a small island of rationality in a wider social order that is predominantly irrational.[104]

As we have stressed throughout, this order is not quite classical, *laissez-faire* liberalism; nor is it a tyrannical, teleological socialism. Neoliberal market governance, from the economy through social security to higher education policy, does not require a crude projection of ideology. Its control lies in the discursive practices of the market, in an art of governing one's conduct and soul. It is *laissez-faire* liberalism turned on itself. Following Russia's integration into this system, the market's unbridled extension in education and beyond represents a tightening of political power, a transition from disciplinary societies to societies of control.[105] Every increase in freedom is conditional on an increase in control: deregulation in finance is matched with regulation of behaviour, while the expansion of university participation is matched with a synthesis of higher education and the economy, amounting to unfreedom perpetuated in the name of freedom. Higher education, as a site of critical, potentially radical ideas, which may enable the formation of a potentially stinging critique of what exists, offers an insight into the bio-

---

103 See Landreth and Colander, *History of Economic Thought.*
104 See Foucault, *The Birth of Biopolitics,* 282.
105 See Gilles Deleuze, "Postscript on Societies of Control", *October* 59 (Winter 1992): 3–7.

political constraints currently in operation. Gilles Deleuze prophesied that this would entail "for the school system: continuous forms of control, and the effect on the school of perpetual training, the corresponding abandonment of all university research, the introduction of the 'corporation' at all levels of schooling".[106] As we have seen in examining market-based changes to higher education in Europe and post-Soviet Russia, Deleuze's prophecy is hardly very far away. As seminars on social theory are supplemented or replaced with CV-writing workshops, the university comes to resemble a business with the students as its customers, and education becomes a commodity to be marketed, bought and sold.[107] Under a global market system, the local, political packaging of this state of affairs may vary a great deal, but the underlying, coercive effects on education and individual behaviour and imagination are a common feature. Marketisation is the *how* of this form of control, and critical reflection on the vast changes occurring globally in higher education provides a partial insight into this polymorphous discourse. It has historically been within higher education and the universities, within the learning process itself, that critical, empowering, thought-provoking ideas and material have often been found. What is needed is not the abandonment of such education, but a discursive-ethical shift, from what Brady calls moral loss to moral reconstruction.[108]

To conclude: it is important to recognise that the binary opposition of a 'free society' based on the market, and a 'totalitarian society' run by the state is anything but clear-cut, the point being that we should not naively accept commonsense attachments to the global institutional triumph of

---

106 Ibid., 7.

107 See Annette Alstadsæter, "Measuring the Consumption Value of Higher Education" (NHH Discussion Paper SAM, April 2004), http://repec.org/esAUSM04/up.172 98.1075484224.pdf (as of 29 November 2016).

108 See Norman Brady, "From 'Moral Loss' to 'Moral Reconstruction'? A Critique of Ethical Perspectives on Challenging the Neoliberal Hegemony in UK Universities in the 21st Century", *Oxford Review of Education* 38:3 (2012): 343–355, http://www.tandf online.com/doi/pdf/10.1080/03054985.2012.698987?needAccess=true (as of 30 November 2016).

neoliberalism, under which democracy, education and freedom have
reached their highest form. Political power and control is far more complex
than this. Nowhere is this more evident and important than in university
education and the question of the space opened up within it for people to
think, write and communicate freely and critically about the world they
inhabit. Post-Soviet Russia offers a unique insight into the realities
underlying the binary opposite of free and totalitarian. As has been argued,
here an education system has developed that has in theory conformed to the
wider status quo by embracing 'freedom', opening for business and joining
the marketplace, but which in practice also entails many restrictive measures.
History is a battlefield of interpretation and conceptual representation; the
dominant discourse necessarily contains its own counter. As Foucault has it,
wherever there is power, there will always be resistance:[109] the persistence of
critical thinking and practice within higher education demonstrates this. To
think freely and critically, demands that fundamentally important concepts
like democracy, freedom and education remain open to questioning, debate
and analysis. To see their meanings become fixed, one-dimensional and
static, reduced to "weapons in the hands of an administration", while the
"underlying population responds with the expected behaviour",[110] marks
the closing of the discursive universe:[111] the disappearance of important
intellectual efforts to trace words like democracy, freedom and education
back to the ideas they once expressed — and also forwards to what they could
come to express. Our task is to resist, rethink and reformulate such vitally
important concepts, to release them from their association with

---

109 See Michel Foucault, "The Subject and Power", in Hubert Dreyfus and Paul Rabinow,
    eds., *Michel Foucault: Beyond Structuralism and Hermeneutics* (Chicago: University of
    Chicago Press, 1983), 208–226.
110 See Herbert Marcuse, *Soviet Marxism* (New York: Columbia University Press, 1958),
    78.
111 See Herbert Marcuse, *One-Dimensional Man* (Boston, MA.: Beacon, 1963), 101.
    Marcuse here specifically states that his analysis of one-dimensional language and
    the closing of the universe of discourse applies to the pro-market ideas of both neo-
    conservativism and neoliberalism.

marketisation: this task entails considering their relation to subjectivity, scrutinising implicit, commonsense reductions, and going beyond simplistic political binaries, in the hope of realising the potential that always exists within this new world.

SOVIET AND POST-SOVIET POLITICS AND SOCIETY

Edited by Dr. Andreas Umland

ISSN 1614-3515

ibidem-Verlag / *ibidem* Press
Melchiorstr. 15
70439 Stuttgart
Germany

ibidem@ibidem.eu
ibidem.eu